Blessings Lloyd!

ON BEHALF OF INNOCENTS

On Behalf of Innocents

A True Story of a Mission, Faith and a Promise Fulfilled

Caress Garten

Brunswick

Library of Congress Cataloging-in-Publication Data

Garten, Caress, 1949-
On behalf of innocents : a true story of a mission, faith, and a promise fulfilled / Caress Garten.-- 1st ed.
    p. c.m.
ISBN 1-55618-197-3 (cloth : alk. paper)
    1. Liability for animals--Indiana.   2. Dogs--Law and legislation--Indiana.   3. Dog owners--Legal status, laws, etc.--Indiana.   4. Dog attacks--Indiana.   5. Garten, Caress, 1949-   I. Title.

KFI3197.6.G37 2001
346.77203'2--dc21

                                            2001037417

First Edition
Published in the United States of America
by

Brunswick Publishing Corporation
1386 Lawrenceville Plank Road
Lawrenceville, Virginia 23868
434-848-3865
http://www.brunswickbooks.com

This book is dedicated to:

Pat Garten, my husband, who believed in the mission,
nursed the injured leg, and who always told me
I was his princess.

Dr. Frank N. Kik, gifted preacher and pastor, former
senior minister of Tabernacle Presbyterian Church,
Indianapolis, Indiana.

All children and the good dogs who are ours to love,
protect, and cherish.

Acknowledgments

When I was a little girl, I felt the presence of an angel that came to my bedside and watched over me each night. Through the last seven years many earthly angels have uplifted me while I was writing this book.

I would like to thank my editor, Pamela O'Bryan, for her sensitivity to the author's voice and mission, her exacting attention to detail, and countless hours.

I am grateful for the support of: Julie and Eric Smith, founders of the Indiana Companion Animal Network, which focuses on the importance of spay neutering; the City of Fort Wayne Animal Care and Control for their assistance and encouragement; Christina Dickerson of the Indianapolis Humane Society for her enthusiasm and backing of this book; the staff of The Humane Society of the United States Great Lakes Regional office who for many years lent me their expertise, guidance, and aid. My appreciation goes to Police-Inspector Stefan Motmans of the Sint-Truidan, Belgium, Police Service and his partner, Duc, who provided the publisher with a wonderful cover.

Many individuals who played a direct role in the mission's success also offered insightful comments, wisdom, and continued friendship during the evolution of the book. No words can adequately express what they mean to me.

Finally, I have been blessed with the help and talents provided by Dave and Dori Crichlow, Carolyn Neale, Barbara Brandt, Christine Plews, Kathy Dansker, Sally Jackson, Lonnie Spearman, and many others. All are angels who give this book wings.

Table of Contents

Prologue

I felt glad to have finished the first part of my walk on this November day and wanted to go home. I had reached the little rapids in the creek that the path wove by when I first saw them running in and out of the trees. Two fast dogs, running. They ran past me; quickly, closely encircling me, their bodies crouching near the ground. At the last possible moment I understood what would happen as one dog turned his head and looked up at me, its mouth in an almost grinning snarl. It was the meanest expression I have ever seen on anything living.

ONE

Ed

My thoughts flickered like the mid-afternoon shadows that filtered down through the trees adding shade along the path. I would think about Ed as he rested in the sunlight, nestled in the tall weeds along Fall Creek. I wondered if he would show himself to me this afternoon. Many days I would walk by and call for him but he would not respond, making me wonder where he was along the creek and what could possibly be more important than greeting me. But the days he did show himself were spectacular. First you would hear the beating of his great wings, then watch the graceful blue body ascend, head held high as his long spindly legs lifted off the ground. Majestically, he would fly down the creek.

I called the great blue heron "Ed" because I had come to visit with him over the months I walked the path along Fall Creek. We were friends, and some days he would let me watch him as he chose not to fly but remain quiet, letting the waters of the creek lap around him, content to allow other birds to be noticed in the sky. I wondered if he realized there were more people coming closer, for the path I walked today had recently become part of the Indianapolis Parks Department; yet, by weekday mid-afternoons, it was often deserted. The park was beautiful despite the fact that an early summer tornado had toppled many trees. The gentle green valleys that sloped towards the creek softened the storm's damage, and the path itself that wove in and around the creek provided a walker's respite.

I needed a respite. The previous spring I had noticed some trouble walking up the stairs at home, and there was pain in my hips that increased during the following weeks. The doctor told me that I needed to walk every day. I like to walk and found the path along Fall Creek. It was a joy, and on weekends there were many children, mothers who strolled babies, and toddlers who chased the ducks along the creek's path.

After a few weeks I realized faces were becoming familiar because I greeted everyone along my three-mile-walk. I watched the children at play and was reminded of the happiness and comfort I felt around little children. There had always been a special camaraderie I felt with them, almost as if I had not grown up but had remained small. They told me their secrets, and as an adult I realized this was an honor, for unless they feel you will understand they won't invite you to listen. Children are given such honest, wise insight. Perhaps it is because they so recently have been with the angels that these qualities seem to come so easily.

A twig snapped beneath my foot, and a breeze gently blew my hair on today's walk. What was this sense that there was something just beyond my reach? Something was coming—but I was not afraid. It was more curiosity mixed with a sense of urgency. I felt very much like someone who would soon be moving to another state, leaving somehow, an undefinable feeling.

These premonitions were connected with my prayers that I had said today. How was I to serve my Father in Heaven? I knew that my life could and was supposed to touch people, and in some manner I was to be the leader. I was to do something. What was the something? In my heart I knew the mission concerned children. I had tried for years, for so long to understand.

The inheritance from the past pulled at me as I remembered the stories.

They each had two sons as I had been given two sons. One was my great-great grandmother on my mother's side. I could see her sometimes in my imagination. It was 1862 and the Civil War was raging. Grant had been through, and her life in middle Tennessee was in chaos. A husband gone in the war, two small boys to care for, and the Yankees were coming to take what was left. She had taken her little boys down to the Cumberland River and placed them on a raft to go downstream to safety with relatives. Did her hoop skirts rustle in the breeze when she waved good-bye? She would not see them again, for she went back to her home to fight for what was hers and to die.

My great-grandfather was one of the little boys who grew up and became a lawyer and later a judge in the state. His son, my grandfather, became a well-known corporate lawyer. I inherited their genes to reason, speak, and persuade. As a six-year-old I would stand at the doorway of grandfather's library watching the "big boys," who were law students, read the heavy, leather-bound books. I remember the smell of the leather.

The other long-ago grandmother, a young widow with two little boys, from my father's side of the family, had come in 1809 by covered wagon into southern Indiana. She lived in a rough cabin of hand-hewn logs and had to deal with Indians, wild animals, the dripping dampness of spring, the cold of winter. How did she live? Was she lonely and did she worry about protecting her children?

One of the sons would become the father of the first of the caregivers: the doctors that would follow in the family. One was my grandfather who had died a year before I was born. I remembered standing by his grave and looking at the flowered wreath that always appeared on the day of his death. He had been a beloved doctor. I look like this grandfather.

Pictures of his youth showed the same dark hair, fair skin and blue eyes. Did some of his caregiver's intuitiveness and sensitivity, the ability to listen come to me? What talents circled in my soul and what use of these gifts did our Father in Heaven expect? I felt I knew my gifts and my past experiences showed I knew my talents. But they seemed not to connect with one another in any precise focus that I felt was hidden in the puzzle. The talents of the lawyers and the personality of the caregivers. The understanding of people and politics. The deeply felt friendships and commitments with children. Why had I been given the ability to inspire and motivate when I spoke?

My thoughts were interrupted as a child on a bicycle raced by me on the path. Another child quickly entered my mind, a little boy. Donald was seven years old and lived in a burned-out and boarded-up area not far from downtown Indianapolis. Most people hurried through the area as fast as their locked cars could take them. Donald was a second grader at public school #27, and his teacher was a close friend of mine. I had volunteered to be her room mother since the families in her classroom had no time or resources for parties.

Donald sat by the windows, a smart little boy with big blue eyes and sandy-colored hair. He lived with his mother and other siblings in a single room. There was a connected bathroom with a tub always filled with filthy clothes. Perhaps this was the reason along with his mother's exhaustion that Donald was always dirty. He had a large, thick scar over his left eye, "where the big boys threw rocks at me," yet he retained a sweet wistfulness about himself. Watching him, I would be reminded that the Chinese believe children are watched over through their seventh year. There must be truth in the belief, for even in the saddest neighborhoods this age group retains its happiness. Donald was happy, yet he possessed an old soul, for the child had an insightfulness far beyond his years. Once, I started to warn him to be careful while playing close to the street. He knew I wanted to return him to a more sheltered innocence and would let me know through a smile or quiet nod that he understood. The last time I saw Donald he was boarding the school bus at the end of the day and he gave me a smile and a thumbs up. I was struck by the fact that children are so courageous and forgiving of an imperfect world.

I remembered crossing the street from the school to go home. Having been warned time and time again that anything newer would be gone or vandalized, I was driving a ten-year-old, slightly rusted car that belonged to my seventeen-year-old son, Benjamin. I noticed that the stray cat who always sat in front of a boarded-up house where the car was parked had spent the afternoon walking over the old Cutlass, leaving a trail of paw prints. Benjamin would not be pleased, I thought. As I started the car I glanced at the fence by the house and saw one of those orange and black signs bought at a drugstore. It read: "Beware of the Dog." These random memories stayed with me as I continued to walk.

A young woman jogged past me on the path, giving me a brief wave and smile. She appeared content, but I thought so many were not. The women I knew lived in the best neighborhoods, their houses were on the home tours, they had bright children, successful careers, and achieving husbands. Many went to church on Sundays, because they had been raised to go to church on Sundays and that is where it was correct to talk to God. Outside of Sundays, God was almost a taboo topic somehow defining a person as simplistic, an individual who was different. The few times I could remember any conversation on the subject there had been dead silence as if a foreign language was being spoken. I had come to the conclusion that perhaps so many of them had never experienced a closeness, a personal walk with a great and good God. It was a part of my life that I took for granted. That closeness had developed over time through simple prayers and conversations. I had also heard the Voice who gave answers with great clarity and perfect truth. You could never tell when the answers would come, but when they did there was no mistaking Who was talking. Sometimes He answered immediately, other times only after a while. I decided there were reasons why He waits silently sometimes.

I first heard Him when I was twenty after asking for the answer since I was sixteen. The Voice that spoke to me came from deep inside with the most loving authority, conveying what I immediately recognized as absolute truth. He simply told me, "You love him very much." This was the answer as I watched Pat walk across the parking lot under my dormitory window. Patterson Garten was academically brilliant, wise, funny, good with people, and had the luck of the Irish without being Irish. He was that combination of gifted person who is going to succeed in any situation yet retain humility and a deep sense of personal honesty about himself and with others. He was and is someone who people recognize as having a rare sense of balance. He loved me, and I understood that I really could not marry someone just because I thought he was a good catch and there was a friendship. Was this love and could I commit myself to him? I prayed for the answer to understand what I truly felt and the answer came. Because of the answer I married the right man. He is also a wonderful father who has always had time for our children, Benjamin and Matthew.

My mind returned to the present. My two sons had recently returned to school. Indiana is so dry at this time of year, and today the creek was down along my walking path. On this late August day, acorns crunched under my feet and the first leaves fell from the trees into the creek, signaling that autumn was coming. I looked for Ed, the heron, but he was gone. I would have to be turning on the path soon, it was time to go home, school would be ending for the day. I liked to be home when the ten-year-old Cutlass pulled into the driveway.

My thoughts were disjointed. Donald, where was he this summer? Would I see him as a grown-up third grader?

I stopped to give a friendly terrier a sniff of my hand and a pat on the head. There were always the same loose dogs. I had decided that they must live close by because they seemed to spend a lot of time in the park.

Another bicycle flashed by me as I remembered being lifted into my mother's arms. Two years old, I was playing in my sandbox in the backyard. It was a hot day, like this one, and I was watching the soft, fine grains of sand slip through my fingers when I felt a thump and I was on my back, an enormous German shepherd head looking me in the face. Then a big long tongue started licking me. His face was bigger than mine! I remember screaming and not being able to get up. I felt myself being lifted, my mother's blond hair in my face and her patting my back. Was this one of the reasons for my camaraderie with children: the understanding that they have their secrets and their worries? Although I never mentioned my worry, I knew by the time I was five or six years old that I would need to conquer the fear of the thump and the big tongue. There were always those doggies who met me while walking to School #84 and playing in the neighborhood. I would offer a nice smile and a pat on the head, wondering if my furry friends knew I was worried. I must have been convincing to myself as well as the neighborhood canines because slowly my fear diminished. Years later, I vaguely recalled that memory, and that was good news for Chuck N. Garten.

Chuck had probably been tied up to some tree or fence in an inner city neighborhood when the rope broke and he left. He found himself lost after awhile with only an old rope around his neck and no tags. He was anything but beautiful, instead rather a scraggly terrier mix, dark fur, his legs, ears, and tail all too long for his body, and he was tired because he had run a long way. Chuck could go no further, so he had decided to walk down the middle of the street and stop each car, place his paws on the front grill, pull himself up, and stare at each driver. The car would slowly start, and

Chuck would pull his paws back toward the pavement and walk to the next car. I was hoping someone would get out of their car and help Chuck before he got to my car. No one did and there he was—upset, looking for help, his paws on the car. My thoughts flashed back and forth. If you do not help this animal, he is going to get squashed. If you do help this animal, you are going to have to keep him because he is so ugly no one is going to adopt him. We already had a dog, Boomer, and a cat from the Humane Society. I had never thought of being a two-dog family.

I watched as my hand slipped from the steering wheel and placed itself upon the door handle. The door opened and an exhausted and filthy Chuck crawled inside. We made the short trip to the vet who claimed he had never laid eyes on Chuck. We advertised that Chuck had been found and his owners could come and get him. Nobody showed. He was ours and was named Chuck N. Garten. The N. stood for Norton. Norton was Ralph Cramden's best friend on the 1950s situation comedy "The Honeymooners." Norton was a nice fella with his scooped neck undershirt, hat nattily placed on the back of his head, always trying to please Ralph. Art Carney would never know the effect of the role model he created, for it was obvious at an early age fate had selected Norton's foot tracks for Chuck to firmly place his own paws into. Now comfortably entrenched in his new home, Chuck was the king of all he surveyed.

I wasn't sorry I had stopped for Chuck. He loved me so much. I walked faster on the path, passing a small group of rapids on the creek. My hips seemed to be getting better, the walking was helping. The blue in the summer sky was a little darker, mid-afternoon was slowly preparing us for evening. The end of the day was coming, and I wondered if God had been listening to my thinking? I wondered if He ever felt tired of listening.

I had almost reached my car close to the beginning of where I started to walk. It was near the grocery. The thought of dinner entered my mind. What were we going to eat tonight? Horns honked in the parking lot, disturbing the ducks waddling, out of the safety of the grassy perimeter of their pond, in between parked cars. Did all women feel this confusion? Did their lives seem continually pulled in many directions? What was this sense of expectation? I walked down to the banks of the creek before heading off the path. I looked for my friend Ed one last time, down the water until the bend, but there was no great flash of blue beauty. He chose to be as the answers I was seeking, elusive.

* * *

By September my walks were now a faithful part of a daily routine, rain or shine. I took the same route of winding asphalt through the trees and by the creek. The heat of summer remained in Indiana, but everyone knew the season was almost over. The swimming pools were closing, there was a stillness in the neighborhoods and along Fall Creek. The kind of unnatural quiet that comes during the day when the children have gone back to school.

I do know Ed was happier. He didn't have to work so hard to be perfectly still and hidden. I would see him more often since school had started. It was easier to think in the new quiet of the day, and slowly, almost imperceptibly, the prayers along Fall Creek were changing. There was a growing frustration and greater sense of expectation at the end of my walks. Every piece of the puzzle was present, but wouldn't fit together.

Soon I planned on returning to school #27 and seeing the second graders and my friend Donald. They were important to me. I had also agreed to serve Meals on Wheels, an agency that aids the elderly and disabled, by developing an endowment and sitting on their board of directors. However, there were flashes of thoughts I could not quite grasp. A damp pall was falling over the work—and there was a sense—just a sense—*that something would stop me from finishing.*

Despite these thoughts there was yet another project. A leadership series had been started in the name of U.S. Senator Richard G. Lugar to encourage women to enter politics. I did not see myself as a politician, but had always been interested in politics.

The Lugar series requires that within five years of completing the course you are expected to run for public office, or help pass legislation, or receive a political appointment. I filled out the long form, which had required thought, and had asked people, busy people, to spend their time writing recommendations for me.

One of those I asked for a recommendation was my representative at the Indiana State House, Paul Mannweiler, whom I knew very well because Pat and I had gone to high school with him. Paul enthusiastically encouraged me to submit my name for the Lugar series.

Paul Mannweiler had been successful in politics on the state legislative level and at thirty-six had become the youngest Speaker of the House in the United States. He had held the position of Speaker for only a couple of years when the Democrats had a resurgence. In 1988, the number of legislators elected for both the Republican and Democrat parties in the Indiana House of Representatives was fifty members each. Paul, a Republican, became Co-Speaker of the House of Representatives with Michael Phillips, a Democrat from Boonville, Indiana; a man who had wanted to be Speaker throughout his adult life.

Sharing is not the best format for the political process, and the two very different men did not care for one another. There is a bronze plaque hanging on the wall in the chamber of the House at the state house commemorating this historic sharing of power in Indiana history. It is a beautiful plaque, dignified, polished, not reflective of the real mood behind the words, which was anything but amiable. The national political picture aided the Democrats in Indiana in 1990, and that party would gain control of the House and Mike Phillips would become sole Speaker of the House. Paul became the minority leader. The Democrats would be further bolstered by the re-election, two years later, of Evan Bayh as governor. However, even the governor would be reminded that although he belonged to the same party, when the legislature is in session, the Speaker of the House is the most powerful politician in the state of Indiana.

My thoughts took me far away from the blue September sky reflected in the creek's little rapids and clear pools along the meandering walker's trail. Despite the bright sunshine I was in a gray limbo. Recently I had mailed the completed Lugar series form; of the three requirements, perhaps I could get a political appointment. I knew city leaders—maybe one of them wouldn't mind having me around. I remembered mentioning to a friend that it would be unlikely I would be involved with passing legislation. "Can you see me doing that?" I had said in dismay. Running for office also seemed doubtful.

I watched the rapids flow over the smooth, round stones that covered the shallow creek bottom. I had spoken these questions of rationale but had been silent as to my prayers—my intuition—that although I was trying to direct my life—*something else was coming.*

* * *

But what could it be? I thought silently as the doors of an elevator opened a few days later on an upper floor of the Columbia Club in downtown Indianapolis. The interview for the Lugar series had arrived.

"Hello, Caress, do you have one of these?" a voice greeted me as I stepped off the elevator. Sue Anne Gilroy, who headed Senator Lugar's office, was a friend who could also pronounce my first name correctly to the judges: "Karis" with a short *a* like "Paris." Caress is a family name I like, but one people often mistook as "caress," meaning a loving touch. She not only understood my name but also knew I walked. She handed me a little brochure. "Caress, this is for Emily," she said. It was a combined walk or run fundraiser at Emily's old school. Emily was Sue Anne's daughter who had died when she was twelve, from cancer, Wilms Tumor.

Emily, Donald, the children of summer who had played along Fall Creek—walking. All of this momentarily merged together in my brain, and I smiled, taking the brochure.

I stepped into a small conference room and met the interviewers. The three judges were all accomplished women, well known for both their initiatives and their intelligence. I was asked my opinions and thoughts on a number of questions with the last being, "Caress, who has had the most important influence in your life?" Since I was there to be honest and I figured it was fine if they took me and fine if they didn't, I replied with perhaps the most politically incorrect but truthful answer I could muster.

"My husband," I answered. I surmised the panel had not heard this one today. "You see, it's his humility," I heard myself saying. "Always, he has handled his gifts and his success with the most grace, and I have learned from him."

One of the judges later told me that this answer is what they remembered most about my interview. Probably, because they were a confident group, they liked my answer. I was in the series.

The interview ended and I drove home along the inner city section of Fall Creek. I passed through the familiar streets and realized I wasn't far from Sarah's house—not far at all. I knew she would understand my sense of frustration.

I had first met my friend Sarah over ten years ago in our children's school parking lot. It was a small Episcopal school, and Sarah asked me to come and join a small group of mothers that met in the chapel before school was over at the end of the day. This group came together just to ask for patience and guidance as they collected their children.

Over time, Sarah had told me about her family and her sisters. She was the baby in the family. Sarah's big sisters had been valedictorians. She would laugh and say, "And then there was me." But Sarah had been given a greater gift, a different gift, than her sisters. Her father had been a minister, and whether through environment, or genes, or just her own special ability, she could spontaneously say the most moving and beautiful prayer. Sarah had spoken to me about the importance of God and heritage in the black churches. She would say, "You know, Caress, that in slavery days they could take your husband from you, your children from you, everyone you loved, but no one could ever separate or take you from the love of God."

Sarah had what I called "a direct line." She was someone who was naturally in tune with the Supreme Being, and so it was Sarah that I called when I reached home.

"What should I do? I feel nothing is right," as all the hesitations and stumbling blocks were repeated to her.

"I don't know what you should do," Sarah quietly answered after listening to me. "Though I do know, Caress, you must have faith and continue to keep asking God." Sarah was always a comfort to me even without answers. She would remember our conversation.

* * *

I did keep asking God and though the last days of October were busy, they provided no understanding. These days, after school, the house was lively and filled with teenagers accompanied by a constantly ringing phone. So I was surprised when the phone rang and the call was actually for me. Anne Shane's warm-hearted voice came over the phone. "Caress, Steve has a new project. He wants to bring volunteers into city government, and I'd like you to be part of the team to make that possible." Anne was a good friend and advisor to our mayor, Stephen Goldsmith, a Republican.

"When do you want me to come?" I asked.

She paused, then laughed, "Can you come tomorrow?"

The next day I walked into her office at the City County Building in downtown Indianapolis. She had just returned from lunch where she had been in conversation with a state senator. Anne sat down in her chair with a wry smile, repeating the conversation. "Yes, Senator, that race looks safe, in fact it looks good. Yes, Senator, I will keep you informed." Anne laughed and said with some exasperation, "How many more days is it until the election? Senator Garton really doesn't want to lose his control at the state house."

State Senator Robert Garton was from Columbus, Indiana; a pretty, mid-size city in the southern part of the state. As the president pro tempore, he headed the Republican majority in the state Senate. He was the most powerful Republican at the state house since the governorship and the House were controlled by the Democrats. Mayor Goldsmith had asked Anne to help the senator remain in control of the Senate, for it was important to the mayor's plans for Indianapolis that legislation advantageous to the city be successfully passed. I had never met Senator Garton, or, for that matter, any of the state legislators other than those that represented the north side of Indianapolis. I really didn't know much about the state house and had only been in the building once about six years earlier. However, I had always paid attention to Senator Garton when he appeared on the news because, although spelled differently, we shared the same last name.

Anne started to explain the project and the mayor's goals to me. It's a funny feeling to sit with a friend and to feel a distance that you can't articulate. To say you'll do the work, be at the meetings, try hard, but something is saying to you deep inside, just below what is called consciousness that you won't be there. How do you explain that to people? I felt like someone who had been asked to paint rooms in a house that was scheduled for demolition. I saw no alternative, so I continued to work—and to walk.

That day the brilliant foliage of autumn peaked, ablaze with gold and red leaves that had not yet fallen from the trees. The path was a magnet for me in the afternoon. An invisible hourglass supplied with sand from the creek bottom monitored my time. The breeze rustled the leaves. They seemed to converse with me, gently repeating conversations about the path along Fall Creek.

"We're talking about the path we walk along Fall Creek," I remembered explaining at a recent fundraiser for Paul Mannweiler. He was a jogger, and I had suddenly wanted him to know more of the path's appeal. "There's a great blue heron who's become my friend," I said without mentioning I'd named him Ed. "You should try running there," I said, then mentioning one of his little boys added, *"Take Steven with you."*

The breeze took on a different tone as beating wings could be heard coming quickly. Hundreds of geese were passing in the sky. The strongest birds flew at the front of the formation, for they had powerful wings, the first to cut through the air, building a cushion to lift up the weakest birds that flew in the middle. Were the birds in front the decisive leaders or the receptive servants? Maybe the lead birds were like the best of human leaders. They were first servants and then leaders. I sensed their urgency; a need to reach a destination. I wondered if I would be given the chance to be the receptive servant?

I walked faster, faster, my heart pumped harder, for something unknown hurried me down the path. The geese flew on, and their beating wings were replaced with the memory of a question I had asked a psychologist. "I thought the test would show something about children, I'm very good with children." My real unsaid question was: What am I supposed to do for children?

"Well," he said. "You've been very successful with

volunteers, and people who are very good with volunteers are also good with children. They have to be patient, nurturing, repeat instructions, tell them what a good job they've done." I thought he was correct, but his words, or my question, missed the mark. He finished with, "You know, you tested as high as I have ever seen in one area." I looked at him and he said, "It's stability, you almost tested off the charts."

The sun filtered through the leaves, warming me as my lungs struggled to keep up with my fast pace. Time was fleeting, but my thoughts remained reflective. I really wasn't any closer to an answer, I remembered thinking, walking into the back door at home that day after the psychologist's visit. I had stepped over muddy soccer cleats and book bags that had been dropped in the back hall. No matter how many times I asked Matthew to "pick up your things," he just couldn't or wouldn't remember. He was too busy organizing what he wanted to do next to worry about being neat.

Matthew was the family's "John Wayne." I would hear toys being pushed aside as he would search for his cowboy boots and vest, strap on the holsters, and with authority he would place the beloved cowboy hat on his head.

I would tiptoe past the doorway and see a three-year-old who saw himself as a giant among men. Now, at fifteen, he was a soccer star and lived in his high school soccer jersey. He was still the protector of all femininity, a role he had chosen for himself long ago. Matt loved laughter and music and liked to play Mozart on the piano. John Wayne didn't like people to know about Mozart, for it was a clue to his deep sensitivity. At fifteen, he was caught in that teenage twilight zone of late childhood and budding adulthood where everything was fine as long as he appeared to fit in as a teen clone of everyone else.

That afternoon he had been talking to me about his soccer schedule. "Make sure nothing happens to this jersey," he had said. "I have to wear it again tomorrow." I remembered how protectively he handed me the damp, dirt-smeared jersey. "Be careful with it," he pleaded, "be very careful." His older brother Benjamin had been sitting on the kitchen floor, rough-housing with Chuck the dog who was delighted to be rolling around on the linoleum with him. There is something truly unique in the human male makeup that enjoys being down on the floor, growling with a dog, and having a wonderful time. At seventeen, he was still so young. The occasional girl would call him and with nervous unease he would talk. Like his friends, he was more comfortable playing basketball and eating pizza on Friday nights than seeing girls. He was a good student, organized, and had inherited his father's inquisitive mind. Benjamin had become more mature, but he couldn't quite comprehend that next year he would go to college. He was going to have to decide soon about applying.

The gurgling water of the creek returned my thinking to the present along with a curious thought, would I be around to help him decide?

I had been walking without seeing; only taking time to notice the flying geese before becoming consumed in my thoughts. Now I would have to decide where to leave the path. The imaginary hourglass had slowly drained of sand. The serenity and brilliant sunshine around me would be left for another time, another day.

* * *

I guess I was thinking of Benjamin and Matthew and all the other teenage boys I knew, remembering their youthful faces and their innocence when I asked the question. It was the end of October, 1992, and the first session of the Lugar series. I raised my hand immediately when the senator started to take questions. When you feel this urgency that you haven't much time, you do get things done. I said, "Senator Lugar, I have a heavy-hearted question. I have two sons who in six or seven years will both be in their twenties. The war in Bosnia parallels in my mind the beginnings of Vietnam. I fear the time frame." I told him I was worried about the lack of experience of the man we were about to elect president. I remember thinking it wasn't the time for political niceties. We were going to have a new president and the boys who played basketball in my driveway were at stake. Whether Republican or Democrat this new president was going to need help. As for me, I was going somewhere and might not get to see the senator for a long time.

"That is a heavy-hearted question," Senator Lugar replied and told the group he would offer the new president his advice on foreign policy. The senator had heard me, and I believed would remember my concern. Oddly, I felt like I was tying up loose ends.

* * *

Autumn had lost its colorful brilliance, replaced by cooler weather and gray skies. It was the first day of November, 1992, and as a member of the board of directors of Meals on Wheels, I was asked to see what the hundreds of volunteers did daily. The secretary at the main office was going to deliver a route that morning, and I asked to go with her. It was a gloomy day as we drove to pick up the meals. Our route started from Methodist Hospital near downtown Indianapolis. Arriving at the back of the hospital, I noticed a man barbecuing next to the building. He was wearing surgical garb and a hair net. "Is that where our meals are prepared?" I asked with a grin.

"No, we'll have to go inside the hospital to pick up our meals," she answered with a laugh. We walked up a loading dock ramp and rang a bell. As we stood in a large unloading area, the door opened, and a big man in regulation green hospital top and pants appeared.

"We're not quite ready for you ladies, it'll be just a minute," he said politely. Behind him were bright lights and signs labeling the way to surgery.

The place looked efficient, sterile, and cold. "They do a really nice job here at Methodist and usually they're right on time," the secretary assured me as a hearse pulled up to the loading dock. The door opened again. It wasn't our lunches, they still weren't ready, but a cart rolled out with a covered corpse.

The back of the hearse opened as I turned to my new friend the secretary and said with a smile, "This is a good place to stay out of."

TWO

Bended Knee

In some ways it was as if they had been born dead. The pact man made with them thousands of years ago had been broken. They had stood by the cave and man had asked them to enter and sit by his fire. Man welcomed them and had been generous, promising to care for the creatures. They had given their loyalty, but man decided to betray their caring, their friendship, their trust. Evil stepped forth, destroying the positive genetics of generations, creating impulsive killers.

It had escalated with a vengeance, as evil does when it goes unchecked, and spiraled and spread until these dogs had been born. Their heritage began long ago around the deep pits with the screaming Staffordshire coal miners who, consumed with their blood sport and greed, lay wages on which dog would fight with most sport and endurance despite his wounds and until his death.

Earlier they had been asked to fight bulls, whom the men first tormented, and afterwards, without mercy the dogs would be asked to hold and rip apart the animal's groin and nose. They were naturally a strong dog, with jaws that could clamp down and hold. But now the men wanted fast dogs, with strength and dexterity, who could fight each other in the pits.

This new dog could wrap his great jaws around the other dog's leg, breaking the bone like a broomstick. He could rush quietly, but the shattering bone made snapping sounds and brought the howling mob to its feet. He could hold and shake with the front teeth and chew with his rear teeth, producing deep, straight cuts as from a knife. The man who trained him commanded that he leap, then grab the cloth rope, and hang suspended for hours from the tree. When he could finally let go, a cat or small dog was thrown to him to tear apart. He had to remember the taste and smell of blood for the fight. They had called him an English bulldog but now he was something different, for he was allowed to mate only with the faster terriers. He wanted to live, to please the men who cheered his brutality in the pits, but only the fiercest would continue to be bred.

Man had brought him to America as the Civil War began. He was brought not in friendship but for sport, and slowly he began to lose his good dog traits. The traits that God had given just to him that man had found so loving. He no longer showed his moods or weaknesses to anyone, for it was to his advantage in the fight to be a stoic. Now, no warning would be given when he attacked, and the men who bred him would be rewarded, for they wanted a killer. Before, he had attacked only as a last resort, he had stared and snarled over food, his mate, and territory. Now that was gone from him. Now he seemed to kill for no reason, there were no inhibitions that kept him from killing, he was now abnormal, all thanks to those who called him their best friend.

They had come a long way to the man, one from Texas, the other from North Carolina. They were important, for they made the man feel important. He had paid dearly for them, spending well over a thousand dollars. The dogs had come with strong names, Thunder and Hook, and, although a mixed breed, they had pedigrees. There were those across the country who knew about their lineage and they communicated through a rough but extensive underground.

Their trade magazines were run off on cheap paper and sent through the mail in plain brown wrappers. They were known to each other by first name only or by nickname: Diamond Jim, Cuban Cowboy, Milk Man. They were a fraternity, crossing skin color and sex. Admiration ran deep for each other's ability with their fighting dogs, and the best in the business were titled "great dog men." Their grand champion's stud fees could reach five hundred to one thousand dollars. These were men and women who enjoyed the violence of fighting dogs.

They had come to the man as pups, and in the last few years he liked to take them along Fall Creek and let them swim and run. They had grown into the great, fierce dogs they were destined and designed by genetics and training to become. He had made them jump and hold and had asked veterinarians for steroids to make them stronger. There were close calls with people, but the man wasn't really bothered.

There had been the trouble with the neighbor, but hadn't he come outside to take care of the fool? The neighbor worked nights and had been walking to his car. Carrying a heavy dinner pail, he had said good-bye to his wife and walked out the front door. He was halfway to the car when he saw the dogs and had made a break, running for his life. They were coming for him, and he knew they were vicious, for he had watched these dogs. There wasn't time to open the car door before they caught him, so taking a running leap, he landed on the hood, hitting one dog in the head with his pail. He had struck the animal hard, but it hadn't fazed him and now they started to leap, trying to mount the front of the car. He yelled for his wife to get the gun; there wasn't much time. He screamed as she grabbed the weapon.

The man heard the screams and came out of his house, seizing his dogs by their thick, black collars. The wife ran towards them with the gun. "I'll kill them the next time," the neighbor spat.

The man didn't want trouble, but the neighbor wasn't of

much concern. After all, his dogs hadn't done any damage. He'd been right there, nothing had happened. He might have to be more careful, though. Time the places right where they would run. He would also carry a gun. It was important for Thunder and Hook to run to keep their powerful front legs and upper bodies in shape. They had to bring in money; he had too much invested.

The man remembered the path along Fall Creek. It was perfect for their training but now there were more people. Sometimes he would walk the dogs along the path in the daytime, passing the walkers, the joggers, and children. He felt assured of his control, for he was a big man, weighing almost three hundred pounds, towering over others as he passed them on the path. He felt a confidence as he walked, people looked at him with respect. Perhaps, if he took them early to run, before dawn, it would be all right.

Joe had dressed in the pre-dawn darkness. His work as a fireman started early and he had to stay in shape. He loved to cycle to work so he could breathe the fresh air and get some exercise. In the life of a fireman you had to stay prepared, ready, and he was doing just that as he made his way down the driveway and crossed over to the Fall Creek corridor. The dark asphalt path was visible though he could see only a few feet ahead. Joe pedaled confidently, knowing its twists and turns. He listened as the tires made their soft humming sounds and the gears on the bike shifted smoothly.

Joe never heard them as they came upon him, bounding out of the night. Suddenly surrounded, he knew they wanted him. There were three dogs, and Joe, who knew dogs and loved dogs, was scared. Leaping from the bike, he used its frame as his weapon. Frantically, he swung the bike back and forth keeping the dogs from his body as they tried to encircle him. He broke out in sweat—what to do, how much longer could he battle—when the man loomed out of the darkness. He grabbed the two older dogs by the thick collars and the younger dog came by command. Joe had seen a lot of people in his fireman's career, and he knew when to shut up and not argue. He wasn't going to make this massive man with his pit bulls angry in this hour before dawn. The man was silent as he held the dogs while Joe rode away, knowing he had narrowly escaped. Joe felt mind-numbed by the close call, and hated the man for what those animals had become.

The man dragged the dogs down the path. His strong hands were tired of gripping the thick collars as he slammed shut the vehicle's door. So they had chased him, but all dogs liked to chase bicycles. The big man brooded as he drove the dogs back home. He slowly weighed the situation and decided the dogs still hadn't hurt anybody, and anyway, the guy had swung the bike. Perhaps the cyclist would make a complaint, so next time he would wait until dawn to see if anyone was out traveling down the path along Fall Creek. He might take a better look around, but they were "game" these dogs and they needed to run.

* * *

It was Thursday, the fifth of November, 1992. The election was over and there would be a new president. I had worked all day in our breakfast room on my mayoral project. The weather was damp and cold as a gloomy, gray sky produced a fine mist of drizzle throughout the day. A white dogwood tree, dripping with rain, stood outside the window. A friendly looking tree, it was planted in just the right spot for the birds to sit and observe the humans inside. A robin sat in the dogwood that day and he stayed perched, never leaving. The robin, though not majestic as my friend Ed, the heron, or strong, like the flying geese, was someone, I thought, who knew who he was and had a sturdy constancy in his grip. He could sleep without falling and spend the day in gales of rain without moving. Great was the strength in his tendons so when his leg was bent at the knee, the claws contracted and gripped like a steel trap. For all of his commonness he was a tenacious bird, and I liked him very much as he kept me company on his bended knee.

I was almost finished for the day, and I needed to speak with my friend Anne who worked with the mayor. Her office told me she was in a meeting and would have to call me back. Looking at the clock, it was after two, and I needed to leave if I was going to walk that afternoon and get back before school ended.

It was funny to me that I didn't have anything to wear for walking now that the weather was cold. I found some pink cotton slacks that I pulled from the bottom of a drawer. There was a pink sweatshirt that went with the slacks and my pink moccasins. I went down the stairs and put on a new short coat of soft wool and started down the hall. A voice called to me from the kitchen that it was cold and I should take gloves. Geneva Campbell had been my helper in the house since I was ill and pregnant with Benjamin almost eighteen years ago. She was a friend who knew me so well that she could anticipate what I would forget. I found some lined leather gloves and hurried to leave. Going out the back door, I said good-bye to her and that I would be back before too long.

The damp day felt cold on my cheeks, making me want to walk fast and hurry home. The winding path was a dull gray from the wet, and the bare branches seemed desolate hanging from the trees. The water was dark with old leaves that floated down the creek. I don't remember hearing anything but my own rubber-soled feet hitting the pavement as a little bit of rain spat at me. The grass had faded and the rain made the bark of the trees appear darker; they glistened along the path. I had walked almost half the distance to where I would turn around to go back, and as I passed the little rapids on the creek I heard wheels and another walker pushing a stroller. I took my eyes from the pavement and looked up to see a baby boy smiling at me. He was dressed in blue and a little blue knitted hat covered his head. He was seven or eight months old and he was happy, even in the gloom, to be out for a walk. He lifted my spirits, and I smiled at him and his mother as we passed. The thought came to me that they were the first people I had seen; everyone else had stayed away on this gray day.

Somewhere from the direction I had come a door opened and they leaped into the drizzle. Quickly they were off chasing squirrels, trying to beat each other to the bait, ready for the kill. Their strong legs ran with speed and agility. Instinct urged the two dogs on as they wove up and down the shallow valley towards the creek. The man came behind, watching them in the distance.

No one would be out today. Even he didn't want to be out in cold, damp rain. He hadn't seen anyone and you couldn't pen these animals up for too long. He brought his gun with him to shoot the dogs if he had to, if things got out of control, but it wouldn't, not with him, not ever. There were stories about these types of dogs when they ran loose and had found a human. Dogs like them had killed, hanging on until the death. Even when they were shot off their victims, it was usually too late and impossible to pry their teeth apart. Sometimes the bullets passed through the dogs into the victim and added to the agony of death.

He was aware of the danger but he'd keep an eye on his dogs—*it was time for them to run.*

I had reached the section on the path where I turned around close to a massive old tree that had fallen near the creek in June during the tornadoes. Sometimes people wandered over to touch and climb on the fallen giant. Today, I felt glad to have finished the first part of the walk on this November day and wanted to go home. Returning, I had reached the little rapids in the creek that the path wove by when I first saw them running in and out of the trees. Two fast dogs running, I thought, and felt very calm as they ran toward me. They were muscular dogs with their ears cropped back. I smiled at them and slowed down my walk, offering my hand, as I always did, in greeting. The man in the distance screamed, "Oh, my God!" Then he yelled something I couldn't understand. The dogs ran past me then; quickly, closely encircling me, their bodies crouching near the ground. At the last possible moment I understood what would happen as one dog turned his head and looked up at me, its mouth in an almost grinning snarl. It was the meanest expression I have ever seen on anything living.

In a second my body went stiff, I looked up, still feeling extremely calm, still smiling, as the dog looked down and sank his teeth into the muscles right below the calf of my left leg.

The dog had great strength and lifted my leg into the air as if it were an old rag. His mouth closed like a vise grip, encompassing the leg. The animal started to shake his head back and forth as he stood on his two hind legs. I felt like a doll being pulled apart—I slipped. The second dog jumped for the top of my head before I could completely stand. I felt and saw his teeth graze my forehead and the top of my head as blood started to pour into my eyes, down my face, over my ears, and down my neck. Surprised how warm and sticky my blood felt, I gasped and struggled to stand as the first dog snapped his head back and forth, jerking the leg. My hands went to cover my face as a fang penetrated the leather gloves into my left hand. The dog's head came down and tore into my coat. He jumped again high in the air to the level of my face as I watched through my fingers. I pulled my shoulders up around my neck as the "game" dog pulled at my coat and leaped around me. I knew the man would come. I never thought he wouldn't because he had screamed, "Oh, my God!" I watched my leg jerking back and forth, and the pink slacks soaking up blood; then blood being sprayed from the leg. My vision through the wet gloves was disappearing. Blood flowed into my eyes and onto the leathered fingers that were protecting my face. Yet, I felt so calm, and wasn't worried or frightened in any sense. I felt no pain. Blood was covering more and more of the pants leg. I hope he comes soon, came to me but in a very reasoned, calm manner. Almost at once an enormous man reached down and grabbed the dog with my leg in his mouth. He was struggling as he pried the dog's mouth open with a dark long object: a hammer handle. Suddenly, I was standing on both legs, and the man was beside me upright like a ramrod and looking straight ahead. He was dead silent; there was soul-less silence, only the dripping trees and rushing water in the creek. I still felt calm, much calmer than the man, and in control. I felt sticky, with blood in my nose and mouth, but I wanted to say something because it seemed natural that one of us should make that effort. I had the feeling I should be polite and start a conversation. I asked him quietly if he thought I would die? I felt blood pouring from the leg.

"Naw," he snarled like his dogs, "you won't die." I didn't feel as if I would die, but I thought it was something to say. I looked down at the dogs, their muzzles covered in blood. They were expressionless, dead-eyed creatures, totally without emotion.

I said nothing else, just started to walk off the path through the valley towards the street about fifty or sixty yards away. I felt very sure that I would find help, but I remember silence, that deadened silence, while walking in the wet grass toward the hill I would have to climb to reach the street. Dripping trees, pounding heart, limited time, dwindling time, I kept walking. I felt no pain, great calm, and knew absolutely I would find help. I was never frightened. Once, I turned just to see where the man and the dogs were and I saw him hurrying down the path, holding the dogs. I kept my eyes on the street as I climbed up the embankment. A woman in a car drove by; she didn't see me as I came over the hill. The street, normally never busy, was empty, and I crossed the street, walking towards some apartments a little down the road. I started to feel dizzy and blank—I couldn't go much farther—there was too much blood trailing me. I reached the apartment's driveway entrance and saw a small red car coming in the distance. I knew this was the car that would stop. I knew absolutely.

The car was almost upon me when the brakes slammed and the car skidded to a stop. A man leaped out of his car and stood yelling at the top of his voice, "Oh, lady, I almost screamed at you for playing a Halloween trick, standing in the street covered in blood." I sat down on the sidewalk and leaned back in the grass. I asked him if he would call 911. Another car slammed on its brakes and then another until I seemed to be surrounded by men. A slender young man in his twenties appeared by my side in the grass. He was shaking and was so upset his voice trembled and his head hung down as he spoke to me.

"I-I-I watched it happen f-f-from my window," he stammered. "I couldn't come to help you because if I did they would get me too."

I felt quiet inside and asked, "Would you call my husband?"

He was agitated. I told him the number as he ran back into the apartments only to come back immediately. He couldn't remember, would I repeat it again for him and a third time until he could remember.

The Sheriff's Department came. Officer Kelly Palmer had responded to a call that a woman had been bitten by a dog on Fall Creek Parkway. The officer bent over me and, speaking gently, he asked which way the man had gone with the dogs. I heard tires burn as he tore down Fall Creek Parkway. I had the sensation that I was going down a floor on an elevator. My foot felt cold and wet and I kicked off the moccasin that was filled with blood. You know when you are beginning to die, and there is calm understanding, a peacefulness. I realized there were pools of blood on the sidewalk and the men that were around me were watching the horizon. They were looking for the dogs. There was an older man with white hair who stood by my feet. He seemed so tall as I sat on the ground. He had been grim-faced watching me, saying nothing, and slowly he turned and stood with his back towards me.

There is something extremely sad to a person who has been hurt when people can't look at them. It's as if they are a rejected member of the human race. Oh, I thought quietly, do I really look that bad? I felt the elevator go down another floor. I realized the older man was afraid to watch. It was odd, the older man was upset, and I was very calm, understanding what was happening. There is a longing, if people are around, for them to smile at you and hold your hand as the elevator goes down. I remained unfrightened, and if I had bled to death on the side of the hill, I know it would have been very peaceful. Later, a trauma nurse would say to me that she thought people were so afraid of blood and getting AIDS that it kept people from being the Good Samaritan. The older man who stood with his back to me wasn't afraid of AIDS, he was afraid of watching death and through me, facing his own.

"I wonder why the ambulance is taking so long?"

The poor men around me were quiet; they seemed forlorn. The officer returned; he hadn't spotted the man and his dogs.

The ground seemed a vulnerable place to me if the dogs came running loose again, and I wondered if these men would help me if they returned. The firemen arrived in their truck. "I'll tell you the truth, this leg's pretty torn up." I listened to him and just recorded the information, noticing his hands were shaking. He thought the leg was probably going to be lost. I felt surprised that everyone was so upset—the fireman cried.

Perhaps it was because the crime was a different violence, dogs ripping a woman up as she walked in the afternoon, or a deep fear many people feel about dogs combined with sudden violence of the most savage sort. Or maybe, it was innocence that touches people so deeply, but I witnessed the first heartfelt reactions to me and dimly understood that I didn't feel their panic. The ambulance came and I was lifted off the ground, surrounded by people. The doors shut behind me and the motor started. The back doors of the ambulance flew open and a tense voice asked, "My wife?" The paramedics became excited only once, when the elevator went down a floor. They stopped talking and started furiously scrambling in the ambulance. I held my fingers up and crossed my second and third fingers in an X for Pat, which was a sign we had always made for a kiss.

I was taken into the emergency ward at Methodist Hospital. The thought returned to me that when picking up Meals on Wheels, I had recently resolved to stay away. They placed me in a little cubicle where I was hooked up and monitored. As my clothes were cut off, I looked down at my right leg that had a three or four inch injury. It reminded me of ground hamburger. I didn't want to look at the badly hurt left leg. I worried how my face looked. My coat was passed over me, and I saw the gaping holes in the back of the coat. Although I was seriously injured, the coat had saved my life. The bloody shoes, torn pants, and pink sweatshirt were placed into a brown sack. It's an amazing paradox to witness the proof of a savage death you almost experienced yet, at the same time, understand, even as the event happened, that you were not to die. In fact, know you would be in control and find help.

Officer Palmer came to the little cubicle and he quietly asked his questions as if words would hurt me. His hands shook taking notes. The officer wanted to find the dogs and the man. He held up a hammer handle with keys on the end and said it had been found on the path. On television, they were beginning to give bulletins out with the description of the man and the two dogs. The attack had come at the perfect time to make the early evening news. On all channels throughout the evening, they looked for the dogs.

I held Pat's hand in the little cubicle. He never took his

eyes away from my eyes and he provided what people who have been through serious trauma need: loving support. He had left me only to find a doctor after the ambulance arrived. He had also called home and spoken with Matthew.

Matthew had been dropped off at home after school by his brother Benjamin who immediately left for tennis. He came into the empty house—Geneva had gone home—and something didn't feel right. He patted Boomer and Chuck and looked for something to eat. He played music in his room and watched it grow dark. The phone rang. Dad said that Mom had been attacked by dogs on the path where she walked. She was in Methodist Hospital and was going to surgery. He was to tell Benjamin and come to the hospital. He felt confused as if he really didn't understand and went to sit in the den to wait for Ben. Slightly after six when Ben walked past the doorway, Matthew heard himself say, "Mom's been hurt, some dogs attacked her on Fall Creek." Benjamin wasn't sure Matt had the story straight; it sounded so weird that something like this could happen. Ben wanted to see where these dogs had come, and they climbed in his old Cutlass and drove in the darkness over towards Fall Creek. They first saw their father's car where it had slammed to a stop. Ben got out and locked the car. This didn't look like Dad, leaving the car alone and unlocked. They drove about a mile down the road and found their mother's car parked off in the gravel. The cars seemed desolate, abandoned possessions to Ben. Lifeless machines, waiting for their owners who had disappeared.

* * *

The rolling cart took me down the hall to surgery, and I watched the ceiling and felt the cart turn the corners. It was mid-evening. Pat had left and I felt a great loss of security now that he was gone. I waited for the doctor and felt how cold the operating room was and started to shake. Blankets didn't help. It was as if my nervous system had decided to quit. It was extremely important to me to meet the doctor before they put me to sleep. "He'll be here soon," the nurse told me. The doctor came, I touched his arm and tried to tell him the man hadn't meant to hurt me. I don't remember saying anything else, but he smiled, listening to me. Curious, I thought, this is the doctor, but he isn't the doctor. This isn't the one who will be with me. I couldn't think any more; I went to sleep.

Benjamin and Matthew walked into the hospital's new lobby and followed directions through corridors around to the surgery waiting room. They found their father and he explained about the dogs and that their mother was very hurt. It was their father's tears they remembered later, rather than what he was trying to tell them.

In southern Florida, a friend switched on television and heard something about a pit bull attack in Indianapolis. The bulletins describing the dogs had been going out for several hours across local television, and CNN started to broadcast the information. In Indianapolis, reporters started to leave messages on the answering machine at home. A neighbor knocked on a friend's door, "Don't you know her?" she asked as she stepped inside. "I can't believe this could happen to somebody like her. I hope something is left of her face."

Paul Mannweiler watched the screen as the news came on and leaped up turning to his wife Leah, "Did you hear that?" A stranger sat in her office at the Indiana Court of Appeals. She loved dogs, knew the different breeds and their temperaments, and the one thought that kept going through her brain was, "I wonder what she looks like now?"

Benjamin and Matthew found a television set and happened to turn it on as the late evening news started. They saw their mother's blood on the sidewalk and watched police search the path. They saw pieces of the coat and darkness. They changed the channels and watched the story again and again. Benjamin didn't really believe it and tried not to think about it. Matthew was quiet. Someone came to get them;

they were going to the recovery room. They walked with their father, passing other patients. Benjamin saw me first, "She's so white she must be dead." He watched the heart monitor and the oxygen mask and looked at the tubing from the IV. His eyes studied the stitches on my forehead and into my scalp, but it was the hair that bothered him. It wasn't like her hair, matted and tangled in dried blood with a sticky jelly that parted the hair so the scalp could be sewn. Matthew felt his heart pounding and his hands growing clammy. He wanted to leave. Matthew, my sensitive protector, the family's John Wayne, started to faint.

Sometimes the unfolding of a miracle is hard to spot, but that is what was happening that afternoon and evening of November 5, 1992. In a series of conditions, combined with perfect timing, a plan was unfolding with intricacies so detailed that no one could imagine good coming from what people perceived as a personal tragedy.

That first night in the hospital I woke every hour and looked around the room. Despite the mauling, a blood transfusion, and surgery, there was no deep anesthetic sleep.

Towards morning I awoke with a dog leaping into my face, teeth and fur at eye level seen between leathered fingers. It was the only nightmare I would have. I glanced down and noticed a note was on my pillow. The note was from a friend of many years who was a nurse. She was on duty in another part of the hospital, and before going home, she had sat and watched me sleeping. She wrote that somehow I looked so sweet asleep and she would come back later. I felt as if someone was watching through the long night when I could no longer stay awake.

The first day I had energy and could sit up and talk into the early evening. My brain still felt I had to be aware and awake. The room was a busy office as the phone by my bed rang all day, and by late afternoon visitors filled my room, overflowing into the adjoining little hall and sitting room.

They had found the dogs. Late the night before, the

man had turned himself and the dogs in to Animal Control. No one had asked why it had taken so long for him to come forward.

In the early evening the visitors left, and the doctor appeared. He told me it was unfortunate, but he was going to have to leave town and another doctor would take over my care.

That evening I was allowed to die. The death came quietly in the night when the brain shut down and the protective natural endorphins finally stopped. At morning I couldn't lift my head; it seemed to be encased in the pillow. The words were hard for my mouth to form and speak. I could hear but the voices seemed hushed and distant. I understood but couldn't respond, and thinking beyond a few brief thoughts was not possible. Bruises on my face appeared and my eyes had broken red blood vessels. Flowers came into the room and more flowers. A sheet of paper went up on the door for visitors to sign. At around ten o'clock in the morning, my body was placed on a cart and wheeled down to some faraway place in the hospital where the leg would be cleaned. I was propped up in a wheelchair and brought back to where there were steel tubs filling with water. My heavy head bowed, sinking into my neck. I waited.

I first heard the sound of humming coming down the hall towards me. It was a sound I listened to after not being able to process sounds, living in an exhausted shell. Music seemed out of place in a morgue. It was not a tune you would know, more like someone whistling in the night to help them get through the darkness. I never looked up at the doctor, my head weighed too much to lift.

Pat knelt beside the wheelchair and the bandages were unwrapped. The leg was placed in the steel tub and the torn flesh cleaned in the water. The doctor said, "It's like a war wound," and as the leg was handled I began to faint and the wheelchair was tipped backwards. I took some short breaths, and the wheels came back down on the floor. My eyes looked to the side, and I saw the doctor showing me the scar on his leg from a long-ago operation. He began talking to the nurses about a birthday party, his wife's birthday party. I was placed back on the rolling cart and saw Pat looking at me, his brown eyes filled with tears. There was a birthday party and the doctor was telling the nurses. I listened from my anonymity to the story as someone who was far away hearing about living people. He had to be there by noon. I had started to reawaken in the bowels of the hospital hearing about a party. The doctor couldn't dwell too long on me. I felt he couldn't deal with the pain of looking at someone lying in the morgue; he had to sing. However, I knew this was the doctor who for some reason was to be with me, and I never looked at his face.

That afternoon the nurses brought in the first of the papers with my picture. They were like obituaries that had started to be written while I still lived. I didn't read any of the articles. By late afternoon I weakly sat up in bed.

It was in the early evening when I had a growing apprehension that someone was in the bathroom, hiding behind the door. Someone who would kill me, was waiting to kill me. I sat up in bed, staring at the entrance to the room because that is where the killer would come. There was something warm and sticky oozing down my face into my ears and eyes; now down the front of my face onto my neck. The blood had started to run down my face again. This was a wide-awake nightmare. I understood it was due to exhaustion and my unconscious was reliving the trauma. My eyes focused on the door entrance, watching for the killer that reason told me wasn't there, but there was this ooze sliding onto my neck. I was in a battle between irrational terror and holding on to reality. There was that robin I had watched an eternity ago, holding on to the branch in the November rain. His holding power got him through the day and into the night. He was not afraid.

Darkness was making its run towards building hysteria,

but the conscious kept fighting. A nurse entered the room and looked at me; "Are you all right?" she asked.

"I think I need to take something."

"What do you usually take?"

"I don't take anything," I answered. How do you explain there's a killer in the bathroom who is lurking, ready to enter the room, and how did she miss seeing all the blood covering my face? She went to call the doctor to give me "something." The nurse didn't understand what was happening, nor did the doctor. I was given some mild tranquilizer that didn't faze the demon, but the robin was hanging on in the battle. Hour after hour the nurse would check the room to see me sitting straight up in bed, stiff like a ramrod, eyes glued to the entrance of the room. She would watch in silence.

I don't know how people respond who have this experience, if they cry or scream, become demanding, or just sit and stare, waiting for the killer. Maybe stubbornness is the trait that requires you sit and wait in the presence of evil, for there was a battle that evening to make me fearful, to break me, to destroy my hope. I don't know if I was discussed at the nurses' station, but I remained in the thoughts of the nurse checking on me. She was looking for direction and at nine o'clock came into the room. "There's a chaplain in the hall, do you want me to send him in?" The chaplain sat beside the bed and listened as I retold the story.

"The man hadn't meant to hurt me. He pulled the dogs off me." I felt a calming presence for there was no vengeance. The chaplain smiled at me from his chair; and when he left I went to sleep. I slept through the night.

By morning there had been a victory, a victory that came in the night. The hours passed and the waiting killer, the flowing blood, had left in the darkness. They had snaked their way out of the room in retreat. A few times afterwards, I wondered if the nurses could stop someone who might want to harm me, but the wide-awake nightmare never returned.

* * *

Linda Worsham sat reading the paper at her desk. She studied the picture of the woman who had been attacked by the dogs and on impulse stood and pushed her chair away. She walked a few feet into Senator Lugar's state director's office and placed the paper on the desk. "This should never have happened and I can do something about it." Sue Anne Gilroy listened to the aide. Linda had successfully helped legislation through the United States Congress and she knew how to put coalitions together. She also loved animals and despised the humans involved with training and breeding fighting dogs. "I want to put a team together," she said, as she thought of the state house that stood outside the windows. They were exactly two months away from the next general assembly, and this was the time to try for a law to stop these attacks. Sue Anne studied Linda, who certainly had the ability and experience. She would also know the best people to call upon. Caress was a friend and the mauling had been on her mind, perhaps something could be done on her behalf.

Sue Anne made the decision. "I want you to stop what you're doing and go to work on this." Linda turned and left the office; she went back to her desk and picked up the phone.

In Ohio, Sandy Rowland, director of the Great Lakes Regional Office of the Humane Society of the United States, read about the attack in Indianapolis.

It was a serious attack and fortunately there hadn't been a fatality. The H.S.U.S. had been tracking fatal dog attacks in the United States due to a growing concern about vicious dogs in the country. Many dogs were being bred and sold with no thought as to their temperament, and illegal dog fighting was widespread. The fighting breeds had continued to become more popular among owners who couldn't or wouldn't handle them responsibly. There were a half million to a million dog bites reported in the United States every year, but there was no nationwide tracking system in place.

She placed the name of the man who owned the dogs in

the computer and looked through the files. There was no doubt in her mind the man was a dogfighter. The description of the attack sounded too much like a fighting dog. "Game" was the fighting term of a dog with unusually strong jaws and deep biting capability. A game dog could shake its opponent violently when a bite hold was secured. This victim's leg had deeply severed skin and tissues that formed a circle around her leg known to fighters as a ringing. The problem was he probably traded and fought animals under an alias. A dog with the same name, Turbo, appeared in the *Sporting Dog Journal,* a seedy publication out of Georgia that featured game dogs. Run off in a house, it came through the mail, illegally, in anonymous wrappers. This was the new Christmas issue, and scenes of angels and the Nativity were featured above the pictures of fighting dogs. The dog's bloodlines were printed, and if they had won five matches they were named Grand Champions. Their subscribers and advertisers were "fanciers" as they referred to themselves. They appreciated a good fighting dog and they loved the violence.

She had been on the phone asking Animal Control in Indianapolis for help. It was not a city known for being very progressive on animal issues. Indiana had experienced a fatality, a child had been ripped to shreds by dogs, and many others seriously injured, but that state hadn't really been interested in doing anything. What would it take? In Ohio, it had taken the death of the doctor. He was the former chief of staff of Dayton's St. Elizabeth Medical Center and former chief of surgery at the Veterans Administration Hospital. He had been attacked by two pit bulls and had tried to climb to safety on top of a parked car. The dogs pulled him from the car, tearing his clothes. He screamed for someone to help him while he was severely mauled on both legs and his right arm. The dogs' owner appeared and stopped the attack too late. The doctor died in surgery three hours later. The car where he was mauled was covered with so much blood that the fire department had to hose it down. His death was a national news story, and although people had died in Ohio before, there was no doubt the doctor's death pressured the legislature to pass one of the toughest vicious dog laws in the country.

She wondered what the woman in Indiana looked like now. Her files were filled with pictures of people who would never be the same, ears torn off, muscles ripped from arms and legs, jagged scars, missing fingers. She pressed the computer keys, knowing he was here somewhere, hiding behind some post office box or working with some other fighter. I want to nail this man, she thought.

Sandy had a record of success. Only recently, she had been a part of one of the biggest and most successful dog-fighting raids in the country. They had been lucky. A woman, a dogfighter's wife, had called. "I can't stand it any more," she said, telling them the fight would take place in Saginaw, Michigan, with fighters from many states. It would be a "convention": the term used for a major fight. She was finished with it, the drugs and guns that were exchanged, the heavy gambling, dogs ripping into one another. Her story was told at considerable risk to herself because fights are highly secretive and dangerous.

Weeks of effort had gone into the raid, and it had taken fifty law enforcement officers, working with Humane Society agents, to ensnare the participants. They had been successful despite the fact that fighters and spectators were given different locations where they were met by the promoter of the fight. They then were taken in secrecy, a few cars at a time, to a checkpoint where the passengers were identified. The participants traveled on to the pits where a lookout waited to see that no one followed. The promoter for the fight in Saginaw was a man who had trained pit bulls for drug dealers. This was different. This was fun, real sport, for him and he would make money. He was pleased with the crowd as he picked up the admission fees.

Women and children were allowed into the "show" free of charge. This was a family sport, all ages came, the tradition handed down from one generation to another. There was the young honeymoon couple who had traveled from Maine and the pregnant women whose voices became shrill as their favorites did combat. It was a bi-racial fraternity of people who never trusted one another. There was the tub of milk used to bathe the dogs before the match. Each dogfighter had a trusted second making sure poison was washed from the dog's coat. Then the dogs were placed on scales to check the weight of the animal. There were breaking sticks close by the pit used to pry the jaws open, the video cameras lined up to film the match, and trophies were ready for best game dog.

The fight had begun that day with the words, "Face your dogs," then "Release," as the handlers let their dogs "scratch" or rush into the pit. The animals used their weight, leverage, and bite holds trying to win, each grabbing the nose or an ear of the other dog. The crowd loved the nose bites because you could hear the crushing of the cartilage. The dogs, dehydrated before the match to lessen bleeding, became heavy bleeders when a vein or artery would rupture in combat. Once they were "fanged" trying to get a firm bite hold, piercing their own mouths with their teeth, the fight was stopped while the handlers yanked the teeth free.

The dogs fought for the best hold before one became too bloodied and "turned" his head and shoulders away from his opponent. The handlers quickly washed off the saliva and blood of both dogs. The excited crowd timed the fifteen seconds before the gladiators were again released. The dog who "turned" was set free first and had ten seconds to attack or lose. He attacked—this would be a good fight, hopefully lasting a couple of hours. There was pride in the pits among the handlers that day as the dogs fought. There would be no fighting to a draw, that was too unpopular, too much money had gone down in bets. Nothing humiliated a good dog man more than having his dog quit on him in a fight. He lost reputation, his sense of prestige with the other fighters. It would be better to "pick the dog up" and concede. Almost anything was better than owning a coward.

The promoters and those guarding the checkpoints had been outwitted that day by agents who would surprise the frenzied crowd in the packed barn who were screaming at the torn dogs' flesh and blood. The Michigan State Police were surprised by the number of weapons they confiscated along with the drugs. The betting had been so heavy, one man had a hundred thousand dollars in his pocket.

Law enforcement agents arrested twenty-three men and women on felony and misdemeanor charges that day. They tried to run as the agents moved into the barn but were caught. The dogs had been injured and were confiscated. The pit had collapsed with its flooring of indoor outdoor carpeting and wooden sides. Bleachers, built for the occasion, had also collapsed, injuring some of the fans.

Sandy remembered pit bulls held in confinement that were given bowling balls to hold in their jaws. They played with bowling balls like other dogs played with rubber toys. She received another fax and noticed this woman in Indianapolis was getting a lot of attention from the media. Good, she thought, Maybe something will come from it. She hadn't been killed—but something was working in Indianapolis. She felt encouraged.

* * *

The second surgery had ended and the doctor stood over me. "I have some good news and some bad news. The good news is I got one side of the leg closed. The bad news is I couldn't close the other side." He was irritated—I wondered what I had done wrong. I heard him say to Pat, "It would have been catastrophic." I really hadn't thought about my leg, and now I was sick through the afternoon from the anesthesia.

In late afternoon Pat would read to me the cards and notes people were writing. I was beginning to realize the deep impact my attack had made on people. The cards came from the poor, the affluent, city leaders, children, those who had suffered with great tragedy, churches, civic organizations, people who had always known me, people who knew me vaguely, people who had never met me. There was some universal element that spoke to people. I was honored by people I knew and loved and many more I will never meet who so deeply and movingly wanted me to know they cared. I had died, yet I lived, and was given the privilege of hearing the intimate notes that usually only the family of the deceased reads. There were letters from people whose families had suffered great personal tragedies and others whose nightmare I had lived. People were frightened and appalled, they were grief-stricken, they were furious. Others lived the emotions, for I was dead. I felt no pain.

The nurse came into the room to wash my hair. I remember being on my back in bed and being draped with a covering. There was this strange sensation of water pouring over my head while I lay still. I remember that the water being taken away looked dirty and brown because of the dried blood being washed from my hair. I still felt very weak, and it came to me slowly that this was how they washed a corpse's hair. It was the only time I remember tears coming down my cheeks, and I couldn't wipe the tears away because my arms were covered. It took so much water, and for the longest time the water continued to pass by the bedside, brown.

I could sit up and stay awake for very short periods during the day. A close friend sat by my bedside. Kathy came every day for several hours to relieve Pat while he checked on business. Sometimes I would open my eyes and she would be reading, sometimes gently sleeping, sitting in the chair. There was always the most wonderful sense of peace and protection as she sat in the chair. Even when her eyes were closed, I felt deeply that I was dearly watched over.

The flowers continued to arrive, surrounding me, spilling into the hall and the other room. After his accident during the 500-mile race, Mario Andretti was in the same room. The nurses would tell me, "You've gotten more flowers than Mario Andretti!" Sometimes there are no words to explain your feelings. You cannot for you are only an observer. I was a silent witness to the love and care of many people. I was gone, removed as someone who had already left the imperfect world for the perfect one.

Pat greeted the visitors in the hall as they came with their flowers and concern. The nurses stood guard at their station.

Then Sarah came. She was one of the few people who entered into the room. Sarah, my most prayerful friend, the one with the "direct line," sat next to me, close to my head, and held my hand. Kathy, the close friend who stood guard during the day, listened as Sarah spoke softly but urgently to me. "Caress, I had a dream the evening of the day you were attacked. I saw it in a dream, I saw everything that happened. You know how you never wear slacks, you were wearing slacks, and you were all in pink. I saw what you did with your hands. I saw everything and I had the dream all through the night."

I listened, my head on the pillow, and answered, "Oh, Sarah, it's something you saw on television."

"No, I had the dream before I saw anything on television and when I did see television the following day it was on the little black and white set in the bedroom.

"Caress, I know what you are to do, for the children, for the babies. You're to help, you're to make it safer." Sarah held my hand and I understood she was right. I didn't move, I couldn't think, I couldn't get out of bed, I only lay still, molded in the sheets. Sarah said, "Caress, you have to get well now, get well first." I had heard the truth, absolute truth, and when it was spoken, from deep inside me came the knowledge that she was absolutely correct.

* * *

The phone kept ringing at home, and the two lone soldiers spoke to the press. Matthew was asked about the different organizations his mother belonged to, and he couldn't remember. He had gone to school and there were prayers for his mother in different classes. He answered questions all day long about what had happened, what would happen to the dogs, the man, how was his mother? He hated every minute because he could no longer be like everyone else. He wanted her to come home and for this to end. He called the hospital and in a pleading voice would ask, "When are you coming home?" Benjamin was answering questions too, speaking to people on the phone every day after school before driving his brother to the hospital. He tried to be the brother who answered the phone.

They watched the nightly news that carried stories about the dogs being held at Animal Control. They had to be held for ten days to check for disease. There was a $12.50 leash law violation. The prosecutor was looking through state law to see if any other charges could be filed. Matthew, one evening, ordered everyone out of his mother's hospital room. He closed the door and sat close to the bed, "This should have happened to me," he said, "This should have happened to me."

The Good Samaritan came to visit, the driver of the little red car who thought I was a Halloween leftover. His name is Ron Lucas, and he had been to the grocery store and was going home as he drove down the road and found me. He brought a rose and said he just wanted to see me again. Ron was the first of several of the men who surrounded me that November day who would call and had kept me in their hearts.

The November weather continued to be gloom and rain.

I could see out the window, but the weather didn't bother me. It seemed to be a part of another world. I could sit up in bed now during the day but could only concentrate for short periods of time. Once, I was taken down to the solarium at the end of the hall, but after ten minutes I couldn't sit up any more. The television wasn't turned on because I didn't want to hear about myself.

The phone had been turned off by my bed and rang in the other room. The Marion County Prosecutor's office called and said that the dogs could be held until trial. Very worried, I shared a universal feeling of terror that survivors of dog attacks understand. What would happen to the dogs? They were killers! This must not happen to anyone else. In my public effort during the next several months to have the animals humanely destroyed, I never met a single dog trainer, veterinarian, animal control officer, or anyone connected with the Humane Society of the United States that didn't believe the dogs should be destroyed.

There was one problem. The owner wanted his dogs back, and in the United States of America dogs are considered personal property. In this country you can't take someone's property away from him easily, even if the property includes killers. The animals themselves had received a great deal of media attention, so in my case the prosecutor ordered the dogs held until trial. This is usually never the case. Sometimes, even in unprovoked attacks where serious bodily injury has occurred, the dog is quarantined with its owner.

The prosecutor hadn't decided what should be the dog's fate; that would eventually be up to a judge. The owner could be charged with having unimmunized dogs, which carried a one thousand dollar fine. Other than that, there was no law that had been broken. Even if I had been killed or the infant in his stroller had been killed, only a $12.50 leash law fine applied. The Humane Society of the United States was telling the prosecutor the man was very likely a dogfighter given the type of dogs, the nature of the attack, the described behavior of the dogs. Dogfighting is a felony in Indiana, but because of the secrecy involved, very hard to prove in court. Dogfighting has been prosecuted only recently in this state.

The man came to the hospital and wanted to see me. Even though I never thought he intentionally meant to hurt me, it scared me that he was in the hall. He later called the hospital and spoke to Pat. He had worked in construction and laid the path along Fall Creek only a short time ago. He had always taken his dogs to run and swim in Fall Creek; it was the same that day except the dogs were chasing squirrels. The man told Pat he had no idea why the dogs attacked me. They had never done anything like that before. He had never wanted anyone to be hurt and when the mauling began he started to run. He said to Pat over the phone, "My legs still hurt from running." I never thought much or felt any emotion about the man, only that he was a minor player in the drama unfolding. Much later I realized he had chosen to become immune to the difference between right and wrong. He was not able to comprehend that his dogs, through the breeding he sought and training that he contributed to, were made evil. He was the prime participant, and both the animals and I were victims of that evil. Although he knew the injuries were senseless, and bad luck that someone had gotten hurt, it wouldn't change him.

* * *

I never thought about my leg; it simply didn't worry me. The problem was I couldn't put any pressure on the leg and had to make exhausted hops and clutches from doorframe to bedpost to get to the bathroom. However, that was an improvement from not being able to move in the bed, and I remained in no pain. This worried the nurses. They would tell me, "It's very admirable that you don't take the medicine, but it's not good to remain in pain and it's not a heavy medication anyway."

I would tell them I didn't need to take anything. They changed the bandages frequently, for the wound continued to be bloody and needed to be cleansed. In a dog bite, the wound is left opened to drain before it is closed. My legs were elevated in bed to keep the swelling down before the doctor tried to close the wound again. The doctor and the trauma nurse wanted me to look at the wounds on my leg before I left the hospital. I said that I would but I wasn't going to look until the last surgery was finished.

The third surgery was coming as the days in the hospital continued. I had received notes from the second graders at school #27. They had drawn pictures of me in the hospital and told me to get well. One note said, "Dear Mrs. Garten, Please get well and take your pills."

Another second grader wrote, "I hope you will come and read stories to us again and play bingo. If a pit bull tries to bite you again kick it in the mouth and run. My progress report was real good. When you come back to our class we will take care of you. Love, Jazmine."

"Dear Mrs. Garten, The next time a bad dog tries to bite you say, 'NO!' then go stop a car and have them take you right home. Your friend who loves you, Charles."

"Dear Mrs. Garten, When you come back we will have treats for you and love you. I got an A in spelling. Billy."

My seven-year-old friends were thinking about me, and so were the teenagers that played basketball in the driveway. They would be allowed in the room when Benjamin and Matthew would come and visit at the end of the day. They would sit on the floor and ask me how I was and what they could do for me. My teenage friends came every day.

My doctor would come in the mornings to change the bandages. He didn't sing anymore but he was funny. He would sometimes explain that he didn't believe in being too serious in an already bad situation. He also couldn't deal well with being too serious, so he tried to make himself happy as well. He liked to dance around the bed, but his hands were steady when he took out the stitches in my forehead. He had a one-man-campaign going on in Methodist Hospital to stop waste. Every time the nurses would want to pitch the Ace bandages taken from around my leg, the doctor would remind them they were perfectly good Ace bandages, and she would need a lot of them when she went home. He was right, and my stockpile of dirty Ace bandages grew. The doctor was sensitive and he thought about my legs and told me one morning after undoing the bandages, "Pretty legs, pretty legs again, with scars," he added. I hadn't thought about a pretty leg or a leg at all, but his sweetness made me think. He said, "If you say your prayers, I may be able to get that closed without a skin graft." The doctor said this as a hopeful remark more than relying deeply on God.

This was the first I had heard about a skin graft, and I immediately knew I didn't want one and I said so. The day before surgery, I told the doctor I had been saying my prayers. A frown crossed his face as he left the room. He was a gifted surgeon. He wanted to, and would, do the best job he could, but he mistakenly thought it was all in his hands. There is a story in Christianity about a doctor, whose name was Luke, who became a follower, a servant, to the Perfect Healer, so twenty centuries later many miracles are worked through medicine. Luke, the physician, wrote of the scene in the Garden of Gethsemane when the Romans came for Jesus. The disciple Peter, who had been asleep in the garden, awakened when the Roman guards arrived and he had picked up his sword and swung and slashed at the captors, slicing off the ear of a slave. With great grace the Perfect Healer bent down and found the ear in the darkness and reattached it to the head of Malchus, the slave. No sutures, no anesthesia, no scars, no hearing loss, no reconstructive surgery, just perfection and grace.

Luke understood that night in the garden, in ways other disciples would not, that there was no longer any room for pride or despair in his work, that his successes and failures as a physician would be done through Another and never again would be his alone. The doctor closed the wound and he drew a happy face on my hip where the skin graft hadn't been necessary.

Looking at the injury for the first time the next day, I felt little emotion gazing down at what looked like violin strings holding the wound together with little bumper pads inserted around the strings. The doctor asked if I wanted to go home. Glancing around the room that had held my body and where the mourners had come, I answered, "Yes."

"I'll miss you," I said to the doctor with a smile.

He answered, "I'll miss you too."

THREE

Eagle

The farmhouse lay quiet in the gray light of morning as the children rose from their beds to tiptoe over cracking floorboards to reach the heavy front door. Ever so carefully and quietly they had inched the door towards them just open enough for the two little boys to leave their sleeping parents and head into the foothills. They had climbed through the morning to find her nest and the eggs that were nestled between the twigs and small stones on the ledge that protruded over the hillside. The mother eagle circled in the sky as each child grabbed an egg and cradled the stolen goods in cupped hands as they made their way down the slippery hillsides, over rocks, and through the flowered meadows back home to the familiar farmhouse. There they had gone around towards the barn and opened the wire door to the chicken coop, depositing the eggs. Their mother's anxious voice called, "Where were you?" as they ran towards her arms.

It was almost noon when the hen placed herself on the orphaned eggs and several days before the first pecks were heard, the old shells crumbled, and the hatchlings wobbled and fell in the barnyard.

Their early weeks were spent scratching in the dusty earth with the chickens, so they didn't notice the swiftly moving shadow that flew overhead, encircling the barnyard. Weeks passed and as they grew into young eagles, they felt a stirring deep inside them as they moved their wings. They began to realize their destiny, that they were not of the barnyard, and would be leaving. Perhaps they felt momentary confusion and fear, a loss of stability, for they didn't know where they were going, where they would land, but there was no choice, they were to leave. The children watched, and as the powerful wings moved back and forth with great symmetry, the eagles lifted from the barnyard into the heavens.

* * *

The marble lobby was empty as my wheelchair was pushed through the doors into the light. The first day of bright sunlight in over two weeks, it was Sunday. The streets were empty, no one walked the sidewalks. The buildings, the pavement, the passing cars, were crisp and clean in the light, reflecting upwards into a solid blue sky. The day seemed different and dazzling to someone who had been in a protective womb of brick and steel. It was as if I had never seen the streets or the sky. We drove home and I came hopping on one leg, clinging to the red bricks, through the back door into the kitchen. Could I really live here? Everything seemed so new in the kitchen, and there were trays of food that had been placed along the side counter. There was a walker in the kitchen, and I wrapped my hands around the handles and started down the long hall, glancing in the den, slowly lifting the walker until I reached the living room. The room was filled with flowers as was the sun porch. My eyes became transfixed looking into the rooms from the perimeter of the hall. I didn't take the walker any farther; the energy didn't last very long.

Pat changed the bandages on my leg for the first time while I lay on the bed upstairs, my hands over my face. He was such a good caregiver, morning and evening, replacing the bloody bandages, always sweet, always encouraging. He could wrap an Ace bandage with precision over the other gauze bandages, beginning with the foot, wrapping up around the leg. He would sit in the bedroom and wait in the evenings while I accomplished the impossible of taking a bath and not looking at my leg. It stayed propped up against the tiles at the front of the tub, carefully out of the bath water where my eyes never focused. I intended to ignore my leg, which had a grotesque, gaping wound that curved inwards toward the bone. There were deep incisions that almost circled the calf, creating long, deep indentations. I thought that if I really looked for any length of time, my leg would somehow capture me, drag me down, making me unable to concentrate on anything else.

It used to be so simple taking a bath. Now I saw the reflection of my face with the red scars on my forehead in the bathroom mirror and wondered if the scar in the middle of the forehead would stay lumpy. I remembered Donald's scar.

During the following week I watched everyone prepare to leave for the day as I stood behind the walker. They had a system down and working. One would pour cereal, the other orange juice, Boomer and Chuck would be let outside and then in again. Kissing me good-bye, Benjamin and Matthew went out the door to school and Pat to work. The house would then be still as I moved the walker down the hall towards the den to sit in the big, soft chair. I kept the phone on the floor next to me with the answering machine set for four rings before the recording started. Sitting in the big chair, I started to write notes to the friends and strangers who had remembered me. There were around a hundred to write while I watched the last of the leaves fall from the pin oaks only to be blown up again by gusts of wind against the den's bay window. Sunday had been beautiful and blue, but my first week home had been windy and gray. Chuck came quietly down the hall and hesitantly stuck his head around the entrance to the den; he wasn't allowed to come into this room. "Come here, Chuckie," I whispered to him, and a delighted Chuck came right over, spending the day, asleep, stretched out on the Oriental rug right next to the big chair.

The phone was ringing and ringing and ringing. There should have been a recording I could have played telling everyone that I had always felt watched over and had known during the attack that I would be all right. No, I wasn't terrified and I felt no pain. I would go through the mauling, the injuries. So many of them needed to tell me where they were and how they felt when they heard of the attack. I had always thought before that people just remembered where they were when Pearl Harbor was attacked or President Kennedy was assassinated, but now it was also, "when the dogs got Caress."

There are probably many unconscious reasons for this. Certainly one factor was that the Humane Society of the United States estimates one in fifty Americans are bitten by a dog every year. The vast majority of the almost fifty million dogs in the country never bite anyone. However, I was finding something universal even among the greatest dog lovers, that there was, on varying levels, fear. "Caress, I almost died when I found out it was you; I saw your blood, I thought of your face. This sounds ridiculous, but all I could think of was I hope she still has her eyes and her eyebrows."

The phone rang again. "All I could think of was your face, Caress, your face," another female caller told me. I was discussed by people, many of whom had never met or seen me. The thought of my having a severe facial injury deeply distressed others, particularly women.

Men and women, friends and strangers, wanted to talk to me, and I listened as the answering machine recorded phone call after phone call when I was too tired to talk.

I could write notes for a couple of hours and then would feel exhausted and stare out the windows in the den. With exhaustion would come a sensation of danger lurking outside; the fortress on the hill protected me, but the day would seem gloomier and there would be a sinister sound in the wind. When I was stronger and exhaustion came less quickly, I knew the danger would fade. Some moments I wondered how would I change anything? I couldn't walk very well or think for very long. However, there was a penetrating confidence, deep and undeniable, that through me, the plan would unfold. No matter how frightened, and sometimes I felt very frightened, there was a trust that would always be affirmed, stronger than the fears, growing with me daily, never leaving.

The outcome of this trust was prophesied centuries ago by a good man named Isaiah. I am sure that while sitting in my Episcopal church, if I had heard this passage from the Old Testament in a sermon, it would not have meant a great deal to me. I would have listened, but then the Old Testament was so long ago and I only vaguely knew who Isaiah was anyway. What struck me now was what Isaiah said: "But those who hope in the Lord will renew their strength. They will soar on wings like eagles; they will run and not grow weary, they will walk and not be faint." It was a promise that he was to record so thousands of years later I would sit with a tape recorder and cellular phone, relating to this man across the ages.

There was only one part of the plan I understood and that was to keep the story alive. I would talk to anyone in the press when they would call. Many of them had been to the path along Fall Creek after I had left in the ambulance. They all felt they knew me in a way and would share with me their feelings about their own children, their dogs, my well-being. One reporter told me he had been moved by Officer Palmer. "Caress," he said, "it's so unusual to see a law enforcement officer visibly upset. It's not that they don't care, they just see so much. We all want to know how you got up the hill on that leg? People want to know how you are." I would tell them I was on a walker, doing better.

"No, I'm not in pain," I would repeat. I would talk to

them about the mauling, the baby I had passed. I tried to explain my feelings, that I had a role to play. "No, I don't think about the dogs' owner and I don't want to sue him." It slowly dawned on me that in my conversations with these men and women they were really listening to me. I believe when the press realized I felt no vengeance and I deeply believed there was a mission for me to accomplish that those feelings alone seemed to make me different. The basic facts would appear in the paper and on television as to how I was getting along, but something else was happening. The people in the media wanted to help me, and somehow, some way, they had come to like me.

I was clumping towards the den on the walker when the phone rang. A protective Chuck was in the way, too close to the walker's legs. I had a funny feeling about this phone call, and as the first ring ended I tried to pick up the pace of the walker. The second ring started; there were two more rings before the recorder would answer. Get the phone, my brain commanded. I fell to my knees, dropping the coffee cup I was carrying, and crawled like a combat veteran, grabbing the phone on the fourth ring. It was the Associated Press, and the reporter wanted me to tell him my story. He wanted to know my memories about the mauling and to include the point that I didn't dislike or fear dogs. The story, which was printed throughout the state of Indiana and surrounding states, laid an important foundation. It was a very personal newspaper story, and strangers across the state began to feel as if they knew me. Animal lovers understood I was not on a vendetta to punish people's pets.

At the end of this first week at home I began trying to reach Paul Mannweiler. In addition to being a friend, he was also my representative at the state house and the one to reach if I should try for a law. When Paul's deep voice came over the phone, I began telling him the story of the mauling, the feeling that I would find help. I wondered if he remembered my talk to him about the path last October. He remembered and I told him, "If you had gone jogging and Steven had followed you…," I paused, remembering the child's blond head bobbing up and down as he stood peddling his bike; Paul in shorts and Tee-shirt jogging in front, "and these dogs had appeared, grabbing Steven's legs, there would have been nothing you could have done to save him. Had you clubbed them, kicked them, it wouldn't have helped; only something to pry their jaws apart, or a gun." I remembered the coat being handed over me in the emergency room and the gaping hole in back. I thought of Paul's back clad only in a Tee-shirt as he would have stopped and turned to save his son. I finished my story with, "Had they killed Steven, you, me, or the baby I passed, the penalty would have been a $12.50 leash law violation."

"There was a dog law introduced, but I can't remember why it was defeated," he said thoughtfully.

"Paul, I want to change the law," I told him flatly.

My tired mind had made the statement not knowing what this bill would say or having any clue as to the pitfalls in writing legislation.

"Caress, let me ask Legislative Services what's on the books and also what other states have done."

"Paul, how does it work?" It was an innocent question, an earnest question, to me a plausible question. I can only remember silence, dead silence, because he was speechless. If I had asked a heart surgeon, "How do you do a triple bypass?" I would have received, maybe not a complicated answer, but some procedural explanation. Try asking a politician to explain how you get legislation through a state house or the nation's Capitol.

The Indiana State House has a little map of how a bill becomes law that is passed out to the thousands of school children who pull up in the yellow buses from across the state to see government in action. The map stars a round-eyed, happy-faced bill. The walking piece of legislation wears shoes and marches from different committees, through the

House and Senate, right up to the governor's office to become a law for citizens in the state of Indiana. Easy to explain, except that's not how it works, not really.

So, my friend, Paul Mannweiler, the minority leader of the Indiana House of Representatives and former Speaker of the House, who sincerely wanted to help me, mumbled something like, "I will call you, Caress." It was now the last week in November.

* * *

I was moving around the house on two walkers, one upstairs, and the other downstairs. Upstairs, I would clump along to the landing, crawl to the first downward step, sit with my legs in front of me, and go down the stairs one by one as a toddler, unsure of her footing. I would go up the stairs at night the same way only backwards. There would be a thump, thump on each step and I would hear Pat laugh and say, "I think I hear Lurch coming."

I needed to hear his laughter, for my prayers would fade midway through saying them, I would feel so exhausted some days. The mornings and the evenings melted together. Pat would hold me in the big chair in the evenings, kissing the scars on my forehead and changing the bandage on my leg.

Benjamin and Matthew were tired of casseroles for dinner that the good friends kept bringing. Matthew's mother was home but she wasn't home, and he missed her not being able to be like herself. The newspapers were still writing stories, the florist came daily, and everyone at school still asked him for updates. He just hated the fact he could no longer melt into the walls of the high school because his mother was a celebrity.

It was hard for the family to understand that I never thought about the dogs' owner. There was a much bigger picture to focus on, and when they felt anger, or hatred, it was very hard on me.

In the last days of November my leg was slowly able to bear more weight without the walker. Many people still called throughout the day. Afterwards my tired brain couldn't think through any more plans of action. Everything I knew to do was already being done. My thinking resembled the grogginess of someone who was awakening after a deep sleep. Moments would come where everything seemed clear, then the haze would return. The sensation of urgency was returning to me.

The feeling was as if you were crawling into bed with the flu, nauseated, weak, and on an impulse raised your head, eyes glancing across the room, through the window, across the lawn, where there seems to be a moving piece of color at the end of the driveway. Your nausea is forgotten, your eyes focus, you watch a toddler walk into the street, the busy street, a street where cars seem to fly down as they round a blind curve. The child stops and sits down on the asphalt. You tear down the hall, the stairs, people try to grab your arm. "You're too sick, you can't go outside." The doorknob turns, you're running down the driveway, you see the baby, he looks at his hands, then turns his head towards you. You hear the traffic approaching the curve, your feet hit the earth, lungs suck in air. The vision ends, the baby fades, the feeling subsides.

* * *

Late November and it was the first time I had been out of the house. A friend was driving me to the doctor. I calmly looked over to where my car had been parked the day of the attack as we traveled over Fall Creek.

I clumped into one of the examining rooms. My doctor had waved at me across the room as I came in to his area. "There she is," he said, walking in to see me. "How have you been?" he asked, looking at the walker and glancing back at me.

"I've been doing all right," I said quietly to him. "Pretty

much home alone." There must have been a trace of sadness in my voice, for he was a sensitive person and his shoulders fell. I was tired that day in the little examining room but glad to see him. He took out the stitches on one side of the leg and left to find the original doctor. "Will you come back?" I asked him.

"Oh, you bet I will," he said. My first doctor broke into a big smile when he saw my leg. The work had been well done.

He was a man in a hurry to return to his side of the building, but stopped on his way out of the little cubicle. "I saw the Associated Press story while I was up in Gary," a northern Indiana city close to Chicago. He had also heard the discussion in the press for a pit bull ban in the state. "You don't want to get rid of all the pit bulls because there are some good pit bulls," he told me with certainty. "And— if two poodles had attacked you, nobody would really care." I didn't say anything and he left the room. My doctor stood quietly, looking down at the floor.

My first doctor was a talented surgeon and he ran the operation at his center, but he didn't know much about dogs or how to talk to me. Some who own the mixed breed called pit bull do feel they own a good dog, but a pit bull's jaw strength and the amount of damage they can inflict makes them as different from other dogs as their genetic makeup does. There have been pit bull owners whose dogs never hurt anyone, and other owners who thought they had a good dog until the dog turned and mauled a family member. I didn't know what my goal was at this point, but it was not a war against pit bulls.

The time with the doctor was the only place I spent time looking at the wound. I looked better to him, some of my coloring had come back, all the dried blood was gone from my hair. I felt if I could keep coming back, I would somehow be all right for another week.

There was something else about coming back I could not even begin to explain, but it was similar to my assuredness about keeping the story alive with the press. I had to come back for my doctor who joked and showed me once again the long scar on his leg. There was something about him that made me certain he was to hear my story and to learn.

It was not quite a week later when the phone rang in the morning. "Caress, my name is Linda Worsham with Senator Lugar's office. I've been working for some weeks, since you were attacked, on a plan. A plan to pass a vicious dog law in the state of Indiana. I would like to drop a copy of the packet I've put together for you to read. I'll place it in your mailbox so not to disturb you. I hope I get to meet you sometime." She didn't explain very much about herself, but her voice stayed with me throughout the day. I was amazed by the phone call. Here was a woman who did not know me but had felt this closeness to me and had worked on my behalf. She did not know Paul or that I had gone to him for help. Paul had to start from ground zero because he had no expertise with legislation dealing with animals. Sitting in my chair, day after day, I asked God if He really wanted me to serve Him in this mission. He had to show me, for I was weak. He knew I couldn't walk and I couldn't think very well and my time was filled with the hundreds of people who wanted to talk to me.

The upstairs and downstairs walkers had been returned to the rental store. Finally, I was able to place enough weight on the ball of my foot to hobble a few places. That same afternoon I watched my doctor take out the stitches where the greatest injury had taken place. The jagged tear was still wide open even after the stitches came out and was bound back up with gauze and the Ace bandage to keep pressure on the scars and the healing open wound. Wounds to the lower leg take longer to heal because the blood circulation is not as great. The doctor talked about scars and how they changed over time. He wanted me to come back in a week to check the open wound. I was glad he wanted me back the next week.

There was a large white envelope waiting in the mailbox

at home. I went inside and placed the envelope on the breakfast room table, then hobbled down the hall to the den. Too tired to read anything, I couldn't seem to remember much about what the doctor had just told me. I listened to the answering machine and stared out the windows, watching the afternoon pass.

November was over; it was now the first of December. The next morning the white envelope on the table appeared in my peripheral vision as I passed the breakfast room. It was there waiting for me to read. The envelope was heavy as I opened the seal and pulled the papers out.

The wondrous stranger had done a great deal of research. Her card was stapled to the first page with her phone number at the senator's office. I glanced through the pages and realized the last eight or ten pages dealt only with me and my attack.

Newspaper articles and more newspaper articles that I had never read and continued to think of as obituaries. I decided to read the other material, not looking at the stories about me.

She had pulled the most useful information together quoting Dr. Randall Lockwood, a nationally recognized animal behaviorist and the leading expert on vicious dog attacks in the United States. Her research showed that the United States was in the process of recognizing that our laws pertaining to dangerous dogs, inherited from centuries old English common law, no longer adequately protected people. Now, throughout our country there were serious problems with the owners of dangerous dogs because many dogs were bred and sold with no regard for their temperament. Dogfighting remained widespread in the United States and the fighting breeds, including but not limited to pit bull type dogs, had become increasingly popular. Indiana, the information stated, needed a law that would place the burden on the irresponsible owner who was usually the direct or indirect cause of dangerous incidents. The most brutal attacks in Indiana had been from pit bull types: Rottweilers, boxers.

Most of these dogs had been bred or trained to kill and were considered lethal weapons. Many of the pit bull types and Rottweilers were used in the drug trade.

I felt someone was explaining the background of my own attack to me and the psychological profile of the human being involved. Only a few short weeks since the attack, and I was given information that many people, even if they survive a serious mauling, never learn. I turned the pages, and my eyes fell on some material labeled "victim profile." Looking down at the page, a bolt went through me. Before my eyes, there it was, provided for me in black and white. Children, the script read, are the principal victims of dog attacks. I reread the line. Children are the principal victims of dog attacks with the greatest risk to children between the ages of five and nine. Children, because of their size, are more likely to be bitten on the face than the leg. The American Medical Association estimated that 44,000 children a year receive facial injuries from dogs with 16,000 of these injuries severe. There was a closing sentence. In the United States the vast majority of fatalities in dog-related deaths are children.

I sat very still in the breakfast room, overwhelmed. For the last twenty years of my life I had been asking what was I to do for children? Not the teacher, not the medical caregiver, not the social worker, not the lawyer. The answer had been given, my beloved second graders, my favorites, the seven year olds, were in the highest risk group. There had been the baby in his stroller on the path who had been shown to me, but now there was no question about my role. I didn't understand how it would be accomplished, but I began to realize that for most of my life I had been in preparation. I had been chosen for this role on behalf of children in Indiana, and with this understanding came the knowledge that my every gift would be used to fulfill this deep inner longing.

* * *

A television truck pulled up outside the man's house, and the reporter stepped out onto the sidewalk. It was a pleasant enough neighborhood, he thought, with small well-kept homes. There had been other members of the press at the initial hearing that morning down at the city county building, but he was the only one who had gotten an interview with the man as he left the courtroom. "Do you want your pit bulls back?" he had asked the man.

"Yes," the man had answered. "I want my dogs back." The most serious charge against him was that his dogs were unimmunized, which in the state of Indiana is a misdemeanor. There is a one thousand dollar fine per dog. The county prosecutor had waited for the report from Animal Control before he had stated there would be no serious charges. Criminal recklessness could not be charged because, according to the report, there was no reported history of violence with these dogs. He could only bring charges if there was evidence.

The reporter was walking toward the house when his eye caught something and he went around towards the backyard. Cages, dog cages for transport. He went to the front door and the man appeared. "Get off my property! Get out!" he yelled at the reporters. The reporter saw more paraphernalia around the yard. There was no doubt the man was a dogfighter. The reporter sat in the television van and thought the man probably had a lot of dogs, moving them in and out with a partner somewhere else in the city. The situation was frustrating, infuriating, and he wondered why Animal Control, when they had collected the dogs, hadn't been looking for the signs of a dogfighter. However, today he had gotten the earlier interview with the man; now he would try and call the victim.

"Would you let us come over and interview you for the evening news?" The reporter was courteous. "It would be a much better story if you would respond to the man leaving court, and something else—people really want to know what you look like. How you are."

This, I knew, was absolutely true. Up to now I had been talking on the phone to reporters, and it worried me a little going on television because I still felt weak, and this was stepping out a little further. "Don't feel any pressure," he added. "But this man does want his dogs." The moment I hung the phone up I knew the march, the mission, had started in earnest.

The television lights went on as the reporter asked me several questions; they would pick just a line or two from everything that was said. The reporter noticed the scars on my head. "How do you feel about the attack?" he asked.

"I have my very sad moments," I answered. "On the whole, I'm all right."

"Will you sue him?"

"No," I answered quietly, "that really wouldn't do any good, and I don't want his money or to ruin him. I want to change the law." I hesitated after the comment, and the reporter sensed I was worried and stopped filming. I felt the media might lose interest in the story if I announced I wanted to change the law. I still wasn't sure what would interest the press. The reporter told me if there was a new piece of legislation, they would cover me at the state house. The lights went back on and I appeared totally in charge, announcing, "People have a right to be safe in their parks as they walk and play. I will seek legislation to change the law."

"Caress, the man's a dogfighter," the reporter told me when the interview ended. "We've all been over to his house where he told us to get out. It's a crime of great secrecy, but I don't understand how Animal Control missed all the evidence here."

Animal Control was commonly referred to as the Siberia of the police department in Indianapolis. The current head of the department knew almost nothing about dogs. In a recent newspaper article, he had stated I had done the right thing by "staring down the dogs" as they came toward me. The statement frustrated those who knew better, for dogs view eye contact as aggression. The reason children are so vulnerable is that they are often eye level with a dog. In my case there had been no time to stare. I had but briefly glanced down as one dog looked up a second before the attack.

I didn't know anything about dog fighting, but I sat and listened while knowing it was not my mission to deal with the man.

As the reporter and the cameraman prepared to leave, the cameraman thanked me for doing the interview and asked, "I hope you're not afraid of big dogs."

"No," I told him, "I'm not afraid of big dogs."

"Oh, that's good because I've always had Labradors and they are the sweetest dogs, wouldn't hurt anybody." I understood people were very protective about their animals and that I would have to continue to assure them I wasn't out for the family pet or afraid of dogs, even big ones.

The television set had been turned on in the early evening darkness of December. Linda Worsham sat watching the news when the story came on with me speaking from the sun porch. She listened, realizing that I wanted to become involved in fighting for the legislation. She contemplated the picture on the screen and picked up the phone to call another member of the team.

Newspaper and television media were calling me now, wanting to know my reaction to what the man had been charged with that morning. I tried to tell them my feelings, that something more had to be done in the law. That evening I placed the phone beside me. A state house correspondent for one of the newspapers called; he too wanted to know my reaction to the charges. "I know what laws we have," I said for what seemed the one hundredth time, "but I want to try and create a law to make this less likely to happen to other people." Then I decided to ask him, "Do you think I will be able to change anything?" The man on the other end of the line was resigned because he'd heard it all and he'd seen it all.

After a pause he started, "Tell you what, I've been covering the state house for years and there is something you ought to know. In Indiana, there's an unwritten law that there will be no legislation passed that undermines what they see as their personal freedoms when it comes to their guns, their booze, or their animals."

This wasn't what I wanted to hear, but I heard myself say, "I hope I can be the one to change part of that."

"I hope you can too," he said, "but don't count on it."

I hung up the phone and felt the familiar sense of urgency as I started to unwrap the Ace bandage around my leg. I stared at the gauze that still became bloody by the end of the day. Pat came into the bedroom and pulled out his supplies of gauze pads, paper tape, and ointment that he kept in a paper bag on the floor at the end of the bed. I put my hands over my eyes as the bloody gauze was removed and listened to Matthew practicing the piano downstairs in the living room. He was playing Mozart, and the music radiated a joyous, uninhibited, elegant spirit in contrast to my numbness, wondering how God would circumvent the sacred cows of the Indiana legislature: guns, booze, and animals.

Early the next morning the phone rang. "Did you see the editorial in the *Star*?" a woman's voice asked. The paper was still in the mailbox at the bottom of the hill, so I didn't know what she was talking about. "If there's one thing we don't need, it's another law." She spoke with absolute assuredness as her voice came crackling across the phone. "We have too many of them as it is," she continued. "The Dobermann pinscher is known for his loyalty, they used to live in the trenches with the German soldiers, protecting them." She jumped back to the law, "There are too many restraints on our personal freedoms now. You see, there was this man, he was a runner and he jogged past our front yard, and naturally Kaiser ran after him, barking, but he stayed in the yard. My husband was out in front and the runner stopped, waving his hands and screaming about Kaiser barking and running along the property. Kaiser didn't like the man waving his hands and screaming at my husband; they're so loyal, you know. Kaiser went out to the street and bit him. It didn't really hurt him that much," she added, "but he started yelling, 'I know my rights,' and 'I'm not going to put up with this.' So, he did press charges and I had to pay a fine, only a little one though." With a quick pause she added, "How are you doing anyway?" She wanted to stop me. She possessed an all-consuming passion for her animal. These people's personalities are different from the millions of dog owners who love their pets and consider them part of the family. These are people who have emotionally crossed a line. She could no longer reason very well when it came to her own animal, and, now, this particular dog also had a record and the owner was worried. In fact, she was fearful of me. I was glad she was on the other end of the phone.

I sat that morning in the breakfast room with the work from the senator's office in my lap. For me, it was a visible, concrete sign that there was a mission. I started to read the material again carefully. There was a copy of the dog bill that had failed last year at the state house, House Bill 1053, to amend the Indiana Code concerning animals. Then in large type, "Carmichael January 7, 1991, read for first time and referred to the Committee on Public Safety." All I understood was that it hadn't worked.

What I didn't know was that the Indiana State House had been descended upon by frantic dog owners, kennel clubs, and farmers from all over the state as the legislator attempted to introduce the bill. Representative Marc Carmichael was from Muncie, Indiana, and a Democrat, which had helped his bill pass out of the House of Representatives, where his party held a majority. However, his bill never received a hearing from the committee it was assigned to on the Senate side.

Senator Pease, a Republican who headed the committee,

was from a rural section of the state and had wanted no part of the bill. I wondered what had happened in Indiana that had moved a legislator to attempt tougher laws, to try to move the stone wall on regulating animals? I didn't know then and I wouldn't know for some weeks, but there were reasons, very terrible reasons.

* * *

Marilyn's light brown hair swung back and forth, framing the pink cheeks and tomboyish smile as her ten-year-old legs pumped up and down. The grease-smeared chain hummed, while rubber wheels hit the ruts on the country back road almost bouncing her off the bike. She grabbed the bicycle handles more firmly, shifting her weight, correcting her balance. She was her grandma's favorite and loved visiting the small farm with its little garden, picking the sweet raspberries that grew in abundance. There were miles of rural roads for Marilyn to ride that wove between small farms and towns near Paoli, Indiana, in the southern part of the state. She had never thought to be afraid as she sped along, passing the occasional farmhouse, pedaling close to the home where the old man and woman lived. The couple that harbored an assortment of mixed breed dogs.

The dogs roamed over the farmlands together and had taken on the ancient genetic traits of the pack. Perhaps the strongest dog, the leader, viewed her as prey that day as he watched for signs of weakness in her childlike movements as she pedaled closer. He would be the first to strike as he led the others into the chase and continued on as the killing began.

The dogs left the couple's yard and bounded out onto the road, surprising the little girl. Her heart pounded as the leader lunged at her and the others encircled the bicycle that was slowing down. They leaped and tore at her coltish legs, their barking disorienting her and camouflaging her screams. At some point she must have known that no help would come for her and she would die beside her bicycle. Her mind wouldn't focus on the flashing teeth or her blood on their muzzles as she turned inward and lost consciousness.

There was nothing to be done, no one could bring her back, there would be no penalty, no one would be held responsible. Nothing done as a warning to others demanding that the couple be held responsible for the animals they harbored. A little girl lay dead in the road, had died a savage death, and nothing was done.

There was only one law in the state of Indiana that dealt with the action of a dog. That law stated that a farmer had the right to shoot a dog that entered his property and harassed his cattle. Indiana had a law to protect its cattle, but not its children.

* * *

I stared down at the failed bill not knowing enough about why people would object to bother reading it again. The copy of the bill was like holding something that was once alive, had been subjected to battle, and had lost the war. Even though I had never been down to the legislature, I realized there had been passion connected with this piece of legislation.

Sometimes during the day and early evening I would ask God once again if He really intended me to play this role. Did I really have the understanding I seemed to feel? I was beginning to understand that in Indiana injuries and deaths caused by dogs were considered terrible, but just something that happened. Everyone owned a dog, or in rural areas, harbored a dog. I had already heard fear from a dog owner. Later I would learn a child had died, and there had been definite reluctance to hold anyone responsible.

Is it me that You want to step out and through You move the mountain? Keep showing me, Father, and I will do what You want me to do in Your name. These were my prayers as I continued to grow stronger.

* * *

I was driven one last time to the doctor's appointment on the other side of town. A nervous apprehension spread over me because I had been coming every week since I left the hospital and now the time was right for me not to come as often.

A car passed us, coming close to my side of the car. There was a vague sense of someone trying to polish me off. The traffic frightened me. I would later call a trauma nurse who explained this was a very common feeling and happened about six weeks after the injury. For people who have been in a life-threatening incident that involves injury, doctors are also important. They are protectors for people who have been hurt, and their patients feel attached to them as they try to regain normalcy in their lives. I also didn't know how to tell my doctor what was happening, that he was part of a miracle, a twentieth century miracle. The doctor unwrapped the gauze and looked at the still open wounds. The leg was covered in dead skin, and he looked and scraped around the recovering wounds. I watched the flakes of dead skin cover his navy blue pants and then watched as he brushed off his legs. He gave me a little brush to take home to remove some of the dead skin. "It's really soft," he told me and added "but then, it's not my leg."

"I want her to come back in two weeks," he said out loud to me and the nurse who was standing in the little room.

"No, I have to come back next week," I told him. He was on his way out of the little room and stopped. "I'm going to change the law. In this state dogs can kill you and there is nothing to be done." I never doubted my role, so looking right at him, I said, "I was *chosen*."

"No," he gasped, stepping backwards, not wanting to believe that God would intentionally let this happen. He had no way of understanding the depth and complexity of my preparation.

The doctor, arms hanging by his side, looked at the same time both worried and amazed. He quietly spoke to me that he was afraid that I would be devastated if it didn't work out. I was trying so hard to convey something I understood to be absolute truth that it never occurred to me there might be disbelief. The one who was questioning was also the one who was supposed to watch. The one who was not a naturally gifted listener was the one who needed to listen.

The good news was that I was coming back again the next week. I felt relieved that I had accomplished the immediate goal. I didn't know how it would all work out, just that I was called upon to continue trusting.

* * *

The dogs had been placed in the cages down at Animal Control. The keepers didn't want to come close to either animal because they would throw themselves against the sides of their cages with such violence that they broke off their teeth. The fact that they continued to be held past the ten-day quarantine period was a testimony to the amount of attention that the woman they had attacked was receiving from the media. There would be no rehabilitating these dogs. The handling by their owner had only reinforced their genes—they were killers.

I sat at home with a piece of paper listing a phone number of the Marion County prosecutor. Jeffrey Modisett was a very bright man and a good man; he knew the law but didn't know a great deal about dogs. The prosecutor was unsure if the dogs should be put down for fear that animal lovers would protest. He didn't realize that these dogs were killers. The prosecutor was a Democrat and not originally from Indianapolis. I didn't know anyone who knew him, so I thought perhaps I should find a lawyer who was also a Democrat.

I decided to call Jeffrey Mallamad, the personal lawyer to Jeffrey Modisett and to the governor, Evan Bayh. A friend had told me, "All three of them are real good buddies." The firm's receptionist connected me.

"Jeff, my name is Caress Garten and I was recently attacked by two pit bulls while walking in a park—"

The lawyer stopped me and with deep feeling said, "I know who you are, and I will do anything for you," then added, "there will be no charge." A lawyer, no charge. I thought God was working overtime. "I'm a jogger and felt so much for you when I heard on the news what had happened."

He was very kind, enabling me to tell him what I wanted. "The prosecutor feels there is a loophole in the law of the state, and I want to try and correct that at the state house. Jeff, I need someone to explain to the prosecutor that these dogs are trained fighters—killers—they should never be released."

"Caress, I will do that, the prosecutor is always interested in the victim's opinions, but he doesn't have to go along with those opinions. The prosecutor has to separate himself from other lawyers, but I will write to him immediately and talk to him personally. Caress, maybe there are people in my law firm who could help you research the law and understand the legislative process."

I mentioned Paul; that hopefully there would be some bill introduced. He pondered for a moment. "There's a man by the name of John Hammond who's part of the firm and he has a good relationship with Paul. He's a lobbyist at the legislature. Let me talk to him about what you want to do." Feeling all that could be done was in process, I thanked my free lawyer for his kindness and for caring about me.

Mid-December was dreary and rainy. Christmas was coming, and the tree stood in the living room, decorated, its lights shone through all the silver tinsel. I had stood a little while by the side of the car in the mud and rain as Pat, Benjamin, and Matthew picked the tree. The Garten men had decorated the tree while I watched from the living room sofa. Sometimes during the day I would sit in the living room and look at the Christmas tree. The smell of the evergreen and the shining lights against the dark green branches always soothed me. For Christians, the light of the world was once again coming to be born. The remembrance of His birth always meant the rebirth of hope. I felt Him close to me, and, just as the free lawyer had appeared to smooth the path, so would others. I gazed upon His Christmas tree and asked that I be able to accomplish His purpose.

I answered the doorbell. The flowers had now turned to holiday fruit baskets. I thought of the blooming plants on the sun porch, in the kitchen, pantry, and breakfast room. I liked looking at their blooms of pink and white. They were referred to with black humor as my pit bull plants, but always the thoughts of the caring souls who had sent them comforted me.

Now, five weeks after my attack, I still hadn't seen many people. Today I waited at home for the stereo repairmen to arrive, and now they stood in the hall. They went around the corner into the den when suddenly one reappeared in front of me—it was his eyes that caught you. He was excited, horrified. "You're the lady who the pit bulls got aren't you?" he blurted. "I was out in California when this little girl was playing in her yard, and I tell you those dogs found her— just chewed her up alive," he said feverishly, "You know, lady, I don't mean to be rude or anything, but there have been women those dogs attacked during the monthly trouble. Those dogs, lady, can smell blood." Leaning against the banister, I listened to this man barely able to cope with what had happened to me. He kept glancing bug-eyed at my leg while explaining the ongoing debate in California over pit bulls.

I remembered thinking of Matthew as a little boy, worried about sharks, as he stepped into the ocean. He was fascinated with different kinds of sharks, and his greatest fear was that one of them would actually grab someone. I was the someone these land sharks had grabbed, and there were people who were terrified.

Now sitting on the stairs, my voice was quietly speaking to the repairman, "I was watched over. I was never afraid. I don't even think about the attack. It was only something that happened to get me to another point." He could not grasp the fact I was not afraid because he was so afraid. I turned to hobble up the stairs, trying to get him to think about the stereo. "It's okay," I told the stereo repairman, "it happened for a reason." There were many people like him, both men and women, who harbored this fear of a mauling by a dog, and pit bulls were their equivalent to Matthew's great white shark.

Matthew was on his way home from school, and Thursday afternoon meant he would go to piano. He didn't mind going to the lesson, but none of his friends were very musical so he stayed quiet about piano. Matthew walked in the back door with his brother. "Who's going to take me to music?" He was tired and not very interested in anything except finding something to eat.

"I'm going to take you today." I told him, "I have to start driving again sometime."

"I don't understand the religion," Matthew said as he went to the living room to collect his music.

"What do you have for homework?" I asked him.

"We have to answer questions for religion and I don't get it."

"Have you tried to get it?" I asked.

He scowled at me, "Yes, but I don't understand different parts."

"What are you supposed to read?"

"It's in the Bible." It was time to go to music now, so I told him to bring the Bible and I would read the section. We left the house and wove through traffic and rain to the piano teacher's home. He hopped out of the car, slamming the door, leaving me in the driveway while he sprinted inside, the rain had turned to a downpour. The Bible was next to me on the seat and I looked up the passages.

I was raised as an Episcopalian and one thing about growing up in the Episcopal Church, or at least my church, is that you are taught very little about the Bible, which is a funny thing to say. What you really know about is the Book of Common Prayer that Episcopalians use in their services.

Now, while the rain streamed down the car windows, I tried to find Judges in the Old Testament. Matthew's religion class dealt with only the Old Testament and this was the first time he had asked for help. I found the passages he didn't understand.

There was a man, from an unimportant family, who was hiding in a cave from enemies. He was trying to exist with barely enough grain to live when he looked out from his cave and saw an angel. The angel spoke to the man and told him God was going to ask something of him. He would ask the man to restore the one God to his people and tear down the altars of the idols that the enemy worshipped. The man, whose name was Gideon, found it hard to believe that this was happening to him. Did God really want him? Gideon needed proof and he needed assurance and more assurance. God continued to show the man, who hid in his cave, that He would never let him down until, in time, he gained such confidence that he led an army to defeat the enemies of the one God.

Here was a man who had no confidence, no human help, no resources, and he couldn't go very far in the beginning of his mission without proof.

I had never heard of this long-ago warrior, but we were so much alike.

From the depths of my being there was a clearer assuredness that I had been prepared in myriad ways and now, the mission. A woman, a stranger, had the day after my attack taken time from her job to go to work on this law. I now had her work as proof. There was a legislator who cared about the legislation and personally cared about me. There was the dream and the vision of a very close friend who had confirmed and understood what I must do. I also had a free lawyer.

Here was this man who lived thousands of years ago, asking for proof that God really did want him; assurance, help in his time of need, that he not be forgotten. Now, there was I, sitting in a car, in the rain, at the end of the twentieth century, asking for assurance and more assurance.

I was physically weak and sometimes felt emotionally vulnerable. Did Gideon ever feel the anxiousness of rescuing the baby who sat in the street? Did friends tell him to return to his cave and forget all this angel stuff? Gideon was asked to make new altars to the one God and to slay the infidel. He was given the authority and the ability; he had only to step out and obey.

Caress was asked to change the law, not kill anybody. Change the legislators' minds and their hearts, then tell the people. She had only to step out and obey.

The car door opened and music pages fluttered down around me. "Let's go," Matthew said as the rain blew inside the car before the door slammed shut. "Mom, did you understand what the religion was all about?" He didn't care about any deep discussion, he just wanted an answer or two. My hand turned the ignition key, and the car started backing down the driveway in the rain.

"Yes, Matthew, I understood," I answered him. "I understood it perfectly." I proceeded to succinctly tell him the story of Gideon, the warrior, who won his battle for the one God.

"That's all I need to know," Matthew answered, not interested in any further religious discussion.

The answering machine light blinked on and off next to the phone. "Would I be a part of a feature article that was being written for the February edition of Indianapolis Monthly?" the message asked. The magazine was subscribed to throughout the state, and the February edition would be on newsstands sometime in January. The editor told me to call the man who was writing the article. She seemed to understand the importance of the mission, assuring me with her words that he would present the story the way I wanted, and it would come out at just the right time.

The writer, Dan Denny, asked me to tell him about the mauling for the article. He was interested in the fact that I spoke of having no pain. "Do you think it was shock?" he asked. I told him I really didn't know, but I would have been in shock for a long time because, although the leg was stiff, I never experienced pain, not even in the hospital. The distance that was covered and the hill scaled after the attack would have been impossible for me had there been pain because my tolerance is not naturally high. People were interested in this fact, but for me it was not particularly important. We discussed the hoped-for changes in the law and my mission that God had given to me. There are people who are placed in the right position at the right time, for this writer never doubted me. Now, there was confidence that the story would be kept alive for the next few months in a publication that would be read around the state.

That evening Pat helped me lower my leg into the tub and use the soft brush from the doctor to remove the dry skin that had collected over the past weeks. I kept my eyes looking straight ahead since the scars were almost closed but still became runny by the end of the day. Deep, taunt scars in parallel bands were on one side of my leg, and on the other side where the dog's lower jaw shook and tore out the muscle, the scar was long, deep, extremely jagged. There the leg would remain concave and misshapen.

Pat carried the burden of telling me how much better the leg looked and that I was still the prettiest girl he knew as the dead skin floated around in the water. He dried the leg, taped the gauze bandages on, and wrapped the Ace bandage up around the leg.

He too had been inundated with pit bull stories. One salesman had gotten out of his car in a rural part of the state and had been walking toward an old barn when a pit bull had come running through the barn doors. The salesman leaped back into his car, slamming the door shut as the dog bit deep into the front tire, tearing, hanging on and shaking its head back and forth. The man relived the fear with Pat who was experiencing and hearing people's terror. They spoke to him at business meetings, during phone calls, as he walked about downtown Indianapolis, and traveled through the state. Pat understood my experiences in dealing with people's fear.

* * *

"Try and gently rub the scars and the leg won't be so sensitive." The doctor looked at my leg and rubbed his hand along the jagged scar. The nerve endings weren't used to being touched and my body flinched. He pushed back on my feet trying to assess how far my foot would flex. He spoke softly to me. "We talk about you, you know." I remembered his concern, amazement, and disbelief. "Do you want to talk about your feelings with someone?"

"No," I told him and remained silent. He was concerned about me but didn't really understand. He wanted me to think and talk about anything else. The doctor was to hear the story, but God had to figure out how I was going to communicate enough of what was happening to him. Perhaps it wasn't for me to ever know why, but the man was searching and had despaired in his life.

The comedian Lily Tomlin once said, "Why is it when we talk to God we are said to be praying, and when God talks to us we're said to be schizophrenic?" He wasn't sure what to think about me. My doctor felt he should be careful with me and I felt I should be careful with him.

Crossing his arms, he leaned against the wall and spoke about his family and that Christmas was coming soon. I listened to him talk, wishing he would listen to me. I had the feeling this must be the wish of a lot of people close to him.

He bent down again and looked at my leg. "Do you want to go to physical therapy?" he asked.

"No," I answered as the nurse asked, "Just one time, maybe?" I shook my head no to her. I had decided there was no time or extra mental energy to go to physical therapy. My plan was to go when I was finished with whatever was going to be asked of me.

"Will it always be so stiff?"

"Always stiff," he answered, stroking my foot. This was a sad answer, for I had hoped that someday the leg wouldn't feel so much like a piece of petrified wood, but I couldn't think about it now—there was the baby in the street looking for me.

I left the medical facility that day for a shopping mall. Christmas was close and salespeople had helped me on the phone, so my trips to stores were simple and brief. It was a rainy December and the elastic bandage stretched out the soft-soled shoe I wore. The shoe sometimes flopped off my foot, and I walked through the department store trying to keep my shoe on, feeling a little dazed and unfamiliar among so many people. Strangers recognized me from my pictures in the paper. I continued to be surprised as they stopped me and wanted to talk.

A man in his thirties turned from a counter and touched my arm. "Caress," he said, "my name is John Hammond; we've never met, but Jeff Mallamad told me you called him at the law firm. I lobby at the state house and if I can help you in any way I want you to call." A little boy by his side, John Hammond IV, was a member of Pat's Boy Scout troop. I remembered Pat telling me he was a pistol, a feisty little boy who stood his ground. Today he stared at my leg.

I had never met any of the family and I guessed John recognized me from the papers along with the telltale Ace bandage. I thanked him for his kindness and his offer of help.

There were thousands of people shopping around us that

day at the shopping center, a week before Christmas, but in the brief period I was in the store, I met John.

* * *

The Christmas parties were like attending Irish wakes—filled with people there to be happy and joyful while tenderly remembering the departed. These parties were the first time I was seen by many people who knew me. Because I was the one who had departed but had not died, had been the object of grief but stood smiling at others, everyone wanted to talk. I stepped into a den so all the discussion around me wouldn't be a damper on the party. I stood comforting others while telling them of the wonderful mission placed before me. I could see Pat in the other room fending off questions, but he could turn the topic away only for a while before someone else would come towards him. He kept glancing toward me as the evening passed and sometimes would stand by me for a while, but I was the one people wanted. I had been standing in the den for a couple of hours when a woman who had been watching from the other room came and stood beside me. I recognized her expression having by this time seen the look before. She was trying to think how she knew me and had suddenly realized by a word someone said or a fleeting image that it was from the newspaper. "I have been praying for you," she said to me so quietly as if in a whisper. "Since I read about the baby, I have prayed that something might be done." She was a very gentle person, fragile, though she seemed to have a quality like a willow, someone that could bend in the wind and stand upright again when the wind became a breeze. I had never met nor seen her, but she seemed a special and promising messenger to me.

"Pray that I will be able to do something," I asked her.

"You will," she said. "You will."

It's so strange to leave a party hungry and exhausted. As we drove home past the glowing Christmas lights, in the darkness I said, "Pat, do you remember what the doctor said to me last October? Stability. I was so stable I almost tested off the charts." He was driving and I looked over at him. "Now, we're going to see if he was right." He slowly nodded his head.

"Yes, we are," he said. "Yes, we are." We both felt shell-shocked.

FOUR

Cathedral

"**D**oes Representative Mannweiler want to include the civil clauses or does he want to leave them out?"

I had no idea what she was talking about much less what Representative Mannweiler wanted to do about including or not including anything. The voice sounded young and she needed direction as to how she should proceed. Only hearing a voice similar to Margaret Thatcher's would have assured me that the bill was being written. Now it was the beginning of the third week in December. The days were slipping by, and time was growing shorter before the 108th Indiana General Assembly began the first week in January.

Christy was a lawyer with Legislative Services at the state house. Her job was to help legislators draft their bills.

"There really isn't much of anything on the books about dogs or any animals," she told me.

She had found the law that dealt with the farmers' cattle and vicious dogs, but that was all she had found, proving correctly that farm conscious Indiana had almost no restrictions on animals at the state level. "I haven't done anything toward writing the bill," she admitted.

My own soft voice may have seemed without authority to her as I explained the importance of what she was doing.

She listened quietly. "I don't have any answers for you, Christy. I just don't know what Paul thinks."

"Cathy," I told Paul's secretary, "Christy sounds unsure on what exactly she's to do; does Paul know her?"

"He's used her before in writing legislation, she'll be all right, Caress."

"Can he talk to her?"

"He's in Washington right now, until the end of the week," she said.

All the air went out of me. Paul had a lot to think about, many decisions, more than this one bill.

"Caress, Paul cares about you and he will not forget this bill. He's going to call at the end of the day, and I will tell him that you're concerned."

She was a very kind person, someone who didn't know me, but was empathetic to the voice speaking to her on the phone. "I'll call you back after I speak with him, Caress, towards late afternoon."

The call came right on schedule near five o'clock. "Paul wants you to know, Caress, that he has told the governor's legislative aide that this is one of the bills he wants let out."

Of course, I had no idea what "let out" meant except that it sounded good and was comforting to me. Paul had not forgotten and he was working on the legislative process that seemed a mystery to me. He was going ahead though not one single word on the actual bill had been written, and the lawyer drafting the bill was confused.

Paul was already confronting what he saw as the politics of the legislation, trying to weave the dog bill successfully out of the House of Representatives.

The Democrats were the majority party in the House and controlled the governor's office, but some Republican bills would reach the floor for a vote. There had to be some cooperation, not only to avoid gridlock and to please the public, but also because the governor's party needed the support of the minority leader on some issues. Each party also knew they would not always be in power, and there were some long memories at the state house.

One man who had a long memory was the current Speaker of the House, Michael Phillips, who for years had watched his legislation be "shot down" by the Republicans. As Speaker, he had the power not to assign the bill to a committee. If he did assign the bill, he had the power to kill the legislation just by giving the execution signal to the committee chairman. Paul was doing his best to circumvent the Speaker by telling the governor's aide this was one of the bills he wanted to advance.

However, there was a problem. Mike Phillips also understood and manipulated the politics of the state house. He had more expertise in state house politics than his party's governor and, on occasion, just ignored the decisions by that office.

There was no understanding of the politics on my part as Chuck slept at my feet in the breakfast room the next morning. My fingers touched the stack of papers from the senator's office for assurance and hope.

Four pages into the manuscript were the names of the team members Linda Worsham had gathered together from across the state. There were five names, all women, who were listed. She had stapled her business card with her address and phone number to the top of the papers. My fingers dialed the numbers to reach Senator Lugar's office.

Linda was in a meeting, could they take a message? My name and number was left for her to call.

Benjamin and Matthew had a separate telephone line in the house, so the main line was left free. This rule was routinely ignored as they tied up both phone lines talking to their friends at one time. This morning they were off to school, so the portable phone with the second line came into the breakfast room with me as well as the regular phone.

The second name on the list was a woman who worked for a judge. The judge's name was listed, but there was no indication what kind of judge he was or where his chambers were located. Leaving the main line free for the senator's office, I used the second line to call an operator who helped me find the municipal judges, and we went through the names at the city county building. The operator tried several other numbers. We couldn't locate this judge and he wasn't listed in the phone book. While going through the different courts on different government levels, about forty-five minutes had passed before the main phone line rang.

"Caress, my name is Velda Boenitz and you have been on my mind for the last week." Velda worked for the *judge.* Still holding the portable phone, I thanked the operator, telling her the person we had been looking so hard for had suddenly called me. "Linda Worsham said she watched you on TV a couple of weeks ago," came the pleasant voice over the phone.

Still stunned she had called while I was looking for her, I stammered, "Where is your judge, Velda?"

"He's at the state house, Caress." I listened while she told me that the team intended for Senator Teresa Lubbers, a former Lugar aide, who was a new state senator, to be the chief sponsor of the bill.

"Velda, I've already called Paul Mannweiler," I said with some concern, "when I first came home from the hospital, before I ever knew about your work."

"That's fine; he can be the main sponsor," she told me calmly. "Teresa can still play a role."

She heard my story of the mauling and my desire to change the law to protect others. She listened to my concern that Christy in Legal Services needed guidance. "Well, Caress, you come on down here and we'll write some legislation," she said with steady assurance. Velda was one of those people when you're in trouble you hope will be there with their confidence and knowledge.

* * *

It was a gray old December day as we drove the few blocks toward the state house. The Ace bandage wound around my leg, partially covered by my dress and coat. My eyes seemed to alternate between the state house that rose in the distance and the leg. Pat turned in to the parking lot, telling the officer he was just dropping me off at the steps. "I'll call when I'm finished," I told him. If Pat couldn't pick me up, someone else from the business could.

Opening the car door, starting to get out, I heard Pat say his affectionate expression for me: "Good luck, Buster."

I began climbing the limestone steps, entering through the massive north doors. My feet moved across the marble floors as my eyes looked up into chandeliers of gleaming brass that descended from the ceiling of cream, gold, and royal blue. The rotunda on the main floor lay one hundred feet beneath a stained glass dome of vivid blue, while marble columns stood as knights, protecting an institution precious to a free people. The building, built toward the end of the nineteenth century, is the most majestic in the state. Five days before Christmas the building appeared empty. The warm glow from the chandeliers and the rich color reflecting from the great oak doorways gave the building warmth and a sense of expectancy as the melody of "Silent Night" softly drifted from some open office door and echoed through the state house.

No one could have entered this building with a more beautiful welcome than I that third week in December. Seeing no living soul, my intuition told me to go up the marble stairs. On what is called the third floor, but appears to be only the second, a lone janitor directed me down the hall to the south end of the building where Legislative Services was located. Walking past the supreme court and the Senate chamber, the building's history and beauty seemed in perfect harmony with my timing and mission.

I would hear Velda say in the weeks that followed: "You know, Caress, the state house is an Italian prince's palace."

She could see the Medicis strolling under the gold and blue moldings, comfortable with their elegant trappings of power, while Venetian waters lapped at the state house steps. We differed in our thinking, for the idea of a palace wasn't possible for me. I would always answer her with the emotion of how the building first welcomed me.

"No, Velda," I would tell her, "the state house is a cathedral."

That afternoon in late December the cream-colored marble floor led directly toward the heavy doors of Legislative Services. The old building proved it was designed in another era with the cumbersomeness of its doors; they reached toward the ceiling, seemingly designed for giants to pass through, dwarfing mere mortals.

Walking inside, I found there were people at work here after all. The place reminded me of a beehive with cubicles, people peering over books, seated behind covered partitions— kind of a hodgepodge of organization that had developed over the years.

Christy Megna came down some narrow stairs descending from the book stacks. "You're the first one here," she said to me as we went into a little makeshift room of partitions that was completely filled by a large table and chairs. Christy sat down at one end, ready for ideas to help her in the initial draft. She had a friendly personality and was liked by the staff. Behind me another woman entered.

"Caress, I'm Velda, the others are coming, it's nice to meet you." A combination of happy energy and efficiency, having worked for an appeals court judge for almost twenty years, she knew Indiana law and the state house as well as anyone. Velda had a quiet second career at the state house and had for years discreetly overseen the legislation that involved the animals she loved.

Two more women came to sit down. One of them wore a pin of a greyhound on her lapel and held a folder with U.S.A. Defenders of Greyhounds printed on the material.

Sally Allen loved greyhounds and had led the fight at the state house to defeat greyhound racing in Indiana. The elegant, but fragile dog was used for its speed then routinely, cruelly discarded after a short life on the racing circuit. She led rescues into other states to save the dogs often left for dead. Sally seemed someone who was all business.

Belinda Lewis' curly brown hair and slender build didn't appear to belong to a policewoman although her voice had an edge of authority. She ran Animal Control in Indiana's second largest city of Fort Wayne, which was the best in the country, according to the Humane Society of the United States. She was also known for her ability to build a criminal case and work closely with the prosecutor in the northern part of the state. Belinda smiled at me, then at Velda; all three women of the team seemed to know each other well.

"You know Carmichael's bill failed for the second time last year," Velda mentioned to the two of them.

"I read the bill," Sally said, "but didn't bother to follow the legislation because it wasn't going anywhere. He asked for everything in that bill and the Farm Bureau was obviously out for him." Sally sniffed, for wasting time wasn't part of her agenda.

For years the Farm Bureau had fought any legislation that might restrict the farmer, and that included the farmer's dog. "There are reports from around the state the Farm Bureau might cooperate this year and support a vicious dog law," continued Velda. She was the state house expert on lobbyists, legislators, and timing.

John Baugh was the lobbyist for the Farm Bureau at the state house. A mild-mannered, round-faced, middle-aged man, who resembled a substantial banker in some mid-sized American town, he walked the halls in his suit and tie. He was one of the few lobbyists who, weeks later, I never saw use a cellular phone to contact anyone. Maybe John didn't need to talk to anyone, for he had single-handedly beaten Representative Carmichael's dog bill. He would melt into the walls that lined the halls outside the House and Senate chambers, always watching who was talking in the halls and how the votes were cast. He controlled the political lives of many legislators in the state house who depended on the farmer's votes and money from groups supporting farm interests.

In Indiana, the problem was not the farmer's dog but the issue of private property. A man's home was his castle, and if a dog wanted to kill you while on his own property, even if you were a small child, that could not be made unlawful. The victim's family could sue, if there was anything to collect, but it would never pass the legislature as a criminal offense.

"We need to get more than public property through because, although Caress' attack was in a park, most attacks occur on private property," Belinda said knowingly.

The group quietly glanced at one another.

"We can try for private property other than property where the dog lives, and if the Farm Bureau doesn't like it we drop back to attacks only on public property," Sally offered.

"We'll have to see what the chief legislator thinks he can get through," Velda said softly, looking at the thin partitioned wall. "Is there anyone working around us?" she muttered to Christy who was busy taking notes.

"No, we're alone. One advantage to working right before Christmas," smiled Christy. "If this dog bill goes through, I'll tell you I'm really going to clean up my act. I have this cocker spaniel and he sometimes runs loose. He's pretty good around people, but I'm not going to take any risks with him if this passes."

"Cockers, they frenzy," Velda mentioned to her. "Humane Societies see cockers returned all the time. They've been so overbred they can "snap" or "frenzy" in kind of a dog psychosis. It's really sad, but there are a lot of them that aren't good family dogs—I'd never have a cocker around children."

"Well, I'm worried about this legislation and it only

protecting people who have been mauled on public property," Belinda interrupted the cocker conversation. "We need tools to help prosecute the owners of these dogs."

She lived with her husband on a quiet street with an unlisted address in Fort Wayne, a city Hollywood could use as an appealing mid-sized, Midwestern city. Yet her life had been in danger a number of times because she dealt with criminals who used dogs to protect their drugs and who had used dogs as weapons.

Belinda loved dogs and owned two rescued Rottweilers from the shelter in Fort Wayne. Her ability with animals had helped make her pets, a breed with fierce potential, two of the best-mannered dogs in that city. However, she knew the potential of dogs bred and trained by criminals as well as irresponsible people. She had seen plenty of blood and muscle tissue that had been torn from victims.

"There are many maulings when a victim has been chased from the street onto a private front yard, where the attack actually has taken place." She looked around the table. "If the bill is passed applying to only public property, the law won't be able to help a lot of people. There are also cases of terrible maulings, plenty in Indiana, where victims, often children, are seriously injured while playing in their own yards." These were familiar cases to Animal Control officers.

One of the most poignant stories nationally had involved a little three-year-old boy who had arrived for a birthday party. The children were playing when a dog entered the backyard and started to grab the children's clothing. The child was taken to the ground and killed. There was no law to protect or avenge him.

The group seemed unsure how much to press the legislature.

Perhaps unseen angels stood around the table aiding the good Samaritans and prodding me, for suddenly the feeling of urgency returned to me.

"Even if a bill passes that covers just public property,

that will be more than what's there now." I feared no law being passed because of the private property discussion. "A law affecting public property would have covered me or the baby in his stroller," I told the listeners at the table. With great assurance and knowing next to nothing about the political process, I told Belinda, "This doesn't have to be the end, we can come back again." It was as if someone guided me, the novice, in my speech and she understood.

"If we passed a law, would it apply to the man in Caress' attack?" Sally asked as Velda shook her head no.

"The law's not retroactive."

"This law would apply to the future," added Christy.

"What's important to me is not the man," I said, adding quietly, "I don't care about punishing the man. I don't even think about him, but I know his dogs make him feel important—almost an extension of himself. He feels powerful with them—I just want to keep this from happening again."

"Caress, you know another real problem in writing this law is that there's really no way to legislate what is 'vicious,' " Velda said as she watched me from across the table. "That's always been the problem and the frustration with this legislation. Even if you pass this law, you want it to hold up. That is, when it's tested or enforced the constitutionality of the bill must hold."

"I'm sorry we're late; Sandy's flight was a little delayed but she wanted to be here," a voice interrupted.

"There they are," Velda said happily.

Someone from out of town would fly in to meet me? Amazing, I thought, watching the two women enter the little makeshift room.

Linda Worsham, who had put together the original material from the senator's office, was a petite, pretty woman with light brown hair. She joined the others with her love of animals, salvaging greyhounds, working to control the animal population in the city. She was, as they all were, committed.

Sandy Rowland was with her from the Humane Society

of the United States. Sandy was moving energy, speaking quickly to the others, then looked at me.

"Caress, you don't know me, but I know a lot about you. Almost since the hour you were attacked we have been following your story. On our computers we're trying to find the name of this man. I'm convinced by the nature of your attack and the fact that he had two pit bulls with him that he's a dogfighter. You rarely find people with more than one of these animals who's not into dogfighting." Her eyes were intense. "What I mean by finding out his name is that dogfighters go by aliases, and we're trying to find out what is his alias. The H.S.U.S. also cares about this legislation and that Indiana passes a vicious dog law. That's what we're here to do today, Caress, to decide what to ask for in the legislation and arrive at the basic points that will successfully pass the bill." Sandy packed a punch with her rapid-fire words.

They talked among themselves, always very careful to include me in the final decisions. They were all caring, even protective, of me as they spoke. All strangers to me, they were also good Samaritans who watched over this unknown woman who had been hurt. They all had perspective and logic and, as dearly as they loved the animals, they did not place them before people.

The group simply hated dogfighters. Each woman had little use for people who trained a dog to be vicious. They all believed owners should be responsible for the actions of their animals.

They wanted a bill that defined a dangerous dog and that would include all breeds. The law would apply only to dogs that kill or injure human beings, not other animals.

"Injuring or killing other animals will just never pass," Velda said assuredly. "One of the red flags that a dog may eventually severely maul a human occurs when a dog kills another animal," she explained to me.

Representative Carmichael's bill had included civil penalties, monetary fines, which Velda and Christy thought made the legislation more complex and difficult to pass. "You can always sue someone," Velda stated and the rest of my new friends agreed. There would be only criminal penalties that included misdemeanors up to a felony, depending on the injuries or death of the victim. "Whoever carries this legislation is going to have to decide on the level of felony. What they think they can get through," Velda said decidedly. The group also agreed the attack by the dog must be unprovoked by the victim.

They were an amazing group of women—one's expertise worked to aid the other's thinking and vice versa.

"What about the dog being put down?" I asked.

"The H.S.U.S. recommends that any dog that severely or fatally injures a human being in an unprovoked attack should be put down," Sandy said. "Sometimes it's a judge's decision what to do with the dog. Other times, when there is no law, the animal is returned to the owner for that decision."

The group became silent. They all knew the dogs that attacked me were killers. They understood the chilling fact that were it not for the publicity, along with the ensuing public outrage, the dogs would have been returned to the man after a short quarantine period.

"Caress, our law is descended from English common law and dogs are considered personal property. In Fort Wayne, we had a situation involving some children in the inner city, two six year olds, both little boys, who would walk to school together. Every day they would pass a fenced yard where there were two German shepherds and the little boys would run back and forth yelling, waving their hands, teasing the dogs. Then, one day, going to school, they stopped to run back and forth when the two shepherds leaped over the fence. The children took off screaming, running, as one shepherd chased down one child and the other chased the second child, and when the dogs caught them, they ripped off their backs."

Belinda solemnly continued, "In Fort Wayne, it was

decided that the dogs were to be given back to the owners, who wanted them back, because the dogs had been provoked."

For some moments there are no words, and I had no words to convey my feelings, slowly saying, "But they were children." I felt unspoken horror for a society whose laws returned dogs that even in a provoked attack savaged children, injuring them for the rest of their lives. Incredulous, my mind thought about the kind of human beings that wanted animals like that back.

"It was controversial to many people, Caress, but this is the United States of America and you just cannot take people's property away from them if they have not broken the law. Inner cities are where most of the bad dogs live. The children who live in those neighborhoods often have no one to teach them how to treat animals. Just another fact of life where they are the victims."

The remarkable group of women was my protector, but I was the child-oriented person. My mission was for children, and it was terrible to me what those little boys had suffered, running screaming down a block in Middle America. Perhaps my unconscious also saw the gaping hole in the back of my coat being passed over my body in the emergency ward. The wind was knocked out of me understanding the law was not always compassionate, but sometimes brutal.

I watched these women around the table and the lawyer filling her legal pad, and at the end of two hours this team of women had listed the basic tenets of a new law. There was never a disagreement among them, and on each proposal they glanced at me for the nod of my head.

"Do you think we can change the law?" I asked all of them while pushing my chair from the table to stand.

Velda looked up at me, and in a mock country twang, one that would make me laugh for the next few months, said, "Caress, they're going to look at you and say 'Gee, she doesn't want any money, well, sure Honey, is this all you want?'"

I glanced over at Christy; the once worried lawyer had a

smile on her face and a page of notes. We both had needed guidance and assurance.

For the past twenty years of my life I had been in meetings with both men and women, volunteer organizations, hospital boards, school boards, but never in a meeting like this one. The personalities were different—each woman had her own opinions, but they rationalized and deferred to one another in order to create a piece of legislation that just might make it through the state house. They had swiftly made one difficult decision after another in a process where the overwhelming majority fail.

I hesitated, wanting to tell them how much they meant to me.

"I have wanted to meet you all for so long."

The table was quiet in the little thin-walled room when Sandy Rowland spoke up and softly said, "Caress, we've all waited years to meet you."

* * *

Walking down the little corridor, passing by the crowded desks, I was out in the marble hall again where Christmas carols still softly played.

Alone among the cream-colored marble columns and golden inlays, I felt grateful for understanding the miracle of the moment. I was to be the public one, the one the legislators would hear and the public would continue to know. Walking past the chambers of the chief justice and down the east hall, I rounded the bend toward the House of Representatives. The door was unlocked, and walking inside, I stood in the darkened chamber. The legislators' seats and desks were empty; only a dim light shone on the seal of Indiana that hung on the front wall. The podiums, the microphones, the voting machine whose lights recorded each representative's vote were lifeless. The visitors' gallery that ringed the House was quiet. The chamber, though empty of its members, seemed a place where battle was done. Turning to my right, walking into a narrow hall, I saw pictures in ornate gold frames lining the passageway. Past Speakers of the House peered out from their portraits, a pictorial history of Indiana politics. Paul's youthful face hung next to a smiling, jovial picture of the present Speaker, Mike Phillips.

Sticking my head around an open door where a receptionist worked at a desk, I asked if this was Paul Mannweiler's office. She looked up at me with a big question mark on her face while chewing hard on a piece of gum. She didn't utter a word, only pointed across the chamber to the doorway on the other side.

I had stumbled into Mike Phillips' offices. Across the dark chamber to the opposite side, a doorway led into a similar narrow passage. I entered an open doorway. Paul's secretary Cathy Parise was working at her desk. "I know Paul's not here, but I wanted to know how to find his office," I explained to her.

"Come in and sit down. How are you?" she said warmly.

"I'm doing pretty well," I answered even though my strength was rapidly leaving me for the day.

"How did the meeting go with Legislative Services?"

"So well, I can hardly believe it," I said to her, smiling. "Christy is going to report to Paul."

It was nice not having to introduce myself. Everyone seemed to know what I looked like and felt as if they knew me. Cathy had been my conduit to Paul, she was already a special friend.

"Caress, I could show you rooms where hearings are held, but I think they're all locked up right now. Come on back and see Paul's office."

The office of the minority leader matched the Speaker's. Paul had a large brass eagle sitting on his desk that peered across the room towards a conference table and a collection of Republican elephants. Tall glass windows looked out across the state house lawn past the statue of Oliver P. Morton, Indiana's Civil War governor. The windows looked as if every bird in the state of Indiana had made an extra effort to tell him they were in control. "Aren't they terrible?" Cathy laughed.

"I hope it's not just Paul's windows they're not washing," was my comment back to her. Walking out of the office, I noticed a picture of Paul's young daughter Gwen hugging her two little brothers. I remembered my second graders and missed not being with them.

"He'll be back from Washington in a few days, Caress, and I'll have him call you," Cathy promised.

I called Pat, telling him I was ready for someone to come get me. My first working hours at the state house were finished.

* * *

Christmas was four days away. In the kitchen a present had arrived—a miniature Christmas tree three feet high, covered with little red bows and tiny lights. The little tree was placed in the den, where it remained shining through the nights before Christmas. The little artificial evergreen remained after the holidays, through the winter months, a glowing reminder of peace and hope.

Sometimes, during the day before going out, I would glance at the little tree standing in the den. I needed to remember my Christmas tree and its sparkling lights as I returned to the medical facility.

The doctor looked down at my leg. I wanted to tell him about the miracles unfolding, but there was always limited time.

He looked at the scars and announced, "We can take off the Ace bandage."

"I'm going to wear it when I testify," I told him decidedly. He sat in front of me and held my foot.

"Oh, milk it for all its worth; are you still doing that?" He hadn't thought too much about the dog bite lady's mission.

Nodding my head yes, I began to tell him my fear that the dogs would not be kept by Animal Control but returned to their owner. He interrupted disgustedly—"Dogs." I ignored him as he sighed deeply and crossed his arms in front of himself.

"I have a plan to reach the prosecutor with a new lawyer; he's a friend and personal lawyer to the governor and the prosecutor. The lawyer told me there would be no charge. It's a miracle." The doctor smiled and listened a little.

I began to tell him about the Christmas carols in the state house; helping to write the legislation. "Oh, some bill being stuck in a committee somewhere?" The doctor didn't have much faith in the Indiana legislature or in the fact that heaven was involved. He didn't want me to be hurt.

"I think if you're going down the road at eighty miles an hour on a motorcycle, you should have something on your head, and that didn't get through," he said with disgust. Obvious to him that if a law like that was defeated, this stood little chance.

He looked at the issue from a doctor's perspective, one who watched people die in the emergency ward or go on to live out their lives in a nursing home. My doctor wouldn't understand about Gideon, the protectors who had gathered at the state house, the lights on the Christmas tree, the feeling of urgency, the timing of the media. I couldn't tell him I asked in my prayers, "Is it really *me* you want?"

Sometimes silence was best with him, saying only a few things each visit. He was stubborn—but I was stubborn too.

On the darkened sun porch, I would sit watching the glowing Christmas tree lights in the living room as I asked for strength and assurance and more assurance. As I knelt by myself in an upstairs bedroom, a door would open and Chuck would join me, licking my hands as I talked to God. Surely Jesus, who was born in a manger with the quiet rustling of animals standing watch, would never forget Chuck and all the dogs. He would remember them along with the sparrows when they fall.

The spirit of Christmas did not touch everyone's life. Terror remained a part of people's lives. A woman told me of her terror over the phone.

"I've told Tom I never go out without my butcher knife. I'm watching him 'cause I saw what he did with the man who comes to see that *dog*. They took a raccoon out of a sack, placed him on the ground. Tom's dog tore that animal limb from limb." I heard a quick breath. "Those men liked watchin'."

"They sound very cruel," I said.

"Tom's a mean man; lets that dog run the neighborhood. A fella down the street saw the dog get his cat. I worry 'bout something more 'cause that pit bull's always out. There's an old lady walks to get her paper—that dog's gonna find her."

The voice dipped lower, "I've told Tom I keep a camera close by and I'm gonna prove he lets that animal run."

"Have you called anyone for help?"

"I've called everyone I can think of, Humane Society says they don't take care of that kind of thing. Animal Control comes out and Tom says his dog never runs loose. He tells 'em I must be crazy, have somethin' out for him."

"Will your neighbors help?" I asked.

"Naw, they're afraid of Tom. I went down to the city county council, talked to their public safety committee, complained that nothing was being done 'bout this dog. I told them about the cat—that everyone's afraid. One seemed bothered and asked me if there were any children in the neighborhood. Most of 'em didn't care though. I'm for getting rid of all those kinds of dogs," she said with steel in her voice. "Some weeks past, I sat on the front porch when Tom's dog ran around the side of the house into my yard. I saw him looking out a window, just watching me, waitin', so I didn't get up, just stayed sittin', rockin'. His eyes stayed on me so I never looked over towards him; I just real slow raised my arm with that butcher knife."

A woman waiting on her porch to kill a dog if he came that Christmas. The man in the house who watched from the window, he was the real terror.

If the dog killed her, he wouldn't be held responsible, for, after all, the dog had done the killing. He could get another animal if he lost this one. He didn't care about dogs and he didn't care about people.

Calls like this one stayed with me as the candles glowed in church on Christmas Eve. People came from across the aisles to greet me and tell me of their prayers for me. I watched Matthew in his acolyte's robes light the candles and thought fifteen-year-old soccer players can look angelic. His continued wish was normalcy at home as he unwrapped presents and made his famous Christmas crab dip in the kitchen.

Late that Christmas Eve, I looked at the fragile silver and golden birds sitting on their branches in the Christmas tree; they were my favorite ornaments. Not as beautiful as Ed, the heron, or as sturdy as my friend the robin, who had sat outside the breakfast room, but special, for they illuminated the beauty and grace of the season.

* * *

The Indiana Legislature would begin its 108th legislative session in ten days. Some states have year-round legislatures whose representatives work full-time addressing their state's concerns. Indiana has what is called a citizen legislature that meets yearly in January with some sessions lasting several months into the spring. The citizen legislature was typical of the conservative nature of the state. Hoosiers didn't want to spend money to support politicians year-round at the state house. They preferred that their neighbors and friends, teachers, businessmen, realtors, and homemakers commute for a few months to Indianapolis to deal with the state's business.

When the assembly did meet, they had a year's worth of business to cover. Because of the short period of time and the pressure for hearings, the power of the chairman increased as to what bills would be heard.

A friend had stopped me shortly before Christmas on one of my short trips in and out of a department store. She had lobbied at the state house and cautioned me, "It might take you three years, Caress." I didn't have three years; it would be this year if I would just step out and obey.

John Hammond had also talked to me on the phone before Christmas, going over names of legislators. He lobbied at the state house as my free lawyer had told me. He was thoughtful, careful, and exact in his comments. He was exceedingly kind and wanted to help me, spending hours over the phone discussing legislators and their backgrounds.

He came from a family that had talked Indiana politics around the dinner table, and as a little boy had absorbed the stories and the backgrounds of the political personalities around the state.

I would hear his children in the background as he calmly spoke, considering possible names of Democrats who might be a good balance to sponsor the legislation along with Paul.

I wondered if I should try to speak to Mike Phillips. I wanted the Speaker to understand that children were involved. The urgency of the matter was important, for in an arena where every piece of legislation was political, this was beyond politics. Surely he would hear me.

The Speaker lived down at the bottom of the state close to the broad Ohio River that separates the Midwest from the South. Immigrant families had crossed the Ohio River from more settled parts of the country into the rolling hills of southern Indiana. There, for generations, these families had gone to work in the coal mines and lived simple lives. In time, unions would become powerful in the southwest part of the state as the mammoth industrial plants were built near the river and hired descendents of the pioneers. They were river Democrats down at the end of the state, a conservative brand of Democrat on many issues. However, they were union, and the unions would speak to government about their needs.

Mike Phillips was a family man with several children and he enjoyed being with people. The Speaker was loyal to his friends, considerate, friendly, even soft-hearted to those he didn't have to deal with politically. The people who lived along the Ohio liked Mike Phillips.

Mike had the working man's common touch. He could roll up his shirt sleeves and sit his massive frame down in the union hall, celebrating the wedding of a constituent's daughter. He was also well educated, a lawyer, and understood people who were affluent.

Speaker Phillips was a man people noticed, big-boned, a large, square face with heavy jowls and thick lips. His size alone could intimidate as his heavy frame, always erect, lumbered down the halls of the state house. The Speaker looked more like a Chicago ward boss than a lawyer from rural Indiana. He had represented his border district in the state house for over twenty years. Early in his political career he had gained power inside the Democrat caucus at the state house and had successfully held together the diverse coalitions of backgrounds and interests from around the state. The Hispanics and black legislators from around Gary combined with the Poles, Croats, and other eastern European minorities were a strong faction in his political caucus. Their names Kromkowski, Matonovich, Villalpando, bespoke their heritage and that of their constituents. Generations had worked in the steel mills whose belching towers of smoke lined the northwestern tip of the state along Lake Michigan. These legislators made up a large Democrat power base in the state of Indiana, but their ethnicity, concerns, location, and temperament were all a long way from Boonville and the river Democrats.

Mike Phillips held them all together by demanding the group unite behind what was important to him and, if they remained loyal, he would remember them and their legislation. He would place their bills in favorable committees and see that money came to them for their campaigns. The Speaker could also find a challenger to run against the non-team member in the next election. Mike Phillips was astute and he remembered who didn't vote with the team.

The Speaker would stand in front of the general assembly, solidly entrenched on the platform, his big arms wrapped around the podium, jaw jutting forward, and on more than one occasion, his back turned to the Republican side of the aisle. Once, a frustrated Republican legislator climbed on top of his desk, waving his hands, pleading to be recognized. He dramatized that when Mike wanted to block you out, you were dead meat.

This was the man I asked my friend Paul about, "Should I go see the Speaker?" I felt I needed his opinion.

"No," he answered immediately, adamantly. "It could even hurt."

He didn't want me to bring the legislation up to the Speaker, to remind him whose bill it was that would be winding its way through the general assembly. Of course, the Speaker would know, but Paul had his own plan.

Paul had grown up on the north side of Indianapolis on a quiet street lined with small, well-kept homes built as World War II ended. He was the youngest of three boys who were raised by their mother. His father had died two weeks after he was born, so as a little boy in the 1950s, an era when "Father Knows Best" played on the television, he was different. He was well-liked and smart, a boy who worked hard. The advantages of working hard and a professional life were obvious to him because the neighborhoods not far from his home reflected affluence and position. He was an Horatio Alger in the most American sense and now had achieved that affluence and position. Friendly, but low-keyed, he didn't like to make waves. You could almost see the wheels turning in his head as people would speak.

He led by building consensus in his caucus; a polished style, a patient listener. Democrats found him approachable and open-minded to work with, although he shielded and controlled his emotions, masking his own thoughts. He was part of the network of movers and shakers in Indianapolis, but also worked well with the small farmer from Macy, Indiana, and the local businessman from Crawfordsville, the retired policeman from Fort Wayne. They made up his Republican caucus. He led a conservative group that wanted the government out of their lives with no new taxes.

Paul's presence was one of assuredness and ease. Physically fit, he looked ready to run a fast three miles and had in all cases of appearance slipped gracefully into his forties. He was loyal to his family and friends, a father who left political functions to be with his children.

Like Mike Phillips, Paul was politically tough. Both men were like a couple of ducks that could take the political banter on the House floor. Barbs and verbal abuse rolled off their backs like water. The two men were cordial to each other, but temperament, geographics, philosophy, and ambition would keep them politically combative.

* * *

Shortly after Christmas I drove down to the state house to go over the legislation that Christy had completed writing and had presented to Paul. The near downtown streets were busy on this drab day. Every light seemed to be red. My thoughts were on reaching the state house as the car approached the downtown bridge that crossed Fall Creek. The light was again red. A young man approached the corner with a pit bull on a leash. He swaggered with importance, crossing the street in front of the car. "Is this a test, Lord?" I said out loud as the green light moved me forward.

My slipper protected the sock covering my foot from getting soaked. The wet limestone steps of the state house were tough to navigate without losing the slipper too small to cover a man's athletic sock. I pulled the doors open and stepped inside as the slipper fell off. To my right came an excited voice from behind a desk. "The pit bulls!" he said, simultaneously standing and yelling. His silver badge gleamed on his chest surrounded by the navy blue uniform. Rick Harris, a young black officer, was with the Capitol Police.

"Yes, it's really me."

"How are you doing, lady?"

"I'm doing fine," I told him as a smile came over my face. "I'm here to change the law."

Rick became my friend that December day, always warmly welcoming me into the state house.

"What a thing to be famous for," Paul said, shaking his head as I told him the story.

"Did you ever think I would become involved with anything so ugly?" I said to him, sitting in his office looking out across the lawn toward the statue of Governor Morton.

"No," he said, gently shaking his head. "No."

"Women have such a hard time with this," I said with a touch of sadness, feeling the strength flow out of me even though it was just mid-morning. "They want everything to be pretty. I'm lucky to have a leg though," I told him quietly. "There was so much blood flying around it was like something out of a *Terminator* movie."

"Who helps take care of the leg, Caress?" Paul asked.

"Pat does," I told him. "You could do it too, and would, but it's definitely true love."

Paul had finished reading the material that had been sent to him by Senator Lugar's office. He understood who the women were that had met in the little room over in Legislative Services and the basis for their ideas.

Christy entered the office as Paul read over what she had prepared. He made a few changes but the group's ideas and goals remained.

"Have you ever been in a meeting like that before?" I asked Christy.

"No," she answered, "I never have; it was the most

positive meeting." Her eyes sparkled as if she knew something different, something special, was unfolding at the state house.

Paul walked with me to his outer office. There were messages and calls for him to return. "All right," he said with a smile and added the now familiar, "I'll call you."

I left the state house, saying good-bye to Rick the policeman who placed the floppy slipper on my foot because the rain had started to sprinkle the steps leading down to the legislators' parking lot.

* * *

The doctor had come into the little examining room with a young man and his nurse. He was joking as he bent down and turned the leg back and forth. The doctor was proud of his work.

"A dog attack," he said out loud as the young man looked surprised, uttering, "Oh," nodding solemnly to me in recognition. I looked at the doctor with a question on my face. "This is my son—of whom I am very proud." He was in no mood to listen to any dog hodgepodge today. The doctor was consumed with himself.

These visits were an unfolding scenario—I never knew what would happen. Sometimes I planned what I would try and explain on a particular appointment. None of my plans were going to work this time.

"I want to talk about something medical," I heard myself say slowly to him. "I was wondering if the nurses ever saw any trauma patients because sometimes they didn't seem to understand what was happening to me." I described the man waiting to kill me in the bathroom and the warmth of my blood as I felt it again cover my face and ooze through my hair. The doctor stood still, listening. The words affected him. He didn't like the image of warm, flowing blood. How I sat in bed waiting for the man to kill me. Telling the nurse, I feel like I need to take something. Quiet for a moment, I watched him looking at me. "The next day you marched to the front of my bed scowling, 'If you want a month's worth of tranquilizers—*I'm not your doctor.*'"

The doctor dropped down on the little stool in front of me, wringing his hands together. "I am sorry if your stay was not as comfortable as it should have been."

The doctor remembered—I had pointed out his imperfection. A moment ago—invincible, displaying his to-be-doctor son—now, momentarily stricken.

"Let's go outside and let her get dressed now," he said referring to the stockings that were rolled up in my shoe.

He saw me step out of the room as he turned to the nurse and his son. "I always walk out with her," he told them with some bravado.

I stood with him outside and asked about his son. "He found out he's a people person," the doctor told me, continuing on about his son's progression in life. He lit a cigar and held it in his hands. He spoke about the son, his father, doctors in his family, when the look came back. It was a visible change of expression from confusion, embarrassment, sorrow, back to pride. Contemptuous again toward this little upstart with the dog problem. Rain was now coming down hard. "It's a bad hair day," he said lightly.

"Hair can take a lot," I said. The doctor was silent, remembering the blood-caked hair. He needed to insult, punish, but end on a light note.

It was like stepping out with death into the rain, I thought. I was not to hold on to this mortal man but step out and off the precipice. With the first step into the downpour my courage returned, the dread of death once again gone. God was giving me challenges, but a miracle had been promised, and the words that were put in my mouth affecting the doctor were for a greater purpose. I would be back next week.

* * *

The last day of the year had come and the phone was ringing by mid-morning. Paul's voice came across the line.

"Caress, I don't know how you'll feel about this, but I want to call a press conference next Monday, the day before opening day, to get publicity for the legislation."

"Yes," was my answer, and then in the next breath I asked if I could consult the team that had been put together.

"Okay," he said calmly.

"I'll call you right back," I told him. He was always unflappable and kind. It never occurred to me that it really was Paul's decision whether to call a press conference or not.

Velda answered her phone in the state house. "Caress, I can't believe you said that to him. You know he's in charge—the one that has to figure out how to get the bill through."

"You mean I shouldn't have told him I was going to check this out with you?"

"He probably thinks, 'Who is this woman?'" she said. It never occurred to me that Paul would care, but I realized my naiveté—she might have a point.

"Well, since he's waiting for an answer, what do you think of the idea, a press conference?"

"I think it's brilliant, and I wish I'd thought of it 'cause what he's trying to do is keep your story in front of the public as well as the legislators so his enemies will have a tougher time saying no to him."

"I guess I'll call him back and tell him it's fine."

"Yeah, and don't tell him anymore you've got to check something out with me."

My first lesson in political protocol was learned. Paul answered the phone in his office. "Good," he answered, "and as long as the governor doesn't call a press conference, and I don't think he's going to, we'll be all right."

I felt that the bill had to pass this year and was being assured in my prayers it would, but Paul couldn't understand everything I was experiencing. Wanting to relieve him of pressure, I said, "Paul, I know you will try, but if it doesn't work this year, it will eventually."

"That's right," the deep voice said with conviction across

the phone lines on the last day of the year. "That's right," he repeated again from the state house office as the conversation ended and the phone line went dead.

The weekend passed with many glad to see the old year gone. Cards were sent to me for a happier New Year. A friend sent a little pin of a tiny angel. I believed the prayers guiding me to step out.

Sunday evening came and I called the reporter who had told me the man who owned the dogs was a dogfighter. He had said that if I pursued the legislation the press would follow.

"Jack, there's going to be a press conference at the state house tomorrow, and I hope you can come." I was trying to make sure at least one reporter came.

"Caress, I'm going to be somewhere else, but the press will be there because you're the story."

I am? I thought, surprised because it wasn't me who was in charge, but He Who was working through me.

The slipper flopped past the news truck complete with a satellite dish, parked at the base of the now familiar stairs of the north entrance. There were a few more people inside the building, legislators arriving, preparing for the opening of the general assembly the following morning.

I waved to Rick and the other Capitol Policeman at the desk and climbed the granite stairs to Paul's office. Velda appeared in the hall as I rounded the corner on the last stretch of corridor that wound around to Paul's office.

Velda's timing was always impeccable. She could appear in the halls at just the right moment to find whom she needed and then just as quickly disappear. After twenty years at the state house she was like a homing pigeon, better than radar.

"Are you ready?" she asked me with a smile.

"I hope so," I told her. "Come with me into Paul's office because I know he's waiting for me," I said. Cathy was at her desk, looking up as we entered.

"He'll be right out, Caress," she told me and with that

the doors to Paul's office opened and he stepped out, pulling on his coat.

"I've asked Jeff Modisett to come, Caress. He's going to meet us downstairs." The tall, lanky prosecutor for Marion County, whom I had been dealing with indirectly and directly through my free lawyer, was going to be with us. Amazing, and one more of Paul's strategies, for Jeff was also an important Democrat.

Velda stood with me, watching Paul. "You both look like a couple of movie stars." Velda was enthusiastic. I hadn't thought of it exactly like that, but I decided it was good if she thought so.

I looked at Paul and said, "Do you think anyone will come?"

He was already moving toward the door when he answered, "Let's go see."

The elevator opened on the main floor across from the rotunda. There stood Prosecutor Modisett. "Thanks for inviting me," he said. We walked quickly over the marble floor and around the rotunda when I noticed bright lights flicking on and cameras in the hall, which surprised me. Velda ducked behind a marble column as the prosecutor and Paul kept walking. They were letting me lead the way. Leaning out of a room, there was a cameraman whom I walked towards. In the room waited twenty to thirty members of the press. Every television and radio station in the city, the Indianapolis newspapers and the Associated Press. Correspondents from out-of-state papers were in the room.

Paul went to the microphone and started explaining the bill. The law would hold dog owners responsible for the actions of their animals running loose in unprovoked attacks. If serious bodily injury or death occurred, there would be misdemeanor and felony charges.

The prosecutor spoke about a void in the law. The legislation was needed to protect people from irresponsible owners.

I looked at the press seated and standing in the room.

Velda sat a few rows back next to Linda who had walked over to the state house from Senator Lugar's office.

The prosecutor finished; then it was my turn.

"I want to send a message to those who would let a vicious dog run loose on innocent people." The lights flicked on as my words were recorded.

The questions flew at me. "How did I feel about the man?" a reporter asked.

"I'm very grateful he pulled the dogs off me, but other than that I really don't think about him."

I didn't think I should try and explain that this was a mission I had been prepared for because we would be there for the rest of the day.

Reporters wrote and asked more questions. I tried to explain that vengeance wasn't my purpose. This law was to help other people, particularly children.

Paul asked me quietly if I wanted him to answer because my voice would shake at the end of some questions.

"No, I'll go on," I told him.

"What would you like done with the dogs?" a reporter asked.

"I would like them humanely put down," I responded. Cameras continued to flash and finally the room was quiet. The rows of reporters and cameramen that crowded the doors had officially finished and were now coming to the front of the room. Three different anchors of the local news came toward the table where I was sitting.

"Good luck," each of them said.

One television anchor who had told me he loved dogs, flashed a big smile and nod before leaving. A reporter from the Associated Press came forward. "How old are you?" he inquired.

"I'm forty-three," I quietly answered him.

The tall prosecutor, who was standing by my shoulder, bent down and gently said to the reporter, "But can you say she doesn't look forty-three?" The reporter smiled. Jeff Modisett won me over as a permanent supporter.

I walked out of the doors and down the hall with the prosecutor and Paul as reporters continued walking with us, often stopping for more answers.

Touching the prosecutor's arm before he turned and walked down the opposite hallway, I mustered my courage. "The dogs need to be destroyed," I told him. "They're killers."

"Well, I know we would never return them to the owner," he told me. "The animal rights people might protest if we destroy them," he said.

Jeff didn't know the animal people with credentials were with me. They all knew there was no rehabilitating these animals. My free lawyer was going to have to continue talking to Prosecutor Modisett. This wasn't the place to try and convince him otherwise.

"Thank you for your help, Jeff," I told him as he turned to leave. I felt a new ally was publicly behind me.

We walked toward the elevator as people stopped Paul in the hall. "How are you doing?" they called to me all the way back to his office doors.

Paul turned with a big smile, taking off his coat. He looked like he had swallowed the canary, "Well—that went pretty well," he said, quietly pleased.

I dialed the phone from the outer office asking that someone from the business come and get me.

"We're all watching you on television, Caress," said one of the office staff. The noon news had started, and the first broadcasts of the press conference were going out across the state.

As I walked toward the state house doors, policeman Rick yelled from behind his desk, "How did it go?"

I gave him a grin as my fingers formed an "OK." Smiling back, he pulled open the great oak doors.

FIVE

Brandon Remembered

Velda sat waiting and working at her desk hidden behind
partitions placed there for privacy. They flanked her
desk on the fourth floor of the state house. The sunlight
streamed in behind her, adding much needed heat to the
area where she worked. The tall, narrow windows designed
several decades before heat-preserving insulation did not keep
the chill of early January from seeping through the panes.
Velda's windows looked out on the legislators' parking lot
that was filled that morning. She had been busy working for
the judge, arriving in the early morning darkness. Velda had
green eyes that sparkled when she smiled and a light-hearted
personality that showed itself with an infectious laugh.
Standing five feet four inches, she walked with authority and
a bounce in her step, always in a hurry covering the marble
corridors of the state house. As she walked she noticed the
little things about people that were clues to their character.
Did the legislator notice the people who swept the floors or
nod at the teenage intern? Velda observed everything and
had good friends in all the nooks and crannies of the building.
She never thought of herself as political, but she was naturally
political. "I don't really think about Republicans and
Democrats, Caress," she would say to me, "just who's useful."

Her desk, on the second day of the legislative session, was covered with the judge's memos for her to proofread. The young law clerks that worked in the room outside the judge's private chambers would check statutes, but often Velda knew as much about the law as the novice lawyers. Placed under the briefs that littered her desk was the work of her life that dealt with protecting and loving animals. On the partitioned walls that faced her as she worked were snapshots of kittens, notices for the next animal fundraiser, and the dog of the month calendar, all of which encircled a pencil sketch of Elvis. "Don't you like Elvis, Caress?" she would croon. "I like Bill Clinton 'cause he looks just like Elvis." I was horrified.

"Stop it!" I would say back to her, thinking of all the Republican pollsters fainting because people might vote for the president because he looked like Elvis. Despite her feelings about Elvis and President Clinton, Velda was a shrewd, thoughtful woman, who was a political tactician for the animal world and, luckily, for me.

She had worked for the judge almost twenty years, and the two of them had reached an understanding. They had a professional working respect for each other that had grown over the years into a loyalty and acceptance of each other's personality. Velda had a political antenna. She knew almost immediately the contents of any bill that would affect animals in the state of Indiana. Her boss, the judge, was charged with interpreting the law, and he didn't want to know anything about the legislation that was being made on the floors immediately beneath him. Velda protected her judge. She was sensitive to his position and she made sure he didn't know what she was up to in her animal political life.

Over the years the judge and Velda had taken on a brother-and sister-like friendship. They would verbally spar with one another, but continued to admire and appreciate each other.

The turning point in their relationship had come years ago when the cat stranglings had taken place east of the

Fountain Square area on Hamilton Street near downtown Indianapolis. Fountain Square, a neighborhood that had once flourished at the turn of the century, now struggled. The city neighborhoods surrounding the pretty black fountain in the middle of the square had become rough, and the once well-maintained homes now had a definite seediness. For years, Eldraine Chapman had lived on one of the old, unnoticed streets where she took care of and fed stray cats that would find their way to her back door. One day Eldraine walked around the back of her property and found some of her friends, the cats who had been coming to visit daily, with their throats slit; some were disemboweled. Others had been thrown on top of garages or just dumped where they were killed. Some of the cats were strangled, left with their eyes bulging. Eldraine tried calling the Humane Society and was told there was nothing they could do. She then called Animal Control. They said there wasn't money in their budget to take care of problems with "cat killers." Eldraine loved her cats and she was going to stop the killings in her neighborhood. She continued to call around town, talking to people who might care about the cat killings, working her way along the animal support chain of command until she found Velda. Velda, who knew the law, told Eldraine there was a cruelty to animals statute she could use that stated if you knowingly injured or killed an animal, it was a Class B misdemeanor.

A monetary award was set up to find the "cat killer." Press releases were sent out, and after an article appeared in the local paper, the Associated Press picked up the story. People around the country started to read about the cat stranglings in Indianapolis. Many sent in donations to add to the reward money to find the cat killer.

The judge watched from a distance and was not pleased. Every day Velda would be on the phone concerning the mass cat murders in Indianapolis. The press bombarded the judge's chambers and continued to want stories. The judge, himself, was not impressed. One Thursday evening he was preparing to leave the state house, ready to make the long trip north back home to Warsaw, Indiana. He would not return until the following Monday. The judge was tired as he packed his briefcase with work and made his way past the clerks, stopping by Velda's desk piled high with memos to type. He watched her pick up a ringing phone. "Call me when Dan Rather calls," he said, sarcasm dripping off his lips as he continued walking towards the door. The next day, Friday, at noon, CBS news called the state house. They had read about the cat killings in Indianapolis, and a news crew from Chicago would be arriving in a few hours to interview Velda. Dan Rather wanted to go with the story that evening.

In northern Indiana late Friday afternoon, the phone rang and the judge listened as Velda went through the day's messages and mail. She ended the call as the evening news was starting. "Judge," she said sweetly, "are you watching the national news?" The judge thought he would when they hung up. "Oh, good, because remember—you wanted to know if Dan Rather called," she said demurely. "Well, you-know-what?" She waited a moment as the question sunk in. *"He* called." Velda's reputation was made with the judge.

An embarrassed Indianapolis Animal Control rushed in at the last moment to help, and the cat killer was eventually sent to jail.

The judge recognized Velda's fine mind, efficiency, and loyalty. Velda appreciated his intelligence, kindness, and respect for her opinions. They tried to understand and acknowledge each other's sensitivities.

* * *

It was to the judge's chambers that I tentatively climbed the many unforgiving marble stairs on the second day of the Indiana Legislature. The state house was noisy and busy with people walking the halls. The oak phone booths at the top of the landing on the third floor were filled, while lobbyists patrolled the halls, holding their cellular phones.

I held on to the railing as I climbed one step after another up to the fourth floor. Aides and more lobbyists passed me on the stairs as I pulled the stiff leg up, grabbing even tighter the heavy oak railing to hold me steady. The fourth floor came nearer as I breathed a little faster, not being used to all the exertion. I continued to plod one stair at a time until a large desk started to appear as I came closer to the landing. It was an executive's desk that seemed out of place, sitting by itself out in the hall. The morning paper was being held up by the reader who sat behind the desk. As I took the last step, the paper went down and a big, smiling, ebony face appeared from behind the headlines. "Well, how you doing?" said a deep voice that sounded like gravel being gargled.

"I'm doing fine," I said. "Do you know where I might find Velda?" I asked the now standing man with a blue policeman's uniform and shining badge. Gene was the bailiff that guarded the judges' chambers on the fourth floor, the ivory tower of the Indiana State House, far removed from the political riff-raff on the floors below.

"She's right in that door behind me," he motioned. "I think she's looking for you—she's been out here once, kind of peering over the sides of the railing. How's that leg?" he nodded toward the bandages and the foot covered with the athletic sock.

"It's getting better," I told him. "You know, I feel I was very much watched over."

"Well, I hope you do real well," he said. The big black man looked solemnly towards me as the deep gravel voice started up again. "If I can ever help you just say the word."

Gene looked down the hall toward Assistant Bailiff Randy Rollings who had looked up from the morning paper he was reading at his desk. "Randy, this lady is our guest," he called over his shoulder. The associate smiled and slightly waved his hand. Gene nodded for me to continue on past his desk.

The enormous oak door was already standing open to the first room of the judge's chambers. His name, written in golden letters, appeared high over the door. Dark wooden bookcases, holding rows of law books, greeted me upon entering, and as I followed the little corridor of emerald green carpeting around the standing partitions, I found Velda.

"Well, there you are," she said, smiling with the musical voice that went up an octave with each word. "Sit down." She nodded toward a wooden chair behind her desk. To my left was a little area behind a bookcase where Velda kept her files and the coffee-maker. There was just enough room to stand and turn around in that little makeshift area. Immediately beyond the little storeroom area on the other side of Velda's partitions was the judicial bathroom. On my right was the entrance to the middle room where the law clerks worked for the judge. The clerk's doorway led immediately into the judge's private chambers where he was presently working behind his desk.

Velda stood, calling to the law clerks. "You all, this is my friend Caress, and she's going to be down here this session while we get a bill passed." Kim and Joe looked up from their desks, giving me a smile and wave.

"Will the Judge mind that I'm here?" I asked Velda.

"Naw, don't worry about him," she said, picking up the ringing phone. I was gazing around Velda's command central when a ruddy complexioned, compact man, standing five foot seven, walked by the work area. A quizzical look passed momentarily over his face, and then a slight frown formed. The judge kept walking, and as if some mental telepathy had taken over, Velda hung up the phone. The judge had recognized me. He knew I was a part of Velda's clandestine political world and should be separated from the judiciary.

"You don't want to sit here anymore," she turned and told me, escorting me out of the carpeted office onto the marble floor outside the judge's chambers. Velda sensed the ethical boundaries of the judge's personality and her own politics. "You know, it's time for my break," she said happily, as we left the ivory-towered fourth floor, descending to the floors below where the common herd of Indiana politics resided.

We walked down the long corridor on the third floor toward the center of the state house. A brass railing on one side looked down to the patterned cream and brown marble below. People were going in and out of offices on the second level. "They won't go into session today until one o'clock," she told me, smacking a piece of paper with black type, "that's what the schedule says right here." We turned a corner, and Velda stopped and motioned with her head to her right, "Caress, this is the Senate side of the state house. This is where all the aristocrats preside in our state government; where everything is done with perfect decorum. Senator Garton runs the sessions with straight parliamentary procedure because, after all, they're senators and not like the cowboys on the House side where anybody says or yells whatever they feel like saying."

I remembered the bowling trophy I had noticed standing on a table placed next to the wall in the House of Representatives. A large golden-colored trophy complete with an elephant and a donkey placed on either side. Once a year the House Republicans bowled against the House Democrats, and the winners kept the trophy on their side of the aisle. The Democrats had won the last bowl-a-thon. It crossed my mind that the Senate probably did not own a bowling trophy, and such undignified memorabilia was relegated to the Wild West House of Representatives that was located directly across the gaping rotunda.

The Senate chamber had an aquarium-like plate glass window in the wall so those in the outer corridor, excluded from the business session, could stare in at the senators, watching their every move. The chamber was empty, but the marble room was handsome with chandeliers hanging from the ceiling, lighting the big leather chairs that stood behind the semicircles of desks. There was a raised dais in the corner of the chamber where President Pro Tem Garton oversaw the Senate, and Lieutenant Governor O'Bannon helped to call the bills to the floor. It seemed more intimate since there were only fifty senators compared to the larger House side.

A tall, slender, white-haired man came down the hall, peering over a handful of papers. He carried himself with authority and looked like a man who was preoccupied with business. Velda stuck the schedule in front of me and I looked down, not wanting to stare back at this man who was suddenly taking a good look at me and the bandaged leg. He continued down the hall and Velda told me in a low voice, "It's good for you to be noticed; that's Senator Larry Borst, who heads the Finance Committee. Ever heard of a bill being "Borsted"? I shook my head no that I didn't know what "Borsted" was all about. "That's what it's called at the state house when Larry kills your piece of legislation. The Finance Committee is powerful, Republican, very conservative. Don't worry, though, he'll just 'luv' you 'cause you don't want any money. He also is the only politician at the state house who is a veterinarian and thinks he should be consulted about all the animal legislation. So, when it gets closer to the time for the Senate to see the bill, I'll make sure he knows what's going on. I like him, he's a good person, tough, but we'll make sure he's informed." Velda guided me in and out of the increasingly busy halls to a doorway at the end of a corridor.

"Now here is where people from around the state can call in if they want their legislator to know how they feel about a particular bill." I looked in the entrance and watched a row of women picking up ringing telephones and writing messages down. There were mailboxes behind them where messages were placed for each legislator. One of the women

I remembered having seen before visiting the polls where I voted. She had faded hair that had once been blond or reddish in color and a face catacombed with wrinkles. She was chain-smoking as she wrote down the messages while giving her opinion to each caller. "I don't know if he's gonna check his messages agin' today, but I'll put yours right on top," she was telling the caller. "That bill is starting on the House side so you don't need to tell your senator about it now. If you do they'll just forgit, so call back if it passes the House." She hung up the phone and looked at Velda.

"Is Mark Kruzan in his office?" Velda asked.

Cigarette hanging from her lips and hand under her chin, her lips barely moved. "Haven't seen him but his messages are gone."

"I wanted my friend to meet him," Velda told the row of message takers. "You're going to get a lot of calls about this lady's bill. The press has named it 'vicious dog' but it's House Bill 1218." They all stopped talking and looked down at the bandaged leg. The cigarette went from one side of the mouth to the other.

"Is Representative Kruzan sponsoring the bill?" she asked.

"He's not the main sponsor, that's Paul Mannweiler, but he's the Democrat who's co-sponsoring on the House side," Velda replied.

Representative Kruzan had been Velda's idea as a co-sponsor. I had suggested his name to Paul who had been mentally going through members of the House, trying to find a Democrat who would be interested in sponsoring the bill—someone he hadn't alienated over his years leading Republicans down at the state house. Paul liked the idea of Mark Kruzan. "I get along with him really well," he told me when the name had been mentioned.

Mark was a young man in his early thirties, an associate professor of law at Indiana University who was most interested in environmental bills. He had first met Velda six years earlier as a freshman legislator while trying to help a constituent. He had heard through the state house grapevine that Velda might advise him on a piece of legislation that concerned animals, so Mark tracked Velda down. In his first attempt at running the gauntlet at the state house, he successfully passed the law that ended the use of decompression chambers for the euthanasia of animals in the state. This was an inhumane practice of stuffing many animals together in a barrel-like chamber while they scratched and clawed one another and their organs exploded due to decreased levels of pressure inside the chamber. Velda and Mark had remained friends over the years at the state house.

I wanted to meet the representative from southern Indiana and thank him for helping to sponsor the legislation. Paul had told me he would introduce me sometime, but he was busy now that the general assembly had convened.

This morning, Mark was not at his desk, so Velda moved on past the ringing phones and chain smokers back out to the main hall. "There are some hearing rooms close by, but I don't know where you will testify—maybe one of these," Velda said thoughtfully as we walked. The rooms were filled with men peering over reading glasses, sitting at tables covered with papers. The large oak doors opened and closed as we passed. People in the hall were turning to look at me as I passed, moving the stiff leg on the ball of my foot.

We entered a waiting elevator and descended to the main floor where Velda walked me over to a tiny old room. "This is the bill room, Caress, a real meeting place for people in the state house. A spot where people talk and pass on information." Anyone could come to the bill room and buy copies of legislation in its current form as it traveled through the state house chambers. People were congregated outside the little room. They were all talking and standing by a set of computers that could be used to find out the current status of a bill: if a hearing had been assigned, the time and place. Velda smiled and waved to a few of the regulars but kept me moving, not wanting to stop.

"Now I'm gonna show you the first floor, which is really the basement," she said, whisking me through the growing crowd of visitors and lobbyists toward the elevator that rattled us down to the lower level. Velda had an agenda for me to quickly learn the state house. "This is where the press resides, and there are some legislators' offices down here from the House side. Hearings are also held down here as well as subcommittee meetings." We passed the Associated Press offices and the *Louisville Courier Journal* office and then the local papers. They were small offices separated with prefabricated wallboard. Men and women of the press were talking on the phones, watching their doorways, and seemed interested in seeing me pass. We wove through many small corridors. The whole floor was like an ant colony, complete with underground passages connecting the state house with other downtown buildings in a vast subterranean network. Nothing beautiful or inspiring down here in the reconverted old basement.

Velda stopped at a small counter where candy bars and coffee were sold. "I want a legislators' handbook," she told the coffee pourer behind the counter.

"They're five dollars," the attendant said as Velda handed her a bill.

"Caress, these come in handy." The glossy little brochure held the pictures of all the men and women participating in the 108th legislative session; the one hundred members of the House and the fifty state senators. There was a little diagram showing where each legislator sat in the different chambers, what committees they sat on, and a map of the state of Indiana showing what section of the state they represented. I needed to know each one.

"My coffee break is about over, Caress, so I'm going to quickly take you back upstairs and leave you on the House side." She was hurrying toward the elevators with her bounce and quickstep when she stopped suddenly as if she had run into a wall. "I'm sorry, Caress, I'm probably walking too fast for you," she said, and her face fell, looking toward the leg.

"You're not going too fast," I told her, "just don't run." People came on the elevator and nodded towards me.

"How are you doing? Good luck to you."

"This is great," Velda whispered, getting off on the third floor. "People are falling all over the place for you. Now I want you to stand out in the hall where everyone will see you as they go in to session at one o'clock."

"Do you think they will know who I am?" I asked her.

"They'll know who you are, it's their business to know who you are. You've been all over the papers, television, and radio; believe me, they'll know you." I watched Velda ascend up the long flight of marble stairs back up to the ivory tower on the fourth floor. She turned at the top of the stairs and started motioning me with her hands to move away from the wall. I stepped out into the very middle of the passage and stood there where Velda gave me the "A-OK" sign and then turned and disappeared at the top of the stairs.

I was alone in the middle of hundreds of people who were now filling the halls. The lobbyists had appeared after lunch to catch legislators in the hall before the session began. I held on to the slick cover of the legislators' handbook for comfort since I hadn't had time to learn anyone's picture. The lobbyists disappeared into every little alcove to talk on their cellular phones, eyes watching doors and hallways so they could stop the legislator who was needed, perhaps getting their message across before the session began.

I was a novice in the halls of government. Everyone seemed to know exactly what to do and where to go and whom to talk to. It was like standing in traffic in the middle of a busy intersection, new in town and lost as to direction.

I wandered down the hall towards the main doors, trying to walk right down the center while circumventing frantic conversations. Most of the members of the House had entered through their respective doors: the Republican side where

Paul was the leader and the Democrat's side where Speaker Mike Phillips presided. The door that led to Speaker Phillips' office was closed. I stopped momentarily and stared.

I didn't know, but behind the Speaker's door a conversation was going on among the Democratic leadership with the co-sponsor of the dog bill, Mark Kruzan. The Speaker had a plan. "I've had this press release drawn up for immediate release that Mannweiler voted against this legislation twice before and now he's changed his mind. This is a chance to embarrass him with the press and the public now that he's put his name in as chief sponsor of this bill." A combination of old animosities and future battles fueled the current anger at the minority leader.

"We want the legislation despite the main sponsor," Mark said earnestly.

"I think Mannweiler's name should come off the bill, or at least not appear first," blurted another man in the room.

"But, I don't want to take his name off the bill or for me to be the main sponsor," Mark shot back. "We have a real opportunity for a Republican to convince people, who otherwise would not listen, that no one is going to lose any personal freedom by supporting this bill. It's a matter of people being responsible for their animals, and a lot of people are going to listen to him who wouldn't listen to a professor from Bloomington who is also a Democrat." The angular face tilted as he spoke. Tall, with a full head of light brown hair, he was always somewhat uncomfortable in the small, exclusive meetings at the state house that often decided the fate of a bill. "She is also his friend, and that makes for a committed legislator," Mark continued calmly. "Now, this bill also becomes important to him." The others still sensed an opportunity. The bill could be useful in worrying Mannweiler. Each other's nemesis, Mannweiler and Phillips both knew how to play the game of politics, and, at the moment, Mannweiler had the momentum because of the media attention the woman who was attacked was receiving.

The Speaker's big jaws jutted out, remembering all the legislation he had tried to introduce over the years that had been killed when the Republicans were in charge. Now he was in power and the dealmaker. "Let it move, but slowly. The bill's been assigned to Jesse's committee, Courts and Criminal Code. Drag out the time when the bill will be heard, and let Mannweiler sweat."

Jesse Villalpando, a lawyer who chaired the committee controlled by the Democrats, was Hispanic and came from East Chicago in the northwestern part of the state. Lake County had the largest group of representatives at the state house other than the capital city of Indianapolis. Jesse was a solidly built man in his thirties with brown eyes and slightly receding black hair framing an olive-skinned, square face. He gave many people the impression he was not a man to cross. Chairman Villalpando was every inch the Latino in temperament, and watchers at the state house had seen the volatile, fiery personality. Jesse was also a party man who would obey Mike's wishes and be none too friendly to Mannweiler.

Everyone in the room was aware that the introduction of the bill had received bipartisan support and had the prosecutor from Indianapolis, a Democrat, behind the legislation. It would be hard not to give the bill a hearing without looking personally, politically vindictive. Every newspaper in the state had covered the press conference down on the first floor, and they continued to follow the woman who had been attacked.

The Democratic leadership also knew the history of a previous dog bill, having twice passed the House only to be killed on the Senate side. The Republicans could kill it themselves; after all, there would be some objections, and perhaps a powerful lobbyist or interest group would produce hundreds or maybe thousands of phone calls against the bill. If the bill had any changes, amendments, there was always conference committee where the bill could be lost in the shuffle during the last days of the legislative session.

The woman who had been attacked was in the state house. The press and the House members knew she was there, and that made harassing Mannweiler through this bill more touchy. But in the end, it would be the head of the Democratic leadership, Speaker Mike Phillips, who would decide if the bill would stay alive, at least on the House side.

Unaware of all the intrigue, I continued to stand in the hall, mesmerized, watching the performances around me as people stepped up to desks on either side of the main doorway to the House chamber. They scribbled furiously on the desks' note pads, sending messages with pages who entered the main doors, now closed to the public because the one o'clock session was beginning. Lobbyists and friends from back home peered through the windows, expectantly waiting and watching the reaction of the legislator receiving their notes. Men waved through the windows, trying to attract the attention of a particular politician who had decided to ignore them as long as possible.

Other lobbyists sat along the benches that lined one wall. They were in for the long haul, some looking immediately bored, others merely tired, slouching down on the seat, but they were waiting in the halls for whomever they needed to see. I stared as an older woman wearing a rumpled gray raincoat locked her arm through a legislator's arm. Often the conversations were intense and brief with legislators hurrying back inside the chamber to take their seats. I watched the different representatives not yet knowing their names, but memorizing their faces and where they sat. Speaker Phillips was taking his place on the dais and the session began.

The doorman guarding the doors that led to Paul's offices smiled and nodded to me. He stayed most of the time, sitting on a folding chair, quickly standing at attention when someone looked like they wanted to enter. There was no telling how long Mr. Young had served the state house, but he would always greet me as a regular. He wore the regulation navy blue jacket, emblazoned with the seal of the state on the front pocket of the blazer, along with conservative gray pants. All the doormen at the state house were older men, mainly retirees, who took on the job of screening those who tried to enter the Senate or House chambers. We had become friends when I had passed through the doors to visit the minority leader's office before Christmas.

Today he knew I must be on some official business, and although he didn't know what, he let me through the big oak doors. The public wasn't supposed to be back in the little corridor that ran alongside the House chamber and where I was now walking. There were loudspeakers placed in the little hall and in the minority leader's office. Mike Phillips' deep voice was coming across, giving instructions to the general assembly. I stopped by the first doorway where legislators entered the chamber and looked out over the occupied desks and swiveling chairs. Legislators looked over and noticed the bandaged leg.

I walked a little further down the narrow hall to a second entrance and watched the Speaker of the house in action, gavel in his hand. I hesitated, knowing I was somewhere I shouldn't be at the moment. Paul was sitting in his chair in the front row, eyes glued to the speaker, mouth turned downwards. His chair was rocking back and forth.

My eyes traveled to the white sock that was working its way down my leg. My hand impulsively yanked at the material. I had begun to droop, like my sock. Slowly, I walked back down the little hall and out the large oak doors. I had been watching the players at the state house for several hours and now climbed the flight of stairs back to the quiet sanctuary of the judicial floor.

Gene was gone for the moment as I paused by his large desk at the top of the stairs. Turning around, I noticed the outside of a little building that had been built on the fourth floor inside the state house. Its pinnacled roof looked up towards the blue vaulted windows edged in gold that covered this section of ceiling. I thought there was definitely some truth in calling this floor the ivory tower. The fourth floor seemed to be in the heavens. The judges that quietly worked in their offices, reading and writing their opinions, were the monks of the state house, unseen in their luxurious cells. The little building had photographs on the outside wall. They were pictures of the judges of the Indiana Court of Appeals that spanned many decades. Judges from the nineteenth century with round, horn-rimmed glasses and somber expressions stared from behind their glass enclosures. Towards the back of the little building the current court was pictured, and Velda's judge smiled out from his picture. He wasn't frowning in his picture in the hall, I thought.

"This is what we call 'the shack.'" The musical voice caught me off guard. Velda was returning to the office, having been on an errand to another judicial chamber. "So how'd you do down there?"

"I think I need to study the book," I told her.

"You'll do great," she replied. "Do you want to come in and sit down?"

"Is the judge still there?" I asked. "I don't think he likes me around all that much."

"Don't worry about him. He'll like you fine, and a few minutes sitting with me won't bother him," Velda assured me, noticing my ambivalence. "Caress," Velda said intently, changing the subject, "there is something I want you to do. Linda is our media person; you know she put that packet of information together and brought it over to your house. Well, now we should begin work on another packet to give to each member of the committee who hears your testimony. There needs to be a letter from you to each committee member saying briefly what happened to you and why they should support you. Can you do that?" she asked. "You can speak, now, can you write?"

"I *can* do that Velda," I guaranteed.

"Did you see all those politicians at work down there?" she smiled. "It could be weeks before they hear this bill. Sometimes things move so slowly down here, then all of a sudden there's movement on a bill and things go so fast you can hardly keep up." Velda cocked her head to one side, her eyes sparkling. "You know, all Paul and Mark Kruzan really have to do is put on their white cowboy hats and stand by your side saying, 'Look at this poor, pretty little lady who's been hurt.' "

"Would you stop it," I started laughing. She could always make me smile. "Do you think we will get a hearing?" I asked, jumbling laughter and worry together.

"'Course we'll get a hearing. Don't know when, but the Speaker is politically savvy, and you've gotten so much publicity he'll almost have to assign it to some committee where they will hear the bill." Velda always spoke with such confidence that I never doubted her opinion.

"Well, I guess then I'll call someone to come get me," I told her with a tired smile.

Parking was a problem at the state house when the legislature was in session, so my car continued to be parked at our business a few blocks away. "I'll see you soon, Caress," Velda called as she walked back towards her office. I grabbed the bannister and slowly started down the flights of stairs. They made me dizzy when I first started down, and the slippery sock made me more cautious. The House session had recessed for the day, and men and women passed me on the main floor with their coats wrapped around them, heading to the legislators' parking lot. I stood by the doors and waved over to Rick of the Capitol Police.

"You coming back tomorrow?" he asked.

"Probably so," I told him.

He gave me his big smile and said, "Well, I'll look for you then."

The gusts of a rainy, cold January day came through the

doors every time someone stepped outside. Senator Garton came by on his way to the parking lot. He stopped to light his pipe before going out the main doors. I thought about introducing myself as a long-lost family member with the name of Garten but hesitated, and he continued on outside down the stairs to a silver Avanti sports car that waited in the senator's parking space close to the door. The license plate noted he was a state senator with the numeral one. I watched him reach his car and looked further toward the street wondering if anyone would ever come for me, when I heard a voice directly behind me. "Oh, I wanted to meet you and here you are." The man's voice continued. "You know, I don't know how I feel. This legislation's important, you got your picture in the paper, lots of publicity, it has a good shot now of passing." He was quiet for a moment and his voice lowered, "But you had to get hurt." The brows knitted together and his face was expressive. Mark Kruzan had found me.

"I've wanted to meet you for weeks," I told him. "Thank you for being the co-sponsor of the bill with Paul."

"Oh, I wanted to be a part of this. You know, I've tried to help this legislation through before. Maybe this is the year," he said as he continued on down the wet limestone stairs. I liked him and wondered if he was a runner as he quickly sprinted through the parking lot. My car appeared and I left for the day, going down the outside steps carefully, with the floppy shoe moving up and down on my foot.

* * *

My hands turned the steering wheel as the car moved through the late afternoon traffic and drove down Fall Creek Parkway. I thought of Ed, and wondered if the great blue heron stayed all winter here in Indiana. I understood his confusion with all the people running, walking, talking by his spot on the creek. He wasn't sure what to do with people closing in around him, so he flew towards Heaven to escape.

Ed would have hated the halls of the state house and thought all those extremely immobile brass eagles down there were quite insane. But it was people who were insane. They who made animals killers for sport and money and who had little conscience concerning the lives of animals or people. The dogs who attacked me had been caged at Animal Control in Indianapolis for over two months and were being held until the trial still more than a month away. I remembered Velda's words to me, "Animal Control's keeping those dogs just because it's you, Caress." She would look me straight in the eyes and tell me, "If they had attacked someone who hadn't gotten your publicity, those dogs would be back at home with their owners again." Her voice had been reflective and resigned. "You know our government responds differently towards people depending on who they are don't you? It's not fair and it's sad, but it's true. You're going to get your trial faster for the same reason." She had smiled. "The press is all over this, and I hope the prosecutor understands the public is not going to stand for it if those dogs aren't destroyed."

The dogs were the ones officers had found at the man's home the evening of the attack. Now in cages, they were breaking their teeth off, hurling themselves against the steel bars.

The car passed the side street that would take me down the section of Fall Creek where the attack had taken place and the curb where I began to die. I kept going straight, although I was going to turn off soon and head towards the grocery store. The store was a few blocks away, and since I hadn't been inside there for two months, the time had come for a return to normalcy.

The parking lot was full with people stopping on their way home from work. The path where I walked was empty. It seemed an eternity since that day in early November. Stopping and parking the car, I walked through the automatic doors and entered the store.

The grocery store carts were stuck together in bunches

along the wall inside the door, and after pulling on one cart, it came free from the others with a loud clang. Something seemed strange, and there wasn't time to think through what that was before I lifted my head and realized there was silence in the store. The checkout aisles were quiet, and eight rows of customers stood still. About fifty pairs of eyes were gazing at me, and no one was talking. I looked over at the checkout aisles. It was amazing, they knew all about me and the bandaged leg. I stopped and smiled, nodding to everyone, and one by one people started talking again. It was the first public place other than the state house I had entered since the press conference. People had been reading about the story since November and I had been on television in December, but now it was different. Now they came to tell me how they felt. "I was very much watched over," I would repeat to one person after another who came to wish me well and hear the story.

I would tell them not to worry … that I had never been afraid. When one person left, another would come towards me. Their own fears were always present when they talked to me. Strangers were passionate on my behalf, sometimes showing anger, other times deeply felt concern. "Ever since I saw your picture you have been on my mind," one woman told me.

"There's that lady who went down to the state house," said another who ran up beside the grocery cart. Some deep chord seemed to have been touched with the strangers around me. People wanted to tell me about themselves and their fears and to look and talk to me. I had taken on some dark issue that lay inside many people. Speaking to strangers, I told them I felt it was something I was to do in my life, a mission for children. That I was protected and watched over even as I was attacked. The more I talked, the more people wanted to hear. Starting to feel that I would never be able to leave, I made my way toward the exit, forgetting whatever it was I had come to buy.

I didn't realize it, but there was an aura developing around the dog bill and my mission that was recognized by the public and I witnessed in the grocery; an aura of innocence on behalf of children and animals for whom the legislation was intended to protect. I was the beneficiary of that aura, experiencing overwhelming love and support.

* * *

"Where have you been? I was worried about you," Pat said to me when I walked in the back door. Boomer and Chuck wanted to be fed, so they also greeted me at the back door, wagging their tails.

"You won't believe what happened to me," I said, repeating the grocery stories.

"Well, it's close to where it happened, Caress. I'm sure everyone in that store has thought, That could have been me."

"It wasn't going to be them though, Pat; it was to be me." Pat, as well as anyone, could understood what I was saying. We had known each other since we were five years old, and although no one can ever completely know another person, he saw the events unfolding and also believed. People were also stopping him to talk, and customers were sending him pictures of me from newspapers around the state.

Matthew walked through the kitchen and didn't say much as he continued down the hall. He wasn't his smiling self, and I followed him as he entered the den. He slouched down in one of the leather wing chairs. "It's just this kid, he's such a jerk." He spit out the words. He was angry and stared down at my leg. "I'm not going to talk about it either," he told me. "Mom, everyone still asks me about you and what happened. About all the stuff in the paper." He was upset, separated from all the other freshman and made to stand out. Not only did he stand out, but I wondered with his nature and personality if he also felt guilty.

"You know it's not your fault that this happened to me," I told the former cowboy who once guarded me in the grocery store aisles.

In one of his classes a teacher had started explaining to the room about the law and how the law is made in a democracy. "This is what Matt's mother is doing at the state house," he would tell the room. The teacher would go through the steps in passing legislation, using me as an example. Matt squirmed in his chair, and at the end of class, he asked the teacher never to mention his mother again. He was fifteen years old and still trying to find himself in the murky world of adolescence. He was concerned with fitting in and looking right, making the soccer team. All of this was drawing too much attention to himself, and then there was the jerk who played on the soccer team.

Also a freshman, the tall, muscular boy hustled for recognition and attention. He would stand in the hall, leaning against the lockers as Matt passed. The boy would start to growl, then bark. "She tastes better than dog food," he whispered. Matt stopped and turned. He felt his face drain of color, and his mouth formed a straight, hard line. He hated that kid. The boy would look back and smile; he knew he was in control. Every day it was the same, and Matt was miserable.

Only later would I learn what was being said in the hall at school. Matt climbed the stairs three at a time, closing his bedroom door at the top of the stairs. He asked himself the eternal question "Why?" Matthew wasn't far enough down his own path to understand my feelings. He couldn't appreciate that no event, no matter how bad, can be properly measured on the day it happens or in the weeks that follow. Only in the context of a life will the mission or knowledge evolving from that event become clear.

* * *

The next day Matthew and his brother left early for school, waving to me as they drove by the kitchen window and traveled down the winding driveway. Benjamin was dealing better with his mother's publicity and accepted the situation.

Pat wrapped the Ace bandage around my foot and leg

before he left. Whenever I tried to wrap my leg, the bandage would become separated and loose, and the heel of my foot slipped through. The bandage wasn't needed, but it attracted attention towards the leg, and lighter elastic bandages under the Ace bandage applied pressure on the red scars. After the leg was wrapped, I never thought about it except for feeling the stiffness throughout the day. There was too much to accomplish to spend emotion grieving. The leg curved inward and the shape had changed due to muscle loss in the calf replaced with thick, red, zigzag scars. Two other deep scars on the outside gave the effect of tight rubber bands having been placed around the leg.

Velda wanted me to write about the attack and why the legislators should support me. Thoughts of what should be said started to filter through my mind. Rain poured down the windows while flashes of watching a robin entered my thoughts, the sound of a stroller's wheels, a baby boy smiling—all those things I remembered from the day of the attack. I had an idea to call the *Indianapolis Star*. "Is there a research department, historian, something like that?"

The operator answered, "There's a number for a librarian."

It clicked with me. "That's the number." I listened as a pleasant sounding woman picked up the phone. "I'm interested in stories about dog attacks on people in Indianapolis. Do you have any articles that involve children, say from a few years ago?" The librarian at the *Star* punched in her computer.

"If you'll hold on, I'll check. Yes," she answered as she read, "we do." She paused, "There was a little boy that received a great deal of attention four years ago. I could send you those stories."

"Thank you, I would like those," I told her. "Do you have different articles that involve other children?" I asked. The librarian continued punching into her computer.

"There are other articles on other children, but not as extensive as this one child." She paused again on her end of the line and her voice became softer, "You know, all the other stories are about you." I sat still, holding the phone; a stranger had recognized me by my voice. Reality was sinking in about the number of people who must be paying attention if I was known by my voice.

"What is your name?" I asked her, still not used to people knowing me and my not knowing them.

"Mary," she told me. "If I can help you again just call."

"Thank you, Mary, I will," I said and hung up the phone.

* * *

The rest of the days that week and the next were spent at the state house. I would study the small legislative handbook, slipping into the ladies' room to look up a picture and make sure I had the name right before stopping the legislator in the hall. I memorized their brief biographies, learned their names, what committees they sat on, and their seniority. Which ones represented a rural district, who cared about the farmer and the hunter.

The lobbyists in the halls also were becoming aware of me. Everyone noticed who was talking to what politician. The halls were tightly packed with people, and the noise level was intense outside the House chamber before the daily session began. John Hammond walked down the hall in his dark lawyer's suit, carrying his cellular phone, when he noticed me. He quickly walked over as I stood in the hall outside the House chamber. "Caress, I've spoken to Jesse Villalpando and he is going to give you a hearing," he said encouragingly. "I've told him that you are a very sincere person."

"Do you know when that will be?" I asked him.

"No, I don't, but he told me that he would hear the bill. He also feels the bill has merit."

"Who sits on this committee?" I asked, interested and anxious about the personalities I would have to persuade.

"Caress, the committee has a number of members from the black caucus, and the co-chairman is a new representative named Thomas Alevizos from northern Indiana." John rattled off the members' names as if preparing a game plan. "Alevizos is a lawyer as is Villalpando. Remember, there are eight Democrats and five Republicans on the committee. Dennis Avery from Evansville is concerned with a lot of children's issues as is Michael Dvorak, a lawyer from Granger. Bill Crawford heads the black legislative caucus and is from Indianapolis, and Greg Porter is also a black caucus member, new to the legislature, from Indianapolis. Robert Hayes, part of the House Democratic leadership, is an attorney from Columbus. Then there is Dale Sturtz who, by profession, is an investigator from the northern part of the state." John paused; he seemed to be mulling over each personality.

"Now the five Republicans should be with you since, to begin with, this is Paul's legislation. Only if they have some serious objection would they go against him in committee. I would think their immediate inclination would be positive towards the bill. They also have to know that this will be one of very few Republican bills that is going to get a hearing on the House side. I imagine Paul has requested that this bill be heard, and the Speaker has to hear a few Republican bills. Also, you have the issue, the media, you're down here being visible. I would say the pressure is on them to hear you. The Republicans are also a diverse group. Jack Cottey is a colonel in the sheriff's department. Dan Pool, part of the Republican House leadership, from Crawfordsville, is a small business owner; Ralph Ayres, a teacher. Then you have two prosecuting attorneys from different sections of the state, Dean Young and Ralph Foley. Remember, Caress, you have a very real human issue and you're going to be the one to tell them your story."

I concentrated on what John had said about each man. "Paul says the fight for this bill is in the House," I said, looking at John.

"Well, he's the minority leader and he knows the leadership in the House will do him no favors," John said, shaking his head. "Though I asked Paul if he was committed to this bill, Caress, and he said yes. That means he's going to try awfully hard to get it through." John looked at me as an idea passed through his head. "You know, Judy and Frank O'Bannon are very close to Mike Phillips. I think Frank supported him for Speaker and they live close to us in the Old Northside." Frank O'Bannon, the lieutenant governor of the state of Indiana, was well liked by both Republicans and Democrats. His wife Judy also was popular and was known to occasionally speak privately to legislators on issues that concerned her.

The Old Northside's historic nineteenth century ambiance was sometimes disrupted by the dangerous neighborhoods that came up to the very edges of the freshly painted gingerbread houses, carefully restored by the new pioneers. John thought he remembered trouble in an apartment building close to the O'Bannon's home. He remembered drug trafficking and believed dogs were involved. John thought carefully. "Perhaps if I write to Judy, explaining that I do not represent you and know your husband as my son's Boy Scout leader, she might have some interest. It's worth a try." John was busy representing his law firm's clients while trying to help me. He was patient and thoughtful with every novice question I presented to him. I thanked him for helping me and he touched my arm before he turned, walking quickly down the hall.

Velda looked up and turned in the swivel chair as I peeked around the partitions. "I saw John Hammond downstairs, and he was telling me about the committee members on Courts and Criminal Code." I turned and looked behind me through the clerks' office. "Is the judge in today?" I always felt a little apprehensive visiting Velda no matter how serenely she welcomed me.

"He's been in and out of the office, gone right now."

"I don't want to get the steely stare," I told her.

"He'd better not stare at you," she said adamantly, the

green eyes widening to make a point. The judge and Velda were definitely like sparring brother and sister, but, after all, I wasn't a member of the family. "Walk with me while I do some errands?" she smilingly said to me.

We walked across to the judges' waiting room where Velda had been assembling papers for her boss. "Isn't John Hammond nice?" she said happily to me. "He reminds me of someone who could be my little brother." She spoke with a chuckle in her voice.

"Velda, John told me some weeks ago about groups that maybe should be endorsing the bill and fact sheets that should be included with my testimony. He said something about direct mail to organizations around the state."

"Caress, many of the groups to sign on to the bill are already in place," Velda said confidently. "That is part of the responsibility of this team that is helping you. Your job is to speak and to write about yourself and what motivates you." She stopped walking and looked at me.

"I can do that," I said, relieved. "You know, I was asked to do this and have waited so long, never completely understanding what it was I was to do, not until now."

"But this hurt you," Velda said. "God wouldn't do anything that would hurt you?" she questioned. "I believe this legislation is like the wheel," she said. "When the wheel first appeared in man's history, it seemed to be invented at about the same time in different spots all over the world. Its time had come. That's what I think about this legislation; its time has come."

I didn't say a word, but yes, the time had come and I was the instrument. I had tried to explain to her before that even as the shock of the mauling took place, there was no terror or pain, only assurance.

Velda sensed my thoughts and wanted me to understand her reluctance to accept what I had told her about the attack. "Caress, when I was a little girl I was taken to church where they told me I was a sinner. I don't think I was a sinner," she said with mild defiance. A long-ago child had sat listening to some misguided adult who with perfect precision had told the little girl she was a sinner—something she quite strongly believed she was not. The experience had negated religion with Velda so much that in adulthood she didn't recognize the personal loving God Who was so close to me. Instead, she spoke about her love and sense of nature, the seasons, birds and animals, the energy of autumn and the restful summer.

"You know, sometimes I seem to understand what direction to take for the animals and in my life from a voice that comes from deep inside." She said this quietly, observantly.

"Velda, that's God you're listening to, and He's speaking to you," I said. Her story was a real paradox, for she was deeply religious, and listening to the voice deep inside, had found her mission and her gifts many years ago.

"I guess I'm kind of an Earth Mother, Caress. I really was born too soon 'cause if I had been born a decade later, probably would have been a hippie." She smiled and shrugged her shoulders.

I thought of Velda in a tie-dyed Tee-shirt rolling around the country in an old van with graffiti spray painted on the outside. She was too organized to have ever been a very successful hippie, and in spite of herself Velda was a *believer*.

"Velda," I suddenly blurted out, remembering John Hammond again, "John's going to write to Judy O'Bannon; they've had some trouble with dogs in their neighborhood, and he thought she might carefully approach Mike Phillips about the legislation.

"Good," she said. "Caress, in the end, you never know for sure what works, and I'd say that would be worth a try. One thing to be sure of is that if plan A doesn't work, we will be ready with plan B," she said, nodding her head.

"Well, I'd better start on my part of plan A," I said. Velda's eyes started twinkling as she looked over at me, her left hand placed on her hip.

"Caress, every dirty old dogfighter in the state of Indiana is gonna say 'There's that damned little socialite that has to go ruin everything.' " My mouth slipped into a smile, then laughter, because I liked the idea of the bad dog owners being worried about the little lady down at the state house.

* * *

At home a manila envelope had arrived in the mail from the newspaper. I sat in my chair in the breakfast room and looked at the pictures of an especially appealing little boy, smiling, bright-eyed, a six year old whose school picture was placed on the front page of the *Indianapolis Star.* The attack had happened four years ago as I glanced at the date at the top of the page. I handled the papers gently as though he might be further hurt by my placing the paper down too quickly on the table. Brandon had left his home that morning and had walked down the sidewalk in the cool autumn air towards the stop where the big yellow school bus soon would come to pick him up. He was busy with a lot of new things as the first of the leaves fell from the trees, touching his jacket. Did he jump over the cracks in the sidewalk and think about the other little boys that sat close by him in school? Did he still feel important carrying the new school lunch box now that he was a big boy and went to school all day long? Brandon reached the bus stop and waited.

Not far away they had watched him walk down the street, and when he stopped, they came for him. They were mean dogs, both pit bulls, that ran toward the little boy slightly before nine in the morning. Brandon was merely game for them, no different than a dog they would seek out to destroy. In their aberrance, Brandon was perfect to tear to shreds and to keep tearing until he was dead. They attacked— butting their heads against his six-year-old frame, knocking him down into the street. One set of fierce jaws grabbed him by the head, tearing off a large part of his scalp and his left ear. The other dog tore into Brandon's arm, his legs, and then shoulder. The child instinctively tried to protect himself, but the strength and size of the animals prevented him from keeping the large jaws away from his head. Brandon was on the ground and the dogs were there to kill him. He couldn't see any more—there was too much blood.

A seventy-five-year-old man rushed from his home carrying a club, answering another neighbor's screams. "They had the kid in the middle of the street chewing the hell out of him," he was later to tell the papers. The older man had run with the club towards Brandon. All he could see were the child's feet, for the body was literally being consumed by their jaws. He started swinging the club, trying to kill the animals. He raised the club one blow after another. He had precious little time—the child was bathed in blood. Terror mixed with adrenaline kept the blows coming one after another until the dogs pulled away from the child and turned on him. It was at this time the police arrived, and one pit bull lunged toward the officer and was shot dead. The other dog also was shot. The officer remembered the dogs' muzzles were covered in blood. The head of Indianapolis Animal Control later reported that the police photographs of Brandon looked like someone had used an ax on the child's head.

The dogs' owners, who lived in a nearby home, told the press they didn't know why their dogs had attacked the child. Brandon's mother later remembered rumors about the basement of the house where those people lived. She had heard that was where people came to fight the dogs.

The owners were not charged with any wrongdoing. There was no law—nobody came forward to say that the dogs' owners had done anything wrong. After all, the dogs had tried to kill Brandon, not them. No evidence was ever found to allow a search of the home for dogfighting. The owners never called Brandon or his family. They washed their hands of the incident.

Brandon lay in the street until the ambulance came and

then spent hours in surgery at Riley Children's Hospital where his surgeon tried to reattach his ear and partially repair the scalp. The doctor told the papers that the little boy had been terribly mauled, and unless help had intervened, he most certainly would have been killed.

I flipped through Brandon's newspaper articles, pictures of him returning to first grade, sitting on the ground coloring pictures for Thanksgiving. Two months later he had been able to enter his classroom and see the other little boys and girls that had made it to school safely that early October morning. His head was tightly bandaged and he wore a small cap. He would always have trouble with his hearing and have deep scars on his head. The article stated he was scared, scared of dogs.

I cherished this little boy as he colored his first grade pictures and smiled into the camera.

I watched the rain through the window and remembered dripping trees, the rushing noise of the waterfall on Fall Creek. The silence of running dogs, the strength of their jaws, how warm your blood feels. That I felt no terror, survived the mauling, and was taken care of. Now I prepared for my role to write and speak to this committee of men, who were so diverse and politically divided, on behalf of a baby boy in his stroller and now, also, for Brandon.

SIX

Jesse's Baby

The darkness closed in around me as I lay quietly under the covers. The dogs had padded into the bedroom pleading to go outside. They came to my side of the bed knowing Pat would ignore them, it was too early to get up. The eighteenth century bed was high off the ground, making it hazardous to slip the injured leg to the floor. I lifted one leg out of bed and slowly the other, noticing sleet blowing sideways into the blackness on the other side of the window pane. I pulled the padded cotton robe around me, groping for the stairs in the hall. Half asleep, I came slowly, step by step, dragging the stiff leg. The dogs were running around the island in the kitchen by the time my foot finally touched the linoleum. I grabbed a chair for balance as one dog jumped up to my waist while the other frantically pawed my upper leg. Back and forth they jumped in the darkness. There was a flash of wet pavement and blood, then sinking teeth. "Stop it!" my voice commanded as my fingers found the light switch. Squinting in the bright light, both Boomer and Chuck retreated under the countertop. Never having been screamed at before, they looked wide-eyed at each other then back at me.

"I'm up at five-thirty in the morning because you want to go outside, and you jump on me just like the bad dogs."

Boomer and Chuck bowed their heads close to the floor. "Go on outside," I said in a softer voice, as their tails began to wag before disappearing into the backyard.

I was awake now and walked stiffly into the den, sitting in the big, soft chair. Thoughts drifted in and out of a tired brain. The testimony and the written letter to the committee were waiting to be handed over and placed in the committee packets.

"Dear God, give me what it takes to touch these men, to make them aware that some events, even in their majestic house of rules and amendments, are above politics. Father, you have used me to carry out Your plan to save children. Now, reassure me in my mere mortalness that You are with me. Although my very essence tells me that I am used perfectly, I am weak and cannot stand to fail. Continue to be with me and show me Your Presence."

I remembered that miracles come around you quietly when you least expect them and in ways you might never dream. As I sat in the darkness, an alarm clock buzzed in an upstairs bedroom, and I listened to footsteps as the family awoke, finally coming down into the kitchen. "Why are Boomer and Chuck sitting outside staring at the door?" Matthew asked. Looking through the back door window, their black coats shone out against the early, gray, winter morning. Both dogs hoped Matthew would open the door.

"They were not good dogs this morning," I told him, "and they can stay out there for a while."

I had kissed each Garten man good-bye for the day when the phone rang. This is going to be one of those days that never slows down, I thought. "Caress, I wanted to call and tell you that Mama died last night." The voice continued talking, my brain half listening as I remembered Mama.

Mama was ninety-eight years old and had lived in a health care facility for the last few years of her life. She had died quietly in her sleep. Mama was not a true relation of ours, but Pat and I felt closeness and love for the warm, fun-loving family of which Mama was the matriarch. At eighteen, in a moment of laughter, I had called her Mama, the family's name for her. Mama was thrilled. She had gone from one room to the next telling everyone who would listen that "Caress called me Mama!"

Mama was born Agnes Picken long ago at the close of the Victorian era. Great old trees lined the street in front of the family's twenty-three-room home where she was raised. Miss Agnes was the cherished daughter of staunch, Scottish Presbyterians who joined Tabernacle Presbyterian Church when she was a young girl. Mama maintained a refined outward appearance, but relaxed into laughter among her family. "I'm ninety-eight years old and I've never earned a nickel," she would say with pleasure, for Mama loved her role as the privileged daughter and protected wife. Mama was a character—but a beloved character. Her funeral would be tomorrow.

The lovely, but tiny, gothic chapel at Crown Hill cemetery held Mama's body. Only her family and a few friends came to her funeral. She had outlived everyone of her generation.

The minister had captured Mama's personality in his eulogy. He was the senior minister at Tabernacle, now a large, inner-city church. Dr. Kik's voice filled the little chapel. The Presbyterians, so known for their famous preachers, had another one with this man.

When he spoke a stillness would fall, for people listened intently. This quiet came as he shared with others his conviction of a gentle God that came looking for those who were lost.

That day in the little chapel, the minister caught my eyes as he began reciting the 23rd Psalm, the one that David had written thousands of years ago. "The LORD is my shepherd; I shall not want. He maketh me to lie down in green pastures: He leadeth me beside the still waters. He restoreth my soul: He leadeth me in the paths of righteousness for His name's sake." Sitting very still, the words penetrated me. "Yea, though I walk through the valley of the shadow of death, I will fear no evil: for Thou art with me; Thy rod and Thy staff they comfort me. Thou preparest a table before me in the presence of mine enemies: Thou annointest my head with oil; my cup runneth over. Surely goodness and mercy shall follow me all the days of my life: and I will dwell in the house of the LORD forever."

David's Psalm was my psalm, my walk in the valley with two pit bulls along the still, late-autumn waters of Fall Creek. In the shadow of death I had feared no evil. I had been reassured that God's love would follow me all the days of my life.

At home after the funeral, Mama's family had returned to laughter and good spirits. The minister taped his sermons every Sunday I was told, as the 23rd Psalm echoed in my ears.

* * *

The weekend came and went with somber January weather. Now, in the last week of the month, Paul became concerned. The promised hearing for the dog bill hadn't materialized. The Speaker's wishes to keep the minority leader toned down were being obeyed. Finally, the word came: the hearing would be the following Tuesday morning. "Just come down early and be ready for whenever they call us," counseled Paul's deep voice over the phone.

"The hearing's Tuesday," I told Velda.

"You'll be great," she said. "Now don't worry 'cause I'll tell Paul's office everyone who's lined up to testify. They'll come forward after you've spoken. Everybody's set to come down from all over the state. Jackie Walorski is coming from South Bend. You haven't met her but I know you'll like her," Velda said enthusiastically. "She's the former head of the Humane Society in St. Joe County, did Animal Control up there."

I remembered Velda talking about Jackie who at twenty-six had taken on that position. She had been a former police reporter for a CBS television affiliate out of South Bend. Standing six feet tall with the voice of a media anchor, Jackie was an impressive addition to Animal Control in the northern part of the state.

The cities of South Bend and nearby Mishawaka were currently plagued with organized crime. When Jackie took over, the outgoing director of Animal Control left a warning for her: "Don't ever try to get rid of the dogfighters or their rings."

"Why not?" she had asked.

"Because you'll be killed. Those people don't care about their dogs and they don't care about people."

One set of dogfighters in the area was two brothers, nationally famous for their dogs. Police had taken pictures of pit bulls belonging to the brothers, showing long scars down their sides. They also discovered heavy logging chains used to stake dogs to the ground. Twenty dead dogs had been found on their property, leaving a hideous testimony to a violent sport. It was also why no one wanted to talk.

A world of vicious dogs and sociopaths, the people who had no conscience, that was the world the twenty-six-year-old Jackie had entered. The criminals must have thought she wouldn't be a problem. They were wrong.

The city of Mishawaka was heavily populated with crack houses guarded by dogs. The dogfighters were also drug dealers, and before police would enter a crack house it was Jackie's job to get the dogs.

During this time a group of drug dealers moved to the outskirts of South Bend. They brought thirty pit bulls with them to guard ten crack houses. Jackie, who had built a reputation snaring dangerous dogs, came to clear them out. The Annie Oakley of northern Indiana was successful and would be rewarded by a drug dealer who was going to kill her.

The dealer would wait outside her house then deliver dead

animals, placed on her doorstep wrapped in newspapers. The dead animal would be followed by a telephoned death threat.

Jackie didn't scare easily. Becoming more aggressive, she began to carry a gun. The drug dealer, under pressure from other criminals, decided there would be too much heat if he killed her—there would be another time.

* * *

"I guess I'll meet Jackie then," I said, slowly thinking about my testimony.

"Sure you will," smiled Velda, "and you don't have a thing to worry about 'cause Jackie, she'll be packin'." I glanced up at Velda who wanted my attention, for she was trying to make me smile.

"She'll be packin'?" I repeated.

"Yeah, she always carries a gun."

Velda never missed an opportunity to expose me to new experiences. I started smiling. I didn't know any women who "packed." "Jackie's been in too many bad situations," Velda added, "and she'll be here to testify for you."

"Do you think anyone will testify against the bill, Velda?" I asked, feeling solemn again.

"I don't know, maybe some kennel clubs—but don't you worry, I've got all the experts and big name organizations with us."

"Is this going to work, Velda?" I asked flatly.

"It's going to work, Caress," she responded. Velda wasn't going to tell me all the ways it might not work.

Pat was going to have to leave on business Tuesday and drive to Chicago. He was upset he couldn't come to the state house, but I was relieved. It would be more difficult to speak with someone who loved me sitting in the room.

Tuesday morning was hectic at the state house, for several committees were holding hearings. Jesse's committee had been assigned several bills that were interesting to the press and other state house watchers. I started the familiar climb to the fourth floor to the judge's chambers. Finishing the first flight of stairs, I arrived on the third floor to see one room lit up with television lights. The room seemed large from the outer corridor. I wondered if that was the room where I would speak.

Velda waited for me at the top of the fourth floor stairs. "Caress, everyone is here and ready to go. The committee's packets were put in their mailboxes. Got to them at just the right time. Don't want them to get the information too soon otherwise they'll just forget!

"The most important thing was your written testimony. Linda told me she cried when she read your letter to the committee. Actually, that's good, Caress. Means it's effective. Linda is no wilting lily, she's been around politics too long, and if you can touch her, chances are great you'll be terrific with this group."

"It's the only way I know to tell the story, Velda," I told her.

"I know," she said softly. Velda appraised the blue dress I wore and bandaged leg that Pat had carefully wrapped that morning before he left. "Do you want to come and sit down for a while?"

"I think I'll go on down to Paul's office and wait until they call us."

"Everyone will be there for you, Caress," Velda said confidently.

The halls were bursting with people as I wound through hurried meetings of lobbyists and legislators, finally reaching Paul's office.

"They're running late, Caress," Cathy told me, referring to the committee. "I think they've had lots of testimony this morning that's made the whole process slow. Your bill was scheduled last on the committee's order of business. Paul's aware it will be a little longer before they're ready for you."

The wait went on for over an hour while I watched people come and go out of Paul's office. I thought it was better not to think about testifying, just concentrate on the people around me.

"It's close to the last week of hearings on the House side, Caress," Cathy told me. "You know," she said, "this is one of the few Republican bills to get a hearing."

"I know," I told her quietly. I know, I repeated silently. My ears were filled with the noise from the hall, and I wondered if Velda knew the hearing was delayed.

The door to Paul's office opened; he had his suit coat on. "You ready?" he asked with a smile. Ready or not—here we come, I thought. We walked out into the crowd while Paul picked up the pace down the corridor. "Caress, a lawyer called me who lobbies at the state house. She wants some of the wording changed in the bill." He looked over at me as he continued to walk. "I told her I wasn't prepared to change the bill. I expect her to testify today." I listened, but it was too late now to worry about negative testimony as we approached the doors where the committee waited. A news reporter noticed me and I waved to him. A big smile came across his face as he flashed me the *V* for victory sign. He followed the crowd congregating outside the doors where we were headed. The television crew was leaving, for the Courts and Criminal Code Committee had just finished hearing testimony from women who had been the victims of stalkers. The legislation was in its third year trying to pass through the Indiana State House.

Paul was nodding and smiling to people while not missing a step. Everything was moving so fast. I started to worry if I could create the emotion to tell the story effectively. For the last few hours, I had been trying not to dwell on testifying. *Now it was time.* Like everything at the state house, when the moment came, it happened quickly and there was one chance. The hearing room doors were closed. I felt a little panicky wishing I had at least seen the room. That wasn't possible now because the moment had come, and when the doors opened, those inside would be watching me. Paul turned and nodded to a woman who had approached us. "Caress, this is Micki Wilson," he said as he stopped for a moment because she seemed to want to speak to me. "I'm going on inside," he said in a low voice and immediately went through the doors.

I felt the presence of the woman who looked grimly towards me. Her eyes never blinked, they penetrated with anger. *"Dogs tore my little boy's face off,"* she spat out bitterly—her body shook. Blood drained from my face as I watched this stranger whose eyes now turned toward the floor.

"I am here for him today," my voice uttered back with surprising strength, "and I am also here for you." She lifted her head, eyes meeting mine.

"Thank you for what you are trying to do," she said quietly, her face still grim, mouth set in a straight line. My fingers touched her cheek, and with the other hand I turned the brass doorknob, entering the room. Paul was standing next to the door because the room was packed with people sitting in chairs and lining the walls.

"What's the protocol?" I whispered.

"When the chairman calls for people to testify, state your name and why you're here, then tell the story." Paul looked straight ahead, watching the committee chairman. He wore that enigmatic expression practiced politicians achieve that makes it impossible to know their feelings. I looked to one side of the room and saw Velda standing by the windows. Sandy Rowland was there from the Humane Society of the United States, and so was Belinda Lewis. Reporters on the other side of the room were taking notes. The men and women who filled the room seemed to be waiting for the committee chairman's next move. Jesse Villalpando sat at the head of a long, dark table. The table itself was massive and seemed an appropriate center of power.

The room was a scene out of Indiana history, for many judicial and legislative decisions had been made here since the nineteenth century.

The committee chairman from East Chicago was not interested in the people who lined the walls or the room's past. He was all business. Jesse seemed mildly irritated as he shifted in his seat. The chairman stood out from the other men as he scanned the room, black eyes flashing, fingers momentarily touching the dark hair. I thought he had been sitting a long time that morning, and he didn't want to be there much longer, particularly with Paul Mannweiler. He was also there to follow the Speaker's orders: not to make life easy for Paul.

The chairman's picture had been in the paper a week ago, arms extended, face intense. Velda had pointed the picture out to me, writing in red pen over the picture, "our committee chair." Now I saw the intensity in person. "Are you ready?" Chairman Villalpando asked as Paul took a seat at the table.

"Yes," he answered with a smile. The smile was not returned as Jesse glanced to the end of the room where I stood.

"Is there anyone who would like to testify in favor of the bill?" The committee looked at me.

"I would like to testify," I said, and the room quieted down. Walking a few steps to the end of the table, I looked toward Jesse Villalpando who had stopped moving in his chair.

"State your name," he said briskly.

"My name is Caress Garten, I'm a life-long resident of Indianapolis. I am married to W. Patterson Garten and I have two sons, ages fifteen and seventeen." The room became almost silent, and I seemed to hear even the little sounds of lead pencils marking note pads and papers being folded and placed to one side. People shifted one last time as I began the story of the November walk. I noticed Paul had his hands folded together resting on the table. I entered the world of dripping trees and a gray, wet path. "I remember the baby smiling at me and that he was dressed in blue. When I returned to the place on the path where I had seen the mother and the baby, I noticed two dogs running in and out of the trees. I extended my hand, and half smiled as they passed me then circled close to me. I saw a man in the distance; he screamed, 'Oh, my God.' "

My mouth started to quiver. Stopping for a moment, I sensed one of those silences when a hundred people seemed not to breathe. My voice wavered as I continued, "One dog sank his teeth into my leg below the calf. The second dog began to jump around me, tearing my coat. I covered my face from the dog who was jumping high off the ground. I slipped and he clawed the top of my head and forehead. Teeth pierced through my glove, tearing into my hand. Blood poured down my face and onto my neck. Through my fingers, I watched blood being sprayed from my leg as the dog continued to shake the leg back and forth."

I looked up and saw Jesse moving again in his seat. His eyes looked up, and I thought he seemed tired of blood and guts. His face was expressionless. I looked at the committee, they were listening intently. I continued while my mind hunted rapidly through everything I had read or thought of in the last few weeks—something that would move the man at the end of the table. My voice cracked, and I stared down at the floor for a moment. I jerked my head up—my throat was becoming dry. "He carried a loaded gun with him. He was going to shoot the dogs if he couldn't pull them off me. There was so much blood about me, but I never felt terror." My voice was becoming softer.

"I always knew I would be taken care of and escape." My voice trailed off as I watched the chairman once again. It dawned on me that he had read the written testimony in the packets. He was becoming bored. I needed his attention. Then the words started to come as I spoke directly to Jesse Villalpando of East Chicago.

"I am here for three little boys." My voice became stronger, and the chairman looked up with a little jolt. His ears had perked up—he was listening. I had remembered the newspaper articles. "One little boy who waited in the darkness for a school bus had his ears ripped off. Another, playing in a downtown alley, had the muscle ripped from his arms, and a third, who was trying to cross a street while returning home from school, was almost killed by a dog." My eyes riveted in on the chairman's dark eyes, and a passionate voice emerged: *"I SPEAK FOR THEM."* The firm line on the chairman's mouth was gone, and there was a pained expression for only a moment. The eyebrows knitted together, and the eyes blinked and betrayed themselves. The emotions of a naturally passionate man had momentarily been revealed. My eyes skimmed over the men around the table in the still quiet room.

Feeling weak, I glanced again at Paul's folded hands. His knuckles seemed white. He looked over, calling out, "Good job," as I walked toward the folding chair a man offered to me. I barely heard Paul; everything seemed to be used up inside of me for the moment.

As I sat down in the chair, a hand touched my shoulder, "Good job, Caress, I'm Jackie Walorski."

Another person began testifying. "Executive Director of the Trial Lawyer's Association," she was saying. The woman from the hall was telling her story. Micki Wilson would later tell me, with a light laugh, that her mother's name was Riley and her temper was Irish. Micki Wilson was Irish and angry in her testimony. She felt a mother's grief over her Adam who had been feeding a pair of Siberian huskies when one dog grabbed him, slashing the little boy's face open down his jaw line and shredding his chin. He had been severely facially injured. The man who owned the animals had been previously seen beating the dog with his fists. The owner had asked Adam to feed his dogs. The husky, a naturally strong dog, and the dog most closely related to the wolf, had been made into a dangerous animal.

"There was nothing that could be done," she cried. "The man didn't even want to give up the dogs." Micki's eyes flashed around the table. "We need the civil penalties, the monetary fines, in this bill," she pleaded with Villalpando.

The volatile Irish temper met the emotions of the Latino who chaired the committee as she finished speaking. Paul watched Micki, his mouth set in a down-turned expression.

Some in the room watched as she furiously returned to her position next to the wall. Others had never taken their eyes from me.

A tall, slightly balding man who stood in the corner came to the head of the table. "My name is Jim Trulock," he said quietly, and I'm a lobbyist for the United Auto Workers. I'm not here in any official capacity, but as a private citizen who was in the emergency ward where Adam was taken after the attack." He glanced over at Micki, whose arms were folded around her sides. "This child's face was so terribly injured," he said, shaking his head, "and I'm here to help support this legislation." Sitting in the folding chair, I stared at them across the room as my numbness reminded me of coming out of anesthesia. I was half-understanding what was happening around me as if in a dream. To my left, Jackie Walorski watched the speakers. She did seem tall, I thought, glancing upward.

"There are twenty-seven thousand members in the state of Indiana, and we support this legislation." Sandy Rowland from the Humane Society of the United States was speaking to the committee. Still dazed, I didn't even notice her walking forward. She had traveled to other state houses over the years trying to achieve this legislation. Later today, after flying to Michigan, she would give testimony in front of a jury to convict a dogfighter.

"Cases like the one you heard about today have been allowed to slip by unnoticed for too many years in Indiana. Now is the time for change, and you have the commitment of thousands of our members to make this law a reality."

Velda stood to my right, watching the committee. She was the team's state house quarterback, evaluating the people and the points made.

"Allen County needs this legislation." Belinda began

when Sandy finished. "In Fort Wayne, there was a woman taken to a man's apartment and raped. When she tried to leave, the man had his pit bull attack her. There is no law to charge the man with the use of the dog. Law enforcement needs some kind of legislation to help prosecute criminals." Belinda paused—she seemed to be speaking in slow motion.

For a few minutes I began to mentally drift, staring back at the eyes still following my every move. "Criminal activity … St. Joe County," fragments of a sentence. The tall Jackie Walorski had left my side.

Northwest Indiana was the general area Jesse Villalpando represented. He listened emotionlessly while she spoke in her distinctive newscaster's voice.

Jackie had just finished speaking, when a familiar face walked by the rows of people sitting around the room. Dressed in the familiar banker's blue suit, his round, full face beaming, the lobbyist walked quickly to the front. A substantial-looking citizen of the community was coming forward. My brain started to quickly flip through the people in the halls. Different conversations were on fast forward working through my memory banks. My arms still felt numb; the anesthesia was still at work as this man continued walking to the head of the table.

"John Baugh," the man stated as if greeting a group outside the gates of the county fair. "I represent the Farm Bureau," he said jovially to those around the table. Velda became extremely still by my side. The rosy-cheeked man continued with the confidence of someone who was well-known and powerful. Paul was unreadable watching him.

I felt confused. This bill was cleared with the Farm Bureau, I thought to myself. "I support this legislation," he began. "However, I would like to place an amendment on the bill."

Velda whispered an audible "No," speaking half to herself. The word caught my ear. Velda's positive personality sensed a land mine. The Farm Bureau lobbyist smiled over his shoulder towards me.

"My amendment deals with the state cruelty statute on the impoundment of livestock." What is he talking about? I thought to myself. "I would like to add to this statute that a public health official must be consulted before cattle or horses can be impounded, and the findings reported to a judge before a court order may be issued to confiscate the animal." The lobbyist smiled at the committee as if this was the most reasonable request yet.

"How can you place an amendment that's about cattle on a bill that's about dogs?" I whispered to Velda.

She was silent, trying to listen. He continued on about the importance of the amendment for the farmers. The committee appeared noncommittal while he ended with a flourish, speaking on the rights of farmers. Velda whispered hurriedly to me, "If it deals with animals and the committee wants the amendment, they will let it remain and call it germane." It seemed so absurd to me, sitting there in the metal folding chair, the newcomer to politics, that this could happen. Velda bent towards me. "The only good thing is that he figures this bill with the hurt little lady is gonna make it through." She smiled, patting my shoulder, but Velda was upset.

The history was that a woman in northern Indiana had infuriated farmers by rescuing horses and cows that, in her opinion, were starving. She had gone into the farmers' fields and taken the animals. The farmers took a dim view of this woman who, in their opinion, had stolen their property. The Farm Bureau wanted this amendment to take care of the problem.

The chairman sat slumped over with his elbow on the table, head resting on the enclosed hand. His mouth pulled to one side, he looked like someone not to cross. Jesse pulled himself upright, "Are there any more to testify for the bill?" There was silence. "Are there those to speak against the bill?"

A young woman walked forward. Linda Valentine, an attorney and state house lobbyist, owned and loved German shepherds. This was the lawyer who had spoken to Paul about the wording of the bill. She was worried the law might go too far in holding owners responsible. Several committee members seemed to know her and listened carefully.

I wondered what was next. Linda Valentine continued to speak to the committee. She had good legs. I felt the Ace bandage wrapped tightly around my left leg.

The man who had risen to give me his seat came forward somewhat sheepishly. He represented a kennel club and briefly spoke about how his objections paralleled Linda Valentine's. He looked over towards me then retreated back to the corner of the room.

The committee was silent as the chairman scanned the men at the table and the people who lined the walls of the supreme court hearing room. "Is there anyone else to speak?" he stated. No one came forward. The room was quiet.

Paul briefly commented, "This is legislation that is needed and has the support of Prosecutor Jeff Modisett. I'm sorry he couldn't be with us today." He looked at Jesse Villalpando after mentioning the name of the Indianapolis Democrat. Paul wanted to say as little as possible, for he was much like Daniel in the lion's den. The room became still. There was a momentary pause.

"*Where's the Men's Ray?*" a voice suddenly shouted angrily. The man's face was beet red with a demeanor like a bulldog. His eyes bulged behind the thick glasses framing his round face. He was the vice chair of the committee, Thomas Alevizos.

I didn't understand what he was saying. "Where's the Men's Ray?" he now screamed. Tom's whole body arched toward Paul who sat perfectly still. The mood had turned ugly. Representative Alevizos was a constitutional lawyer and a confident freshman legislator. He was going after the minority leader, the man the Speaker despised.

I was hoping Paul knew what he meant by Men's Ray. What is he talking about? I thought to myself blankly, wondering, Does he mean men's room? Tom Alevizos was referring to the legal term, *mens rea,* meaning "intent." Paul remained unreadable. "Representative Alevizos, we believe the owner is responsible for their animal," he said in a calm, low tone. Tom became quiet, still glaring. I started to squirm in the chair; Paul was not pronouncing the new representative's name correctly. I pulled a piece of paper from my purse and wrote down the name phonetically *AL A VA SOS.* Only the *VA* was pronounced with long vowel sounds, the rest were short vowels. I studied the paper and put it back in my purse. Representative Alevizos had stopped yelling. He realized there wasn't going to be a fight with the minority leader. Well aware he was outnumbered politically, Paul was making every attempt to be cordial.

The statuesque Jackie Walorski moved over next to Velda, whispering, "How can you take anybody seriously whose feet don't touch the ground?" Looking down the table, I saw it was true. Tom Alevizos' little feet didn't touch the carpeted hearing room's floor.

"Well, what do you want to do with this?" Jesse Villalpando bluntly asked the committee, his mouth irritably turned downward. He unbuttoned his suit coat, revealing a wilted white shirt. The hearings had gone on most of the morning with the fate of the bill now resting with those who were enemies of the minority leader.

Probably, it had already been arranged what would happen next. A committee member spoke up that because of some of the questions in wording, it should go to a subcommittee. "Okay, let's do that," Villalpando said decisively, choosing a majority of Democrats and a fewer number of Republicans to serve. He ended with the appointment of the representative whose feet didn't touch the ground as subcommittee chairman. Jesse nodded toward Tom Alevizos with a smile.

The folding chair was becoming uncomfortable. I thought of the Roman Emperors who with a thumbs up or thumbs down could make a decision on a life. This was that kind of feeling. I was merely a piece of a complex web, and expendable. The committee hadn't killed the bill, but they were sending it to what many at the state house referred to as the "graveyard." Subcommittees were convenient places where bills were never heard from again.

"Not a good sign, Caress," one of the team members said to me as the hearing started to end, but quickly hugging my shoulder, added, "It will be all right."

People were coming toward me. Some wanted to offer encouragement, others, often strangers, simply touched my hands as I remained glued to the uncomfortable chair.

My eyes caught Paul standing at the end of the table. I struggled to stand as he was leaving. I heard fragments of a conversation. "You've got to understand," Belinda was saying to the lawyer who owned the German shepherds, "most serious maulings take place with the dog's first attack." She was trying to explain why the traditional thinking of excusing the dog's first bite no longer applied. Now there were many dogs whose first bite was fatal. The lawyer was listening.

"I didn't know that," I heard her say as I hurried toward the door.

Paul had his head down, quickly walking out the doors. I didn't say anything, hurrying to keep up. "Tell them to get someone to talk to Alevizos," he said quietly.

In addition to having a hard time pronouncing his name, Paul quite simply was worried. The Speaker's plan was working.

I remained in the busy corridor after Paul disappeared into his office. The noise in the hall was loud in my ears like a train rushing by me. I felt momentarily unsure as if I were waiting on the wrong platform with the train leaving without me. Perhaps they would kill the bill.

Velda didn't know Tom Alevizos; he was new at the state

house. He represented Michigan City, in northern Indiana, an area known throughout the state as "da region." "Da region" was home to many different ethnic groups. Tom had replaced another Democrat whose last name was Hric, pronounced "Rick" at the state house. Representative Hric was short in stature, and in the words of one representative, "very fat." He would walk up the aisle, huffing and puffing to the microphone. Most members thought he would have a coronary before he retired. Representative Hric had retired alive, and was replaced by Representative Alevizos. Tom was not fat but he was very short, leading Velda later to remark, "I think there must be a strong Munchkin vote up there in Michigan City."

It was obvious politics was playing out its role in the Indiana House of Representatives. Perhaps the dog bill wouldn't even get to a vote in the House this year.

What good could I do? I thought, depressed, as I passed people in the hall and clumped down the marble steps to the main floor.

"You take care," policeman Rick said to me as I waved to him, walking into an early afternoon of late January.

January in the state of Indiana is dismal. The early winter of 1993 was marked with cold dampness and dull days; intermittently there would be a spatter of sleet or rain. The good news was that no snow made wearing a sock in a floppy slipper easier.

The rubber-soled slipper scuffed across the asphalt of the legislators' parking lot. I was worried, mentally drained from the testimony. Glancing up at the long windows on the second floor that framed the supreme court conference room, the emotions came flooding back.

The wet sleet hit the car windows as the windshield wipers started clicking back and forth, momentarily erasing the wet slush. Where was the beautiful Ed? I wondered as all loveliness and grace seemed replaced by anxiousness and fear.

The streets of downtown Indianapolis were busy with

early afternoon traffic as I drove north, crossing the bridge over Fall Creek.

I passed Trinity, my church, with the little Episcopal school where Benjamin and Matthew had attended. I traveled a few more blocks when the gothic steeple of Tabernacle Presbyterian appeared. It was Mama's church, and the church of the minister who had preached her funeral. I wanted to hear the minister again, remembering that he taped his sermons.

The parking lot was almost empty, and the branches of the trees that framed the building's windows were bare and black, standing in dormant winter grass. The cement step into the back entrance was smooth and slightly irregular, a testimony to a working church. Inside, a receptionist sat behind a glass window in a small office. She guided me across the dark, tiled hall to another little room where there stood a stand filled with tapes from different Sundays. "I heard Dr. Kik at a funeral," I told her. My hand left the warmth of my coat pocket touching the cassettes, remembering his voice. "Yea, though I walk through the valley of the shadow of death ..."

"We sell a lot of these; he has a radio audience too." she said cheerfully.

"Well, I've never met him, but I thought he was special," I said sincerely. There were weeks of sermons on tape, but I chose the two most recent Sunday sermons, telling the receptionist, "Thank you."

Leaving, I thought of my special friend Sarah who lived a few blocks away from the church. There was a representative who had sat on the committee this morning, a young black man, a Democrat. He was Sarah's representative. I made a mental note that she should ask him to support the legislation. A shorthaired brown terrier, a young stray, trotted down the sidewalk as I pulled out of the church parking lot. No collar, no tags; too many dogs, I thought. He would probably end up being hit by a car or euthanized at Animal Control. I realized the things I noticed now were different.

It was still early afternoon when I drove up the curving driveway. No one was home from school as I unlocked the back door, placing the tapes down on the kitchen counter. I heard a thud hit the floor as Chuck leapt off Benjamin's bed. He was incorrigible, always the dog of the streets, looking for opportunities to sleep on the forbidden beds. Boomer loved her spot on the backstairs landing; more genteel, she did what she was told. Boomer and Chuck came down the back stairs to greet me. Now, they both wanted to be patted as they told me the wonderful job they had done guarding the family homestead.

"You don't realize what I've been through this morning," I told them, stroking both heads. "I had to talk about the bad dogs all morning." They wagged their tails as I left them in the kitchen.

The big, soft chair held me as when I first came home from the hospital. I dropped the first of the minister's sermons into the tape recorder. I liked his voice; it filled the room, for he was a dramatic speaker. The sermon dealt with Christians handling adversity. He spoke of climbing mountains. I felt he was in the room with me.

I sank into the softness of the cushions feeling very tired, so tired, still numb. The second tape began, the second sermon. The voice of the minister came into the room once again. This time the voice spoke each word distinctly, pointedly. "The man needed assurance, and he needed more assurance. Gideon had been asked to complete a task for God. He was so like us today."

I sat straight up in the chair. *The sermon was about Gideon.* Astounded, I listened to the minister who had so moved me with David's Psalm. He repeated the story I had read in the car a month ago. As long as Gideon would try, God proved again and again He would never fail him. "You don't have to be afraid any more," the minister said over the little tape. "Good news," the voice said confidently. "Best news you've had today."

I watched the bright lights on the small, artificial Christmas tree that remained on the table. Covered with its little red silk bows, it always sparkled through the dark winter days. I am in a miracle, I thought, sitting quietly, no longer fearful but assured. Benjamin and Matthew came in the back door, home from school. I heard the refrigerator door open as I left the den when the phone rang. "I thought of you all day long. How did it go?"

I told Pat of the hearing and that the bill had been sent to subcommittee, saying, "I did the best job I could." It wasn't easy to explain the tension in the room or the doubt that followed the hearing, the mother's grief for her son, or the promise given to me again through the story of Gideon. Some things are hard to explain when you're still trying to comprehend what is unfolding about you.

That evening Sarah listened over the phone as I asked her to call her representative. I had found him in the legislative handbook and was studying his picture as we talked. "His name is Gregory Porter, and he's a Democrat," I told her.

"Is he a black man?" asked Sarah.

"Yes, do you know him?"

"No, but I will call him, Caress. I'll tell him how I have to drive around after Alex on his paper route because of the dogs."

"Will you call me after you talk to him?"

"Right away, as soon as I talk to him. How is everything at home?" she asked quietly.

"Well, fine; Pat's in Chicago but he'll be home later tonight. Benjamin and Matthew are upstairs."

"How are they handling this?" Her voice remained subdued.

"Benjamin better than Matthew, who wants it to all go away. I can't make it go away for him, Sarah."

"No, I know, but you must be on your guard," she said

seriously. I have known you for a long time and, Caress, I believe you were chosen. I heard you last summer when you called, anxious, seeking, waiting. Now, you have been asked to do something for great good, and you may never know all the people it affects in different ways, but there will be the one who will try and beat you." She added softly, "He will try and destroy your family."

Sarah acknowledged that evil existed and fought goodness. Perhaps Episcopalians just didn't spend much time recognizing evil, but as she spoke I knew, as always with her, that she was correct.

Pat came in late that evening; his hand stroked my hair. He had dark circles under his eyes. "You're the prettiest girl I know," he said with a smile. I thought that with a scarred-up forehead and a leg that didn't look so perfect anymore, I was pretty lucky he thought so. "I'm glad it went all right today," he said. I nodded, but it was too late at night to begin to explain the day to him. He was the loving husband who wrapped my leg in the pre-dawn. I thought of him rocking the newborn babies years ago through the night, wanting me to sleep. In those days he would get dressed early, often leaving for work not having slept. God must have understood that I would need someone very special at home to help me through losing a part of my leg. He understood there were children who were depending on me. The children who now slept in their cribs, and others who now waited for the school buses.

* * *

I awoke the next morning with a problem that had been nagging at me. I was still worried that Prosecutor Modisett did not understand how dangerous the dogs that attacked me were. There was still the possibility that he might choose to place the dogs for adoption or rehabilitation.

The prosecutor didn't understand the history on the dogs being held in the cages downtown. The Department of

Animal Control, which he depended upon for information, continued to say in the papers that there was no evidence the dogs were bred to fight, and there was no history of violence. Lieutenant Matt Schneider, the head of the department, had told the papers, "The city ordinance allows a death sentence for the dogs, but in my many years of experience I've never had to execute an animal."

Sandy Rowland was frustrated. Indianapolis television crews had described to her the dogfighting paraphernalia inside the home and in the yard of the man who owned the dogs. She was all too well aware of the training techniques and equipment used with fighting dogs. Just the previous month an important dogfighter had been stopped.

Three days before Christmas, a twenty-four-year-old man and his fifty-nine-year-old mother were arrested in New Jersey after authorities had removed thirty-four pit bulls from their property, in what was described as a major training site for dogfighting. The police had removed guns, one hundred and eighty-nine syringes, animal steroids, electric treadmills, dogfighting videos, and books on how to train dogs for fighting. Cats, chickens, and other dogs were found that had been routinely torn apart by the dogs to train them as killers. The owners had to post twenty-seven thousand dollars in bail. Authorities said some of the dogs might be worth as much as fifteen thousand dollars each. The dogs had been fought in several states in the east and south with as much as forty thousand dollars bet on a single match. Some of the dogs confiscated were missing eyes and had ears torn off.

Now, in Indianapolis, the H.S.U.S. felt they might have stumbled across another major dogfighter through my attack. However, no help came from the department called a "black hole," by other Animal Control officers in the state.

Phoning my free lawyer, I was telling the story again with more information that the dogs were trained killers. Jeff Mallamad listened to me and wanted to talk to Sandy Rowland as well. The court date was approaching in

February, and I stressed again the man wanted his dogs back. Jeff remained empathetic and would continue to be the messenger to the prosecutor.

I gave him Sandy Rowland's telephone number, and now that the conversation was over I sat in the breakfast room again, looking out into the January day. I would go back down to the state house in a couple of hours to talk to Velda and some of the other team members who had testified yesterday.

Benjamin and Matthew had left earlier in the day for high school, and Pat had left even earlier. He still looked tired from the previous day, but his mind was going full speed ahead as he picked up his briefcase, heading out the door in the early morning darkness. Boomer and Chuck passed him on his way out the door. "You be good dogs," he told them, "and take care of Mama," as they wagged their tails, happy that they were the good dogs.

* * *

Velda escorted me through the state house corridors over to one of the packed elevators that took us down to the first floor or, as I called it, the ugly basement. Belinda Lewis had traveled back from Fort Wayne. Linda Worsham from Senator Lugar's office was there, and Sally Allen had returned. We were going to eat lunch and discuss the next move. The group walked through the old basement hall to where the daily papers were sold. Velda paused, dropping money in the stand. "Did anyone look in the paper this morning?" She spanned the little group with her eyes. No one had read anything. Our paper was still at the bottom of the hill in the mailbox. I decided early on not to read the stories in the paper about the day-by-day accounts of my life.

Velda tucked the paper under one arm and took the group through a set of doors that led into a winding tunnel. "Don't know where you are, do you?" she said to me as the tunnel led us under the busy downtown streets.

"Caress," Velda counseled, "we've got to teach Paul how

to pronounce Alevizos' name. That man is smart, maybe a little short, but he wants to make a name for himself."

The group was walking down a carpeted underground slope when I recognized a familiar blue suit. John Baugh was coming down the corridor.

"Smile, Caress," Velda whispered under her breath. John nodded and smiled back as we passed in the tunnel. How could you do this? I thought as I watched him pass. How could cattle be a part of a vicious dog bill?

The group walked in silence, all thinking the same thought. "That's part of the lunch discussion," Velda said. Doors suddenly opened into a world filled with fast-paced people who glided upwards on shining escalators, landing in a food court. People noticed us immediately.

"Good luck, Honey," a stranger called to me, and, "There's that lady," another pointed out while balancing a tray of food. They all wanted to know about my leg.

I finally reached the table where the group waited for me to place my own tray down. Velda, whose reading glasses were on the tip of her nose, scanned the morning paper.

"You're right at the top of the page," she said. The headline read, "Despite horror stories, vote on vicious dog bill is put off until revision." The story stated, "Tearful testimony from the survivor of a dog attack was not enough to persuade a legislative committee to approve a bill imposing criminal penalties on owners of vicious dogs."

"Oh, no, now people are really going to see me as some victim."

"This talks about your soft and steady voice, Caress," Velda pointed out, not looking up from the paper. I never thought of my voice as soft, I thought. Odd how people saw you, often different from how we see ourselves.

"It's a good article," she said smiling, lifting her head, whipping off the reading glasses. She passed the newspaper around the table.

"We've got to find another bill for the Farm Bureau's

amendment to go on," Velda said to the group. "It can't go on the dog bill."

"This is a bill that has to stay uncluttered. The more uncluttered, the better chance no one will kill it or make changes," Sally agreed, touching her greyhound pin on her lapel.

"It's definite though, John Baugh thinks this one is going to make it through; that's why he wants to stick this amendment on," Velda reminded the group.

"He must feel there would be support for him on that committee," Belinda added.

"Maybe I should talk to Dennis Avery," Velda mused. "He's the man who sat closest to you, Caress, at the end of the table." I remembered his silver hair and that he had seemed interested in the comment by the lawyer who owned the German shepherds. "He's a Democrat, so Paul couldn't talk to him. Mark Kruzan could, or maybe—me," she said almost to herself.

"Mike Dvorak wasn't there yesterday," Belinda noted. "I know him and he should be okay." Mike Dvorak, another Democrat, was also concerned with children's issues.

"Let's talk about language," guided Velda. "I'm worried the subcommittee might need help with Linda Valentine's concerns. Also, how could a word or two be changed to broaden the law's use by prosecutors?"

"If an owner is walking the dog on a long leash, and the dog grabs a child running by in an unprovoked attack, is the owner responsible?" I asked.

"If the owner does not have control of the animal because the leash is too long, yes," replied Velda. The language of the law allows for this scenario."

The little group mentioned different cases, people connected with animals around Indiana. I wanted to understand the different cases, but my brain seemed to stop, and exhaustion quietly took over. The energy drained out of my arms; the leg was becoming a cumbersome piece of concrete.

The words continued around me, but I was no longer present. The noise from the food court resonated around the bright neon lights from the different food stands. I was remembering the robin who hung on to the dogwood branch, silent with his thoughts despite the rain that fell upon him.

"You never know what will happen, though, and publicity sometimes aggravates old grudges," I heard Velda saying. My brain returned to the table. Speaker Mike Phillips came to mind and Thomas Alevizos' red face.

"The longer the session goes, the meaner it's going to get," Velda said evenly. "And even though it's good to have a legislator with power carrying your bill—down side is most always what you want passed becomes a political football.

"However," she smiled, "timing is everything."

The little group around me was always so positive. None of them ever told me about the legislation they'd all seen die for political or vindictive paybacks. I was naive about the yearly political disposal of important legislation. The protective little group was not going to let me be aware of their worries.

All of them were again coming back for the subcommittee meeting scheduled next week. They would be prepared to quickly defuse the opposition.

The group was beginning to break for the afternoon. We walked back to the state house where some of my guardians said good-bye. The busy afternoon session had started. Lobbyists lined the bannister overlooking the rotunda. It was a waiting game, and those leaning against the bannister looked bored. The halls were clogged with people visiting the building or returning to an office.

Velda had left me, saying good-bye as she went up the stairs to the ivory tower, leaving politics on the third floor.

My coat had been left hanging on a coat rack inside Paul's office. Mr. Young opened the doors as two twelve-year-old pages came rushing past me out into the hall.

The Speaker's voice was coming over the sound system into the offices as I put one arm into the silk lining of the coat and then the other.

"How are you, Caress?" Cathy asked me from behind her desk.

"I'm fine," I told her. "It went pretty well yesterday."

"Paul didn't say too much about it, but then he's the silent type anyway," she smiled. I stood in the doorway of Paul's office, looking into the narrow outer hall, glancing at the old group photos of legislators taken at the end of the nineteenth century. The woolen coat, heavy on my shoulders, began to weigh me down. One of the outer doors stood open. Mr. Young must be talking to someone and forgot to close the door, I thought, noticing the flow of people in the hall.

Then I saw her. She had moved into my sight then vanished, passing in front of the half-opened door. She was smiling, looking expectantly forward, a pretty young woman with dark hair. She pushed a little dark-haired baby, a boy not a year old, in a stroller. The baby was happy, looking down the hall, little hands gripped around the stroller's bar. I had never seen her before, but I knew who she was and where she was going. I stood still for a few seconds, then barely breathing, walked into the hall. The mother and baby were making their way through the noisy crowd. As I followed her, Jesse Villalpando came out the doors at the far end of the hall. Smiling, he came up to the baby, bending over to talk to him. I walked closer to the mother, not wanting to stop, but to be seen as I passed on one side.

Jesse Villalpando had a baby boy. The ending words of my testimony, his momentary change of expression, the hurt little boys. I glanced back briefly, heading for the closest set of stairs. I had reached Jesse Villalpando.

The main floor, by contrast to the one I had just left, was empty. Suspended on the last marble step, my hand rested on the bannister while I gathered strength for the walk to the car.

"Hello, Caress," a familiar voice said to my side. John Keeler was a friend from childhood, now a lawyer and legislator at the state house.

"Caress, you know whatever happens you can't take this personally," he carefully told me. I watched him silently, for it was personal to me and, after all, there was a mission. John didn't mince words. "I've seen people spend six figures and fail trying to get a bill through the Indiana State House. Paul is trying hard; he's talking to everyone about this bill. The best thing that could happen is for it to pass the House and Senate with no amendments then be sent straight to the governor." He put his hand on my arm. "You remember this," he said softly, "that there are a lot of ways for bills to die." Then, smiling slightly, voice mildly rising, added, "And a lot of ways for them to be resurrected too."

I always liked John.

SEVEN

A Rottweiler in the House

Desolate is rural Indiana in winter. Hawks soar across the frozen fields, and the field mouse hides in the gray light. Shadows fall on rusting tin roofs that cover decaying barns. The damp haze rises from the fields in early morning as the hawk's sharp eyes watch for life stirring below. He is the intermediary, soaring between heaven's promise of warmth and love and the potential of all below.

Indiana's acres of farming landscape in spring are more welcoming as blue skies greet the dark earth, eventually evolving into the golden, tasseled fields of fall.

William Herschell wrote *Ain't God Good to Indiana,* his love of Indiana, the good earth, its reassuring harvests. His poem and his name would become a part of the state house where his poetry is immortalized on a bronze plaque placed in the rotunda.

Since the nineteenth century the acres of black earth have lay waiting in mid-January, never far from the city, still close to the county line of present day Indianapolis.

* * *

Late afternoon had not quite given way to early darkness. Hawks circled over the trees in the front yard. I had noticed them earlier from a window. The paneled wood of the den glowed from the brilliant lights of the little Christmas tree in what was left of the dim day. "Get someone to talk to Alevizos," Paul's low voice repeated in my mind as I sat down looking at the lights.

The phone rang across the room. Surprised and standing quickly, my face smashed into the oriental rug. The leg was weak and my balance was off. My elbows pulled me along the carpet over to the ringing phone.

"Hi, Caress, it's Sarah," said the voice on the other end of the phone. "I called him," she said softly. Representative Gregory Porter, who sat on Jesse's committee, had taken Sarah's call.

"I talked to him about Alex and how dangerous it was delivering papers with all the dogs." Her voice seemed more breathless than usual. "I'm sorry it took me a few days, but he knows who we are now and that he represents us." She added slowly, "I told him we wanted the legislation."

"What did he say?" I asked.

"Caress, he told me he doesn't know how he's going to vote, he's been getting calls against the bill too."

"Oh, Sarah," was all I could say for a moment. A heaviness started to grow in my chest as any thought of defeat began to sap what was left of my energy.

"I don't know what these men think or what they'll end up doing. They've sent this bill to a subcommittee, a graveyard for bills," I said despairingly.

"Caress, sometimes it seems darkest right before dawn." The receiver pressed next to my ear was a lifeline. What was it about Sarah that whenever she spoke to me there was an immediate calming? With those words the drowning effect stopped.

"Will you keep me in your prayers, Sarah?" I asked.

"I will keep you there, Caress."

January would soon end and the bill continued to wallow

in subcommittee, its location yet to be posted. The sense of urgency returned.

I was so tired yet I remembered once again the minister's voice and his tape ministry. I soon found time to drive down to the church. The door was open to the media center when I arrived. "Can I help you?" a tall man with a youthful smiling face asked.

"I want some more of your Dr. Kik sermons. I think I'm supposed to listen to this man."

"Are you a Presbyterian?" he asked pleasantly.

"No, I'm an Episcopalian."

That question now seemed irrelevant. Denominations no longer made any difference to me. I had left those differences lying on the sidewalk, bleeding to death, going down the elevator.

I took my new tapes and left the little office, returning to the car. The question of denomination reminded me of another man's statement of faith.

"Do you know anything about me?" he had asked during a conversation a few weeks before. "I became a Christian in August of 1978." The voice was crisp, energetic as he spoke over the phone. Eric Miller hosted a cable television program that discussed selected legislation. He supported my mission.

Recently, Belinda, Paul, and I had been a part of his television taping. My mind would occasionally stumble over something Belinda had said testifying at the state house and again on television. The issue kept being forgotten, lost among my own thoughts and emotions. It had to do with the use of a vicious dog and a rape. Belinda referred to the crime at the hearing in the state house and the television taping. The press had forgotten the story. The victim was poor, the criminal habitual, and the location was one where people expected those things to happen. These were throwaway people. Occasionally in my thoughts I would remember the story. Something didn't click with what she was saying about the law—but the answer and the issue continued to elude me.

The tapes were in my hands as I walked to the back door at home. Chuck had been running in the yard and was delighted to see me. "You're a mess," I told him. Tongue hanging out, eyes watching me, waiting for the door to open, he didn't care about tracking dirt inside.

Stepping into the kitchen a thought again repeated inside my head. Get someone to talk to Alevizos. Suddenly, the name came to me. Sam Jones.

I stood smiling, thinking of Sam. "Sometimes they forget I'm there," he had said to me at dinner one evening several years before, referring to leaders of the community who would ask him to sit on their boards, then through one comment or off color joke, forget he was in the room and that he was a black man. Now in his early sixties, he had been the head of the Indianapolis Urban League for many years. Sam was a recognized leader and spokesman for minorities in Indiana. It was my honor that somewhere along the line he also considered himself my friend. I didn't know if he had ever been involved at the state house but suspected he would be known by the Democrats on Jesse Villalpando's committee.

It was Pat who ran into Sam at a noon meeting the next day and asked him if he would call different members of Jesse's committee. "You tell Caress," Sam had said, "not to ask me, but to tell me what to do."

I had found an important Democrat who would talk to Tom Alevizos and, more important, Sam would talk to Jesse Villalpando.

* * *

As the week ended, Velda called me. "Caress, the subcommittee meeting is scheduled for next Wednesday. I've called everybody and told them where to meet us. We're all gonna' sit right up front so they'll have to look at you. I think we'll be fine. They won't take any more testimony but you should be there. It's starting to heat up down here, Caress, but then it's no fun to watch unless there's a good fight."

This was a budget year in the state of Indiana, and the budget would have to be cut. The governor, Evan Bayh, a Democrat, had promised a budget that included cutting Medicaid spending. Democrats, particularly those who represented economically depressed Gary, Indiana, were fighting for casino gambling. Gun control and the right of a city to ban assault weapons were also major battles in the Indiana General Assembly. Then there was my bill.

At the end of January, the budget had still not reached the floor of the Indiana House of Representatives. Now into cold, stark February came Wednesday's subcommittee meeting. I waved to Rick while coming in the state house doors and climbed the marble steps up to the fourth floor where I saw Velda peering over the railing to the floor below.

"I'm here, Velda," I said, touching her shoulder.

"I've been looking for you," she said enthusiastically. She had been delivering briefs to another judge while keeping her eyes open for me. "We have about an hour and a half before the subcommittee meets. The meeting is scheduled for a room on the first floor."

"You mean in the basement," I corrected her, recalling the walls painted in men's room green.

Below us, Velda noticed a group of fifty or sixty men standing together, encircling a single man who seemed to be giving directions of some kind. Only the man in the center of the ring was speaking, waving in different directions; the others, standing silent, were listening intently. All seemed to be middle-aged, wearing vested, navy blue suits. Each man held a fistful of papers in one hand. "I wonder who they are?" said Velda.

"They're surgeons," I said.

"How do you know that?" she asked with a grin, one hand placed on her hip.

"Because I walked in behind two of them," I told her.

"They're here about Medicare." Velda looked back down over the railing at the group that was now in something of a team huddle. Her eyes appraised the multi-blue suits that were on the verge of fanning out over the state house.

"They'll be gone tomorrow, Caress," she said matter of factly, shrugging her shoulders, as if the doctors were a gust of wind. The group was breaking up with each man going in a different direction.

"Do you want to come in and sit down, wait with me while I work?" she asked me.

"I think I'll just walk the halls for a while and try to be seen," I answered with Velda nodding her approval.

Leaving the quiet fourth floor to the melee of the political third was always a little like descending into the real world again with its swirl of visitors, lobbyists, and state house regulars. It continued to make me a little anxious. There was safety in the ivory tower, but that wasn't where the law was really fought for, nor was it where I belonged.

A busload of school children from Greene County filed through the third floor. Skirting around the children, I heard my name.

"Caress, I heard they sent the bill to subcommittee." John Hammond came walking at a fast clip, placing his hand on my shoulder. "I can try to talk to some of the committee members," he said as his face clouded. "Also, Caress, Judy O'Bannon called me about my letter to her, and I was wrong about the dogs in the neighborhood. There was trouble with crime in a nearby apartment house, but dogs weren't involved, so I had that wrong. I'm sorry." His face became longer as he paused. "She may go ahead and say something to the Speaker about the bill though she would never say anything to me. You just never know."

I remembered the wife of the lieutenant governor had recently been mugged outside her home and might be sympathetic to the dog issue anyway. "Maybe she will, John.

Sam Jones is going to call members on the committee for me." John's lower jaw dropped.

"You got Sam Jones to call for you?" As I nodded yes, he started to laugh. "Well, you sure don't need me."

"Oh, yes, I do," I added as he left, touching my arm again before hurrying down the hall.

The politicians were leaving their offices and heading to various committees. The halls were becoming crowded as budget meetings were being held and groups of people gathered outside the doors. I seemed to be standing still in the middle of a busy stream with the flow of people passing by me on either side. It was one of those moments when you feel lonely in a crowd. Everyone seemed to have a place or person they were running to see while I remained still, waiting. The stream was expanding into a river as more people filled the corridor. The ball of the bandaged foot touched the smooth surface of the marble; I was momentarily frozen, unsure of which way to turn.

"Mrs. Garten." I heard a voice and turned to see a man coming up at a fast walk behind me. The chairman's expressive, round brown eyes showed some emotion. "Thank you for testifying," he said quickly, continuing to walk by me into the entrance of the House used by the Democrats.

"I hope something can be done," I called after him.

"We'll see what the committee does," he answered as the doorman on the Speaker's side of the House opened the door for Jesse Villalpando to disappear inside.

I didn't know then, but the day before Paul had led the House of Representatives in the first budget debate. Before the document had even reached the floor, the Republican minority leader had irritated the Democrats.

During that session day Mark Kruzan had stood by his seat asking to speak. The lawyer from Bloomington was known for never sitting, always in perpetual motion. He had been dubbed "Representative Cruiser" by members of the House.

Mark considered Paul a friend even though the two men

had philosophical differences. That friendship was one of the reasons his name was on the dog bill, but now the battle for the budget was ongoing.

Paul had finished speaking. "Now I turn the microphone over to Representative Cruiser, er-r-r, Kruzan." Mark strolled to the front of the chamber.

"Thank you, Representative Rottweiler," he said with glee as the Democrats in the chamber erupted with barking while Paul returned to his seat.

Now, the day after the beginning budget battle cries, I watched the closed door Chairman Villalpando had disappeared behind. Farther down the hall, a slender young man stood watching, wearing a slightly wrinkled, gray raincoat. He wants to speak to you, I thought as he walked towards me. "My name is Elmer Borders," he said, sticking out his hand. "I represent the Indiana State Troopers; we want to sign on to your bill." I had learned the more groups you had in support of your bill the stronger it became, and a law enforcement group helping was good news. "I spoke to Representative Mannweiler earlier, and we need to have police dogs in the line of duty exempt from the legislation. We know you have a subcommittee meeting today, and Representative Mannweiler said he thought the committee would accept the exemption. I really hope this law goes through for you," he added sincerely.

I smiled at Elmer. "I hope the committee listens to him too," I said, thanking him for the support of the state troopers. Mr. Young swung open the great oak doors as I walked toward the entrance. I thought it was time to tell Paul I was here for the subcommittee meeting.

Cathy was working at her desk, phone pressed to her ear, as I entered the waiting area, sitting quietly down in the chair next to the door. A man sat next to me reading a newspaper, holding it in front of him with both hands. The pages rustled as he would finish a story then turn the pages with authority. One of the doctors was waiting. He moved in his chair as the corner of my eye caught the newspaper being lowered and a head turning towards me. He gave me one quiet and meaningful nod, slowly raising the paper again. He was first. I didn't know how long he had been sitting there, but this man figured he was in a doctor's office waiting his proper turn. The door to Paul's office was shut. Occasionally, someone would leave and another legislator would enter the office. It was a crowded non-smoke-filled room where some decision making was going on while I waited, becoming anxious about the time. Cathy noticed my anxiety. "You have ten minutes, Caress," she told me, being aware of Paul's schedule.

The door to Paul's office was opening again. In a flash I was standing by the door. "Tell Paul I'm here and going on to the meeting." The movement and voices stopped as my words carried inside. Darting towards the outer door, a sense of urgency was pressing me to find Velda and the others. I heard a newspaper smack the table as I stepped into the hall.

I had already learned something the doctor didn't know. So much business was done in the halls and on the stairways, in the parking lots and standing in the shelter outside the main doors. He would have probably been better off following Paul into the men's room, a place I couldn't go.

The little group was waiting for me. Smiling and businesslike, they walked me over to the elevator. My legs started to feel heavy; a sick feeling was rising inside my chest. The mood was positive, but I wondered if that was for my benefit. People turned to watch the bandaged leg walk past them on the way to subcommittee. This was a building where everyone seemed to know what was happening, even in the remote rooms in the basement. My guardians discussed the Farm Bureau's livestock amendment, wondering if John Baugh would be at the meeting. No one spoke about their worries or if the axe would come down on this bill.

"I wonder if anyone from the DNR will be there?"

mentioned Belinda. I didn't know what the DNR was, feeling too apprehensive about the meeting to think much about what she was saying. She was referring to the Department of Natural Resources, a group that was always interested in any legislation that might affect the hunters' interests involving their dogs. I began to follow the others into the bustling meeting room when an arm grabbed me.

"I just want to tell you that I'm a lawyer in an office with six other lawyers, all women. We have your picture up on the wall, and every morning we say, 'Go, Caress.' " Her eyes just sparkled, and I smiled back at her, astonished.

"You do?"

"Yes, we do, and my daughter has a picture in her room." Wonderful people seemed to appear over and over again at just the right moment.

"Thank you for telling me," I said, still stunned as the hand dropped from my arm and she hurried off down the hall.

Stepping inside the door, I saw Tom Alevizos conversing with a tall, middle-aged, big-boned man. The man rocked back and forth on his feet, one hand placed on his waist inside an open suit jacket that covered an ample, protruding belly.

"I'd like you to meet someone," Representative Alevizos said, smiling at me. Surprised at his friendliness, I wanted to do anything the good representative wanted me to do. Tom gazed pleasantly up at a surgeon from LaPorte, Indiana, who was at least six foot four. "Mrs. Garten is here to follow a bill she initiated," he said. Tom looked smilingly up at me as I lifted my head to smile up at the doctor, who paused for a moment before lowering his eyes towards the representative.

Representative Alevizos was extremely interested, so I was extremely interested and hung on the doctor's every word as my head shifted up and down from one to the other.

Tom began to step backwards toward the front of the room; the subcommittee meeting was already late in getting started.

I followed the representative as far as the first row, sitting down in a seat flanked on either side by Velda and Belinda.

Paul arrived, sitting down at the table. On the other side of the room, John Baugh leaned against the wall, quietly speaking to another man. Belinda's eyes searched the room. I didn't understand why she was worried, but there wasn't time to ask her now.

The lawyer who was concerned about her three German shepherds was present, along with a young man in his thirties. Sitting near the front, they were carefully listening to the committee. Turning around in the chair, I noticed three older women who had been at the initial hearing a week ago. They were sitting together a few rows behind me, all three waved at me at the same time. They were holding their purses, sitting on the edges of the chairs, giving me encouraging nods and grins. I slowly brought up my hand and waved back. It was still so amazing the people who followed me through the Indiana State House. Paul was looking at the new wording in the bill and had already spoken to Legislative Services about exempting police dogs in the line of duty. Representative Alevizos seemed calmer towards Paul, and I wondered if Sam Jones had helped bring this about or if Chairman Villalpando had given orders to stop being the mad dog.

Perhaps Tom just wanted to make the changes and pass the responsibility of the bill back to Jesse. There was no doubt Tom had gone out of his way to be friendly towards me, and now this new civility towards Paul. A few word changes were made making responsible dog owners less *likely* to break the law with the words "knowingly" and "intentionally." The Republicans and the Democrats seemed happy with the changes. It was suddenly a love fest.

Velda noticed the young man the same time I did. He had moved to the edge of his chair, visibly agitated, moving back and forth trying to get anyone's attention on the committee. He was sitting next to the lawyer and was very unhappy about what he was hearing. He wanted to speak and was shaking his dark head of hair back and forth. The committee looked over at him. "Did you want to say something?" Representative Alevizos asked.

"He's not supposed to say anything at this meeting," Velda whispered. But the subcommittee chairman was being generous, and now the young man sprang to his feet.

"I'm a veterinarian with ten years of having animals on the table," he said passionately. "We need to enforce the laws we have, maybe with higher fines. We don't need any more laws." It worried me to have anyone standing and talking against the bill.

"Don't worry, Caress," Belinda said in a low voice, looking at the committee, "their eyes have glazed over. He doesn't understand the legislation."

The room became still, it was time for the vote. John Baugh waited for any word or needed clarification about his livestock amendment. No mention was made about the Farm Bureau amendment as Representative Alevizos called for the vote around the table.

Only nods of approval as the bill escaped the dungeon of the subcommittee and was shuttled back to the Courts and Criminal Code Committee—back to Chairman Villalpando. I sighed with relief, for every step in and out of committees was a little victory followed by apprehension as to what would happen the next time.

"We still need to do something about that amendment," Velda said to the group, walking back up the hall. "It should go back to the committee next week. This is just the kind of thing that could eventually send this bill to conference committee, and it's just better if it finds another home."

By another home, Velda meant another bill for the Farm Bureau to attach itself to for a free ride through the state house.

Belinda hugged me good-bye. She had traveled back and forth from Fort Wayne several times in the last month on my behalf and she could not come back for next week's committee meeting. The others delegated me over to Velda for the following week.

Back home, late that afternoon, I watched from an upstairs window as three young hawks glided high above the leafless trees against a bright, blue February sky. I had read the notes that still arrived for me daily in the mail. Sometimes they came from strangers in different states, other times from long-lost childhood friends, all offering their support and their prayers. I wondered if Heaven was getting tired of hearing about me, but their prayers supported me.

I wondered if the hawks' nest was atop one of the old trees that had stood for hundreds of years in the yard. These birds had been given the gift of vision to see great distances. They could see so much more than human beings as they soared over houses and busy streets—more in a brief flight than I could see with my limited vision from the second story window. The hawk's vision brought me closer to understanding He who made us and His perfect vision overseeing the whole of our lives. I seemed to catch only brief glimpses of the whole of my life, but the mission at the state house was clear even though who would be touched or the reasons why might never be known to me.

Sam Jones called toward the end of the week with the word. "I really leaned on them, Caress," he said emphatically. I knew Sam had helped, but as Velda often said, "You can never be sure what exactly worked."

A few days later, she left a message at home for me, "Caress, Jesse's committee meets next week."

We were now within a few weeks of the bills changing to the Senate from the House and Senate bills coming across to the House. The bill not only had to get out of Chairman Villalpando's committee, it had to be voted on by the full House and be voted on before the crossover.

* * *

With only a few days before the committee's vote, I watched Speaker Phillips walk outside the House Chamber. He wore a heavy coat, making him appear even larger as his presence dominated the marble hall. The Speaker walked toward me, but his eyes never gave any recognition. He saw everyone in the hall, but wasn't going to acknowledge me. I had ironically crossed his path the very afternoon I would try to ask Jesse Villalpando personally for his vote. Although the Speaker didn't dislike me, the bill was political and important as far as tempering the minority leader. He passed, never turning his head, seemingly oblivious, and that was worrisome.

Jesse Villalpando walked hurriedly by, calling out to answer another legislator, "Whatever Mike says," before disappearing into a side door. I didn't know anything more about the conversation Chairman Villalpando was referring to, but the remark alluded to the Speaker's power.

I was uncomfortable. You hope some things are beyond politics, but nothing at the state house purely is, and Speaker Phillips could still ask Chairman Villalpando never to bring the bill before his committee again.

Velda had come down from the ivory tower to look for me, and I showed her the stationery with my name at the top bordered in red. "That should do it," she smiled. She had wanted me to bring some personal stationery to send a note into Jesse rather than the paper tear offs available from the desks outside the House chamber. The House had started into its daily session, and many lobbyists were writing messages to be sent inside.

I had written on my note, "Representative Villalpando, may I please speak to you for a moment?"

"Could you please take this to Representative Villalpando?" I asked, handing the note to a young Asian woman. A mob of lobbyists wanted their cards delivered to Democrats who sat on the House Ways and Means Committee. She studied the messages, pushing the chair away from the desk. Hurrying off, she looked back once before bolting into the chamber as if annihilation would be immediate if she didn't deliver those notes and cards—*now*. I watched her looking for the right representatives. I could see the back of Jesse Villalpando as he sat in his chair talking to the members around him. She returned to the outer hall, but I hadn't noticed her handing Jesse my note.

"Did the message get to Representative Villalpando?" I asked, pushing my way to the desk again.

"He's got the note," she nodded, smiling that she could report something to at least one of the people wanting information. Other legislators were coming out into the hall, but Jesse Villalpando was still in his seat. No one had told me he didn't have to or wouldn't come out to see me. A newcomer in the halls of government, it was slowly sinking in as I stood in the hall that he wasn't coming and that he was sending me a message.

I listened to the Speaker's voice coming over the microphone and out into the hall. He was calling a recess because the two parties were breaking to caucus. They were continuing to address the budget and beginning to do serious battle.

Had the Speaker seen me in the hall outside the main doors? Jesse stood in front of his desk, the red border of the note was lying in front of him. The legislators were exiting the main chamber; the Republicans were filing out to the left, Democrats to the right. Lobbyists in the hall were still having animated conversations with the representatives that had come out to talk. On the other side of the great doors, Cathy was handing Paul a fistful of papers as he noticed me coming in the door. "Sent a note in to Jesse Villalpando, and he wouldn't come out," I told Paul blankly.

He looked at me as his eyes became large and an internal rolodex started working on fast forward. He was trying to think through what exactly he had done at what moment to anger the right people. "I just wanted you to know," I told him.

"He didn't come out," Velda said to herself, "and after you sent in that note with your name on the top." She was quiet, then thoughtful, the normal cheerfulness was gone. "Well, we'll find out what's going on, and in the meantime stay out of Paul's office."

The ivory tower had a calming effect upon me. A slight smile crossed my face, "I know, I've already thought of that one."

There wasn't much more to be accomplished or not accomplished that day so I decided to leave.

The parking lot and outside steps were once again filled with freezing slush. Two Capitol Policeman had left their desk and walked up behind me. "We're here to escort you down those stairs."

I smiled and half laughed, "I'm okay."

"Nope, you're not and you're not going down by yourself." Pat had driven into the legislator's parking lot and stopped at the base of the stairs. The policemen each held an arm until one reached down and opened the car door.

"Thank you, Rick," I said.

"That would have made a good picture," Pat noted as we drove out of the parking lot.

"I faxed copies of the two dogs' vaccination records to Sandy Rowland." Pat had walked over to the deputy prosecutor's office after a pretrial hearing and made copies of the dogs' vaccination papers. "She wanted that information, so I know it's important." One of the dogs had an interstate health certificate that showed the dog had been vaccinated two years ago. A mixed breed pit bull shipped to Indianapolis from Azle, Texas. No name was given to the dog by the Texas veterinarian. The pit bull would have been almost two and a half years old at the time of the November attack. The other dog was shipped to Indianapolis a year ago from North Carolina. The veterinarian in that state had written the name Zeb for the animal whose predominant breed was pit bull. When shipped, the male dog was a year old, weighing between twenty and fifty pounds. Last November, he would have been two years old. A third dog, a six-year-old male pit bull named Turbo, who the man claimed was not one of the dogs involved in the attack, had recently been vaccinated in December. No one knew where Turbo came from in the country.

There was a message waiting at home for me to call Sandy Rowland at the Great Lakes office of the Humane Society of the United States. I hadn't seen her since the testimony over a couple of weeks ago and now envisioned the blond head whirling around in the H.S.U.S. office as the information came across the fax machine.

An excited voice came over the phone. "I want you to know that I took one look at the names on who shipped those dogs to our friend in Indianapolis, and what we have in both Texas and North Carolina are big time dogfighters known throughout the country. I feel this man you ran into has many dogs—if you can really call them dogs," she told me.

"Why is he calling them Thunder and Hook when the name of at least the full-grown dog that was shipped is Zeb?"

"Well," she paused, "often these dogs have many names; that's why they're so hard to track if they're on the fighting or breeding circuit. You better believe these animals are worth money to him, probably a lot of money."

"Could you speak to the deputy prosecutor and Jeff, my free lawyer?" I asked.

"I spoke to both men, the deputy prosecutor is frustrated with Animal Control and says that really the Sheriff was more helpful in collecting information. It's infuriating—I'd love to get more of these people who train dogs to kill," Sandy said grimly.

The man had played a role in an event that horrified people, but I never thought about him. There was the big picture and what I was to do, and he was a very minor part. The fact that very little could be done to him under the law frustrated people. Those that loved animals wanted to punish a player in the brutal world of the dogfighter. Those whose concern dealt with people were just outraged. Everyone but the man wanted the dogs destroyed.

"Caress, something that frustrates me is that I think I'll be involved in a trial in Michigan when your court date comes up."

"Sandy, just as long as the prosecutor knows what you know they'll use what they can."

"They're going to put that guy in jail aren't they, Mom?" Matthew said to me at the dinner table. Both boys realized the trial would be in a couple of weeks.

"No," I told him, "he won't go to jail. He'll probably be fined because the dogs weren't immunized, but he won't go to jail."

"He should," he said, looking down at his plate.

"I don't think anything about him, Matthew," I said, looking directly at him. "I just want the dogs destroyed so they don't hurt anyone else."

"She's trying to change the law so people will be held responsible and go to jail if something like this happens again," Pat said to him.

"It's to keep it from happening to other people, particularly children," I said, continuing to watch a fifteen year old struggle with the situation.

"Will this be on TV?" he said suddenly as if a dreadful thought had occurred to him about the upcoming court proceedings.

"I don't know, it could be," I said with a shrug of my shoulders. "Don't worry about the man anymore, Matthew." He watched me wide-eyed. "You know you can't do good if you're busy hating someone." He heard me but it didn't make him any happier.

Chuck lay on the kitchen linoleum, facing the breakfast room, watching his family eat dinner.

"Look at Chuck," Matthew said as we turned around to see Chuck's eyes alert and ears pick up as he realized he was being discussed. "Can't he have his ears trimmed or something?" Matt asked. "He just looks like a no class dog." Fur that resembled stringy long hairs was hanging down off the end of Chuck's ears.

"He is a no class dog," said Pat. "He wouldn't look right with good-looking ears. Would you Chuck?" Pat said to a wagging tail and panting tongue, watching from the next room. "Chuck's just happy the way he is—running, barking, eating, and sleeping where he shouldn't."

"I wonder if Chuck would like to play in water?" Benjamin the animal lover asked. He was remembering dogs splashing in waves, running loose on an island we had visited in the Caribbean Sea.

Spring vacation was about six weeks away. Early last fall, reservations had been made for a trip to Grenada. That was in a different lifetime, I thought to myself. No one in the family but me was thinking about spring vacation. I wondered if I would be going. The bill hadn't even passed out of the House, and it was the middle of February. I looked at Matthew eating his dinner. He just wanted his mother to be as she had always been—running into the waves, laughing as he shot over the light blue water in rented jet skis. Benjamin would not be with us again on spring vacation because he would go to college in the fall. Pat could go with them, but he would miss me and want me along.

My leg still flinched when my hand passed over the long red scar. The nerve endings remained sensitive to the touch.

Our time together on family vacations was almost over, I thought.

* * *

That day at the state house, Paul had quietly cornered Mark Kruzan. "Should I take my name off the bill?" he asked bluntly.

"It's going to move Paul, they have you worried, that's the purpose. Jesse wasn't going out to see Caress because he knew she would tell you he had spoken with her. I really felt bad. I saw her in the hall when he didn't leave the chamber. I think her eyes were opened to some of the realities down here sometimes," Mark smiled wistfully. He didn't like the games both sides played.

Velda had come down from the fourth floor to find her friend Dennis Avery, a member of Jesse's Courts and Criminal Code Committee.

She successfully spotted him walking at a fast clip, head and shoulders bent over as he scanned a note while moving down the hall. Pulling him to one side of the corridor, she simply asked, "Are we in trouble?"

"It should be all right," he said. "But you know because of whose bill it is, it's going to be played out as long as possible."

"We have a problem with the Farm Bureau's amendment. I would like to find it another home," she told him succinctly. "We don't want any amendments on this bill, Dennis. This is the best chance we've ever had for getting this legislation through."

"It should come up for a vote at the next committee meeting," he told her.

"I hope so 'cause we're running out of time." Velda had gotten her answer. Jesse would hear the bill at the very last moment at the last committee meeting. The troubling amendment would also be voted on at the last minute. She had also left a request with a Democrat who could speak to the other Democrats on the committee.

Velda called me with the information. "Caress, Jesse's committee is going to vote on the legislation next Tuesday. Do you remember Dennis Avery from when you testified?

Dennis is a good man, very concerned with children's issues, so he would relate to what you've been saying. He thinks we're okay, but I also think it's good you've stayed out of Paul's office." Velda half snorted. "Do you know there are legislators that now bark when they walk by his door?"

I wasn't sure what to think about the barking. I could only think how important the legislation potentially could be if it became law.

"Do you think the Speaker will call it to the floor even if they vote it out of committee?" I was worried again about the two men's dislike of one another.

"You've gotten too much attention, Caress, and he would look so bad killing this legislation when all the blame could publicly and specifically be placed on him."

She paused for a moment. "The rules change every year, and I currently think the Speaker has to call bills passed out of committee to a vote. Although, our friend Paul, when he was Speaker, didn't call to the floor a few bills that had passed committee. Caress," as if reading my thoughts, "you've gotten too much publicity," she said again. "There are a lot of Democrats who want this legislation. What we really need to accomplish is keeping that Farm Bureau amendment from being placed on the bill."

Sometimes it all seemed too worrisome and impossible to understand completely. Too many personalities, interests, and personal agendas to keep straight for a novice who didn't understand all the rules or the players. Sometimes waves of exhaustion, mental and physical, would pass over me and I would become silent.

"I want you to do something," Velda began talking again, jolting me back to the conversation. "Linda wants you to write a letter asking each member of the House for their vote. Similar to the letter you wrote to the committee members. She'll copy it and personalize it for each legislator. We'll make sure they actually read it too before they vote on the bill. We've got to think positively and keep working,

Caress. Linda thinks we need to keep you in front of the legislators to keep it personal. They may want to get that mean old Paul Mannweiler, but they really don't want to hurt the little lady."

"Do you want copies of *Indianapolis Monthly;* there's going to be an article about me, the attack, the legislation in the next issue." I hadn't seen the story but suddenly thought it might be effective if given to each legislator.

"Can you get one hundred and fifty copies?" Velda asked. "Enough to cover both the House and Senate?"

"I think so; I know the daughter of the publisher and her husband.

"Who else do you know?" she laughed.

"I really don't know anybody," I said, which is how I felt.

"You could have fooled me."

"I'll write the letter, Velda."

* * *

The third floor of the state house seemed especially busy at the top of the landing. I stepped off expecting to easily round the corner in the normally uncrowded hallway in front of the supreme court. Workmen were bustling back and forth propping ladders against windows that lined the end of the room. Men on the outside of the building were busy with buckets of water and squeegees, standing on scaffolding suspended in the air. "What's happening?" I asked one of the workmen. A rosy-cheeked man with a big smile stopped and placed his hands on his hips.

"Well, we got word that national television is coming in here next week for the Tyson appeal."

"Oh," I said as the windows covered in bird droppings were once again becoming clear. "Well, I know it will look nice," I said, smiling back at him, wondering if Alan Dershowitz was worth all this trouble. He seemed to spend all his time ridiculing the justice system in the state of Indiana. "Are you going to do the whole building?" I asked him.

"No, just this room," he told me as he walked toward the inside ladders. I remembered Paul's bird-blasted window and the view looking out across the lawn towards the statue of Governor Morton. The birds' target window belonging to the minority leader of Indiana's House of Representatives would remain the same.

I stood out in the main hall as Paul walked into the corridor. I had timed arriving close to the beginning of the committee meeting that was to be held somewhere down in the basement. Paul had his file of papers with him, ready for any questions, and he was smiling as he came over to where I waited.

"You know, Caress, last night I took our golden retriever for a walk. I thought of you because I knew I couldn't take his leash off no matter how much I wanted to take his leash off." I looked over at him. "He had the worst case of diarrhea." In spite of my anxiety over the committee meeting, I started to laugh as we passed a group of state senators congregating together. One of them noticing us was an imposing black woman who wore a sparkling rhinestone pin on her suit lapel spelling out the word "Casino." Senator Rogers was from Gary, Indiana, and was crusading for legalized gambling in the state. I saw Paul smile and half nod at the senator, saying in the low voice, "Earline." Senator Rogers may have had other things on her mind, for she did not smile back or recognize Paul. I felt a distinct chill as the elevator doors opened, then closed behind us as we descended to the basement.

The Courts and Criminal Code Committee was important to a lot of different people for many reasons. I sat in a half empty row near the back, and Paul sat down next to me as the committee finished discussing another bill. The table at the front was filled with committee members all in deep discussion with Chairman Villalpando presiding. I noticed Velda sitting near the front in the second row and John Baugh standing to one side close to the committee members. I looked around the room for people holding copies of the legislation. A young blond woman, also seated near the front, held a copy. She was a new one. Worrying to myself, I wondered what she wanted.

It was hard to hear near the back, and unclear exactly what was being said in the front of the room. Paul was looking over the legislative changes from the subcommittee meeting when I heard him say abruptly, "They're getting ready for us. I'm going up to the front."

The chairman turned his head toward those seated in the crowded, mid-sized room. He was looking around when he sat straight up, and the dark eyes became larger. Jesse Villalpando looked surprised when he saw me, then uncomfortable, he wasn't able to look away for a moment. The dark head snapped back toward the waiting committee, and he asked for the subcommittee's report. Tom Alevizos began going over wording and the matter of excluding police dogs in the line of duty from the bill. The men around the table were talking in low voices as they huddled together. The noise from the outer hall was becoming louder, making it even harder to hear the committee's words, adding to my anxiety while waiting for the vote.

A young woman moved across the folding chairs and sat down beside me. "I'm Jane Harrington," she told me, carefully placing my hand in her lap, protectively covering it with her own. It was an unusual gesture, but I felt a real sincerity about her as she sat listening to the committee. She was a news reporter; one I recognized from television. I remembered a story that she had been beaten by a former boyfriend who was a police detective. He had placed a gun in her mouth. She had also prosecuted the man in court.

Jane was there for me and had made a special effort to find the committee meeting in the state house that day. "Can you hear what they're saying?" she asked. I shook my head no, feeling a sickening anticipation of a vote. I strained to hear, for Jesse Villalpando had made a motion. I heard voices around the table begin to vote. First a nay, then another nay, a nodding aye from a committee member, another voice was too low to hear.

More nays, then an aye until Jesse Villalpando boomed out, "The measure is defeated for lack of a majority." The reporter was confused. I felt faint.

"Was that the bill?" she said to me.

I heard the chairman say "vote on the bill," and they started around the table again.

"No," I nervously whispered to my friend holding my hand, "that was the amendment." She smiled with relief before listening again. This time I heard ayes as one member after another recorded his vote. Jesse's turn came, and the volatile chairman with the dark hair and flashing brown eyes hesitated for a moment. He stared toward the back of the room—he was looking for *me*.

Sitting up, I looked right back at him as he clearly pronounced, *"Aye."*

Chairman Villalpando then turned back to the men around the table. "The ayes have it. Bill passes from committee."

"Yes!" the reporter yelled while squeezing my hand.

The room burst with noise. I caught a glimpse of John Baugh throwing his arms up in the air and stepping backward into the wall, eyes wide, cheeks blazing. "Whaahappened?" he was yelling, looking at the committee. Velda, springing to her feet, seemed in seconds to be talking calmly to the Farm Bureau lobbyist. Paul hadn't moved from the end of the table. His eyes were big as a slight pop went off and the blinding, bright television lights came on. He walked towards me at the back of the room.

"They're really following you everywhere aren't they?" he said quietly as we walked into the hall. My new friend Jane placed the microphone up to me.

"How do you like the experience at the state house?" she asked, smiling.

"I want to thank the committee for their wonderful

bipartisan support," I told her, hoping Jesse would watch the evening news or read tomorrow's paper, for a print reporter was busy writing down that quote. Paul was saying something to another television reporter while the camera recorded a long look at the bandaged leg.

I seemed to feel after each successful step that I had momentarily reached a safe harbor. I alone would hear the Presbyterian minister in the halls of the state house tell Gideon's story to me about faith and courage. "You don't have to be afraid anymore," he would repeat again and again.

Paul and I walked back to the elevators. A woman's voice came from behind me. "Could I speak with you for a moment?" she said politely. The elevator doors opened and Paul nodded to me.

"I've got to go on up," he said.

"Is this legislation breed specific?" the voice questioned as I turned to listen to the woman whom I had spotted in the committee room. She still held a copy of the legislation and stood very straight and tall. She wore a navy blazer with a silver head of a German shepherd fastened securely on the lapel.

"No, it's not breed specific," I assured her, observing the concern and the obvious dedication to German shepherds. I had learned from my own support group that if you wore animal jewelry, there was a serious correlation of commitment and concern for that species.

"We've always fought breed specific legislation," she continued, "but if that's not what this is all about then I would say we could support the bill."

She followed legislation at the state house for another kennel club of German shepherd owners. That was the problem, I thought, of trying to get a rogue dog like the pit bull banned. It scared the breed owners whose dogs could be considered potentially dangerous. "I like German shepherds," I told her and she broke into a smile.

"I've followed your story," she continued somewhat

hesitantly. "Actually, we must live fairly close; our house is right on Fall Creek Parkway near where you were attacked. That man who owned the dogs, well, he must have a partner. I've watched a truck pull up and off into the grass before on the other side of the street. They have cages in the back of the truck, and these two men have long heavy leashes, so long they couldn't possibly control those dogs. One of them brings a bicycle where they attach a leash to the bicycle. This great big man sits on the bike, and they make the dog pull him over the grass down to the path and around the bend where I lose sight of them. They must want those dogs to be really strong. Kind of bizarre don't you think?"

"Yes," I said to her, "that is bizarre," thinking to myself. Those dogs were in training.

"Well, good luck to you," she said.

"Thank you," I answered, stepping inside the elevator doors.

Two men stopped talking as the elevator jolted and moved upwards. "That was something 'bout the Farm Bureau amendment." The man was in a jovial mood. "Bet you're pleased." He smiled a wide grin, showing big, square teeth with a couple of gaps along the front. "I don't know if they worked it out ahead of time, but five voted for it, five voted against it, and two of them wouldn't vote. So no majority, deee—feated, yet all the politicians that had to vote for the Farm Bureau got to say their ayes. Congratulations." The man just beamed as the doors opened and I stepped out into the crowded third floor. This is an amazing place, I thought. I felt so light, walking down the hall, as if a major hurdle had been cleared when actually the bill wasn't even halfway through the process. Velda was talking on the phone when I finally peered around the partitions to hand her the promised letter.

"Hi," she whispered. "I'm telling Linda what happened." Velda had a big smile on her face and was moving back and forth in her chair.

"Velda, what did you say to John Baugh?"

"I told him I didn't have anything to do with the vote." My eyes were growing large.

"You did?" I said.

"Yeah, I don't want him mad at me."

I thought Velda must be friends with the three hawks that circled continuously in the February sky. She seemed to share with them keen eyes and a perfect sense of timing, floating high above the crowd in the ivory tower. Like the great birds, she was also an intermediary—one who ran ahead and smoothed the path so the novice with the bandaged leg would not fall.

EIGHT

Perfect Timing

The little hall was narrow with cream-colored plastered walls. Small, dark-framed sketches of ancient churches lined the passage. A normally locked door that guarded the hall leading to the church offices stood open. The door safeguarded the clergy and their staff from those that might wander in from the sometimes precarious neighborhood outside. Impulsively, I walked through the door and tiptoed down the hall toward the minister's office. I had come to the church on my now weekly mission to buy more of the minister's taped sermons when I noticed the open door.

The secretary was not at her desk so the minister's office was open for me to peer inside unseen. Looking into the office, I smiled. Tiny antique cars lined the desk and the surrounding ledges in front of the bookshelves that reached towards the ceiling. In the corner stood a lighted old-fashioned gas pump from the 1930s whose mellow light gave this inner sanctum brightness along with a warm glow, reflecting a personality with a touch of humor. The Presbyterian minister didn't know I existed. He had come to Indianapolis to serve a church and to direct its mission towards the neighborhood. In addition, quite unknowingly to him, the minister was also sent to Indiana on behalf of children and to assure me.

After the first ten days in February had slipped by, there was a phone call from Paul. His deep voice was light and upbeat. "I haven't gotten any notice for amendments on the bill," he said with enthusiasm. The entire membership of the House was now looking at the dog bill. During what was called "second reading," any member could attempt to place an amendment on the legislation. If a member was considering an amendment, he or she had to notify the author of the bill. No one wanted to change the legislation, so Paul was feeling confident. Now, if everything continued smoothly, it was only a matter of timing and the Speaker's cooperation to bring the legislation to a vote. "I think after the bill passes second reading today, the vote will come tomorrow if not the day after." He paused. "When do you go to trial?"

"Next week," I answered.

"Who's the judge?" he asked.

"I think his name is Taylor Baker. He's a black judge, Municipal Court. Supposedly a tough judge."

"Well, keep me posted," Paul replied.

I remembered his upbeat tone, which was memorable because Paul hid his emotions very well, being the good lawyer and politician. People who had known him for years would remark they hadn't known he was irritated at a meeting until weeks later, he so skillfully masked his feelings. He was also a careful person; someone who didn't make statements unless he was confident.

The next time the phone rang it was Velda. "Caress, the dog bill is on the list for third reading tomorrow. Must have sailed through second reading. I predict they vote on the bill tomorrow. The Speaker has it down, so unless he just doesn't call the bill," she paused, "which of course he's not going to do," she added for my comfort, "we should be ready with all the letters and magazines to go out to the legislators. Timing is everything, Caress," she said with conviction. "And after twenty years here, I'm sure of the timing.

"The *Indianapolis Monthly*'s have been delivered to the

state house. I've got them stockpiled away, and now they need to be stuffed with your letter smack dab where that story is with the picture of you." Velda was on a roll. "I'll get the pages to help us deliver them right before they vote. Now you have to get yourself down here about ten o'clock; that will give you enough time to sign off."

"What's sign off?" I asked, feeling as if we were suddenly speaking a foreign language.

"Caress, you have to hand sign each letter," she laughed. "Linda has them all personalized and ready to go. What's great about this too is that those magazines have not hit the newsstand. Those politicians will get the first copies." I was listening, careful not to become too excited. I had learned to take each day as it came, particularly when politics were involved. "Caress, you know somethin'?"

"What Velda?" I returned, half laughing at her tone.

"You're such fun to get legislation with," she squealed, and I could see the devilish smile and sparkling green eyes.

Velda was waiting the next day at the top of the stairs. "I've got you set up in the shack," she said with a smile. "You sign all the letters, then we stuff the magazines during my lunch hour, and we'll be all set."

Entering the little carpeted building, Velda guided me down the narrow side aisle towards a partition giving one end of the shack some privacy. A heavy wooden table held stacks of letters. Dear Representative Alevizos and so on, all neatly laser printed in organized, alphabetized stacks.

"Now all you have to do is sign your 'John Hancock' over and over," she laughed.

"I think I can handle that part," I said.

"You'd better," Velda responded, tossing a pen with black ink toward me. "Come get me when you're finished," she said, grinning, and then turned and walked back down the little aisle.

I picked up the pen and started signing my name, watching the names of the representatives pass as I turned over each letter. I had faces now to go with the names, and, for many of them, also personalities. My eyes glanced past the bookcases filled with century old law books down to the letters waiting for me on the table. The smell of old leather, sweet and musty, filled the little room. Comfort, familiarity, stability—Grandfather. He was with me in the room while I signed the papers.

The letters were in my hands as I left the little building and passed Gene the bailiff's executive desk. Gene sat rocking in his oversized chair and looking up, gave me a beaming smile. A nearby door opened and Velda appeared right on time, pulling a handcart, walking quickly towards me. "I can cart the magazines down to the House mailboxes and have them ready when they check their messages after lunch."

Velda escorted me into the judges' conference room where the magazines had been laid out on a large table. "Caress, we've got an hour to get these stuffed and downstairs. I know they'll vote on this bill this afternoon. I just feel, even though they've got lots of legislation to vote on—this is the day. It'll be a shorter afternoon session 'cause tonight the governor is having all the legislators over to the mansion for dinner. Don't worry, though, he does this once a year, but they never serve any alcohol so none of the legislators want to go over too early. Boring, you know," she said lightheartedly.

Glancing over the table, I simultaneously grabbed an organized stack of magazines, finding the page with my picture and sticking a letter inside with each representative's name appearing just above the closed pages. Velda was placing stacks on the handcart. "I tell ya' again, this is the most fun to be with you," she said, bubbling over. "The timing is going to be perfect. They're gonna sit there and think, *Who Is This Woman?* I only wish along with this you'd sue that man with his dogs. What day next week is the trial?"

"Tuesday," I said briefly.

"I know the judge—been around a long time. I don't think he's someone who just fell off the turnip truck," she snorted.

"Velda, I think of it right now with only one thought."

"What's that?" she asked.

"Relief," I said to her quietly. "Relief, for I know the mission—and that is to get this law and not worry about the man."

It was almost noon when we finished loading the cart, now stacked high with magazines. "This is gonna take a couple of trips, and I've changed my mind about the mailboxes," Velda said to me as we stood ready to go out the door. "I think we'll take these right down to the House chamber." Velda yanked the cart forward, hurrying me out the door and down the hall. Velda left me outside Paul's office as she went in search of pages to place a magazine on each member's desk. Cathy was talking to a tall woman whose silver gray hair was in contrast to a pretty, young face with big, round blue eyes. She was laughing with Cathy and her white sweater sparkled with rhinestones that glittered.

"Caress, this is Diane Masariu; she's Speaker Phillips' secretary." I nodded my head and smiled, wondering if she was a good friend of Cathy's despite the fact both their bosses couldn't stand one another.

"Nice to meet you," I said to the Speaker's secretary. "My friend is out in the hall looking for pages to pass these magazines out before the session begins."

"The pages are all at lunch," Diane informed me. "So, I'll pass them out for you." Picking up armfuls of magazines and noting the names at the top of each, she said, "It's no trouble, we'll get these on their desks before the session starts."

"Thank you," I said. I don't know if it ever entered Diane's mind that it was Paul's legislation. She was helping me and was someone, despite her loyalty to the Speaker, who did exactly what she wanted to do.

Velda was racing up and down the still quiet lunchtime corridors. "I can't find any pages," she said with exasperation.

"It's all right, Velda, the Speaker's secretary is helping pass out the magazines." Amazing grace, I thought as Velda walked towards the marble stairs, returning to the judge's chamber, still commenting to me about perfect timing as she disappeared from view.

An hour passed before the halls became crowded with people interested in the next House session. I walked back into Paul's office where Cathy handed me a list of bills ready for the afternoon vote. Close to the top of the second page read "House Bills on third reading." "House Bill 1218, Mannweiler, bill to regulate the owners of dogs," was halfway down the page. "I hope the Speaker calls the bill," I said warily to Cathy.

"He will, Caress, today's the day." As I turned to go back into the hall, Velda hurried around the corner.

"Caress, I went up to the House gallery and watched everyone in the chamber. They're just sitting there reading that article 'bout you," she crooned.

Tom Alevizos stood talking in the inner hall. Staring up at another legislator, he turned to his side and noticed us standing almost beside him. "We're going to try and get this out for you this afternoon," the representative said as he smiled my way. Velda nudged me.

"Did you hear that?" she said excitedly. "This is good, Caress. Now, if we just don't run out of time this afternoon before they take the vote." I glanced into the chamber and noticed most of the legislators were present and the magazine had been a hit. I also noticed a couple of legislators snickering to themselves as they discussed the article placed immediately before mine that discussed sex in the twilight years.

Paul had slipped into his seat at the front, and the Speaker was gaveling the session to order. "Caress, I have to go back to work but I'll find a way to check on you and what's happening after a while." Velda had the adrenaline flowing while I just wanted this major hurdle of the final vote on the House side to be over. I glanced up at the clock; it was one-thirty in the afternoon. The session had begun on time, but

I was mindful that time was of the essence due to the dinner at the governor's residence.

"I would like to honor this afternoon a distinguished citizen who has contributed a lifetime of service to Indiana." The voice droned on as the platitudes continued. Many legislators were still talking among themselves. The clock now read one-forty and business had not yet begun.

"I would now like to introduce the finest high school debate team in southern Indiana," as the representative from a county in the lower part of the state congratulated a group of apple-cheeked teenagers. Glancing at the gallery, I saw it was almost filled. People were still finding seats and calling to one another. The Speaker's gavel now pounded the podium, demanding silence. Almost half an hour had passed with no business accomplished; I glanced down at the cherry red paper filled with bills to be voted on today. Nervously, my fingers gripped the sheet as someone ready to go on stage and play a role. So many factors could and did kill potential laws. Some factors were political, others personal, and sometimes bills simply ran out of time.

Finally, the chamber quieted and the Speaker was calling each bill on second reading, asking if there were amendments. The bills on second reading had to be taken care of first. I noticed that every bill up for passage to the Senate was authored by a Democrat except for one—the dog bill.

"The fight is in the House," I heard Paul's voice telling me but comforted myself, remembering Representative Alevizos' smile and comment just an hour earlier. I watched the Speaker gaveling bills through second reading. Looking down at the bold black type listing the House bills, I checked each one off as they passed and felt the pressure of the minutes as they continued to tick away.

A leader in the majority party known for his feistiness and closeness with the Speaker came to the microphone. A short, stocky man he wore a bad toupee that from day to day was positioned differently on his head. His legislation dealt with gambling, which was important to his part of the state. A conservative member of the Republican caucus followed, wanting an amendment on the bill to help rehabilitate chronic gamblers. Representative Patrick Bauer relished the politics of the moment, smiling at the futility of those who spoke against his bill. The Speaker had his party voting in blocks and the amendment failed. More amendments came only to be defeated. The clock was moving.

"Do you want a chair ma'am?" the voice of one of the House doormen asked as I gratefully sat down just inside the chamber.

A legislator bent forward over his desk toward me. He was a former police captain from Allen County where the city of Fort Wayne was located. He wasn't very interested in the afternoon session and looked bored. "We'll get to vote on your bill today. You know Belinda Lewis? Nobody was better with dogs than her father," he mused. "She's a fine police woman." He momentarily paused, reached over and casually voted by pressing a small button on his desk.

"She's helping me get this law," I said, "and she's not too bad with dogs herself."

The Speaker had called the first bill on third reading and Representative Bauer was back again before the general assembly, explaining his legislation and loving the limelight. "Who cares about that?" he pondered.

"Well I think he does," I answered, looking toward the Speaker whose hands were folded across the barrel chest. He stood on a raised dais overlooking the chamber, lower lip protruding, gavel in hand. I watched the back of Paul's head as he slowly rocked back and forth in his chair.

The time was now two hours into the session and a happy Patrick Bauer returned to his seat; his bill had been passed onto the Senate. Nine more House bills and it was our turn. We should be able to get the vote in, I comforted myself. A couple of other lawmakers came to the podium. Their bills were shoo-ins. Everyone was a Democrat and the Speaker had decided long ago their bills were going to get out of the chamber.

"House Bill 1127, county park and recreation boards" flashed upon the screen when the chant started: "Rickkk, Rickkk, Rickkk." Representative Alevizos halted coming from his seat, then laughed; the short figure stormed to the front of the room. The name of his equally short predecessor followed him to the podium as the chamber rocked with calls of "Rickkk." The room quieted as Representative Alevizos briefly described his bill. Soon voted on to the Senate, he smiled, quickly returning to his desk.

A representative from just outside Indianapolis passed my chair. Bending over, she whispered in my ear, "Don't worry, but the Speaker is going to drag this out. I think your votes are there, though. The only one who really detests Paul is the Speaker; otherwise he's respected on both sides of the aisle. How is your leg?" She looked down at the brown Ace bandage and slippered foot.

"I'm not even thinking about it right now," I said with a slight smile.

There were now only three bills to be called before House Bill 1218. I felt myself steadily becoming more exhausted with the anxiety of waiting. Now it was after four in the afternoon, and I was still sitting in my chair in the aisle. The television cameras in the balcony were shifting positions to film me watching the vote. A local television anchorman was trying to get my attention. He was mouthing his words, asking if we could talk afterwards. I nodded yes back to him. We both were waiting.

Representative Dobis pushed his seat back from near the front of the chamber. He was another leader in the majority party and a friend of the Speaker's. The vote on his legislation immediately preceded Paul's. Going to the podium, he simply said, "I yield to Representative Dvorak," and then sat down. Representative Dvorak's bill was listed far down the page from the dog bill. I felt betrayed, not realizing that bills didn't have to be called in order. His legislation was also running out of time and he was a Democrat. Mike Dvorak's bill dealt with an emotional issue—requiring children to wear seat belts on school buses. Representatives rose to speak for and against the legislation. The afternoon was quickly evaporating as the vote was called. The gallery cheered as the bill passed out of the House and on to the Senate where it would die, never receiving a hearing from the fiscally conservative committee to which it was assigned.

It was now quarter of five and the Speaker called the next bill. "Pass," called out the legislator. The Speaker drew himself up at the microphone. "Tonight, we will be the guests of Governor Bayh for dinner at the residence." He paused, looking around the chamber. "So today's session will end somewhat early." I felt the blood draining from my body as Velda slipped behind me.

"He's gonna call it, Caress."

"Are you sure?" I said, feeling wilted. Velda leaned over.

"The timing's right, I can feel it; just look at those TV cameras. The Speaker knows you're here, he sees you, and doesn't want to look bad publicly."

Paul had stopped rocking in his chair. "H.B. 1218 regulates owners of dogs" appeared on the voting machine. I felt the rest of the blood in my body leave me. The roller coaster had left its safe port, and I didn't know if I could live through the ride. Paul stood up and turned, walking quickly across the front of the chamber and down the little side aisle toward me. "Caress, I have to assign the bill to a senator if it passes. Do you approve of Teresa Lubbers?" I nodded yes to him.

"Paul, do you think anyone will get up and say anything?" I looked at him as if we were both ready to go to the firing squad. A wry smile came across his face.

"Oh, I don't think they're going to let me off easily." He turned and was back up the little aisle, reaching the podium. Paul's face was unreadable as he began speaking. "This is legislation that has passed the House twice before, and there have been no amendments to this bill. I would like to see it passed today."

Paul had decided to make it short and sweet. The magazines rested on the legislators' desks; some were looking at the pictures again. Several members wanted to speak. Mark Kruzan strolled to the front of the chamber.

"Well, we're here today to vote on Representative Rottweiler's bill." Paul laughed with the rest; he was the good politician. There was no laughter from me. If a friend was making a joke, what would follow from his enemies?

Needing the waiting to end, I felt only tension, and called upon angels to be present, for there were children to be saved. "His friend is here today," Mark was saying as eyes in the chamber turned. "This is legislation we have seen before and seen defeated. If we don't vote for it this year, I guarantee you it will be back next year with another victim." Paul stood quietly watching Mark. The Speaker stood immobile and stoic.

Mark Kruzan was not one of the Speaker's soul mates. This effort would not help the cruiser come one step closer to leadership in his party under the current Speaker. Mark smiled at the chamber and walked away from the podium as another legislator started to walk up the aisle.

Douglas Kinser was a Democrat from industrial New Castle, Indiana. He was the only Quaker in the Indiana House of Representatives and had impressed me as a thoughtful man.

"Representative Mannweiler," he began, "we have had this legislation before in the House. You must remember?" he said, pausing. "I think it's legislation that does have merit," he added agreeably, looking over at me sitting in the aisle. He glanced up at the gallery, then at Paul as a sly smile crossed his face. "Look up to the gallery, Representative," he said to Paul. "Former Representative Marc Carmichael is visiting today. You remember him don't you?" Paul looked bemused. "While he was in the general assembly he was my seatmate.

Do you remember that, Representative?" Paul nodded his head. "One tries to vote for their seatmate's legislation, and I always tried to vote for Marc's. This was his legislation, remember?" Paul again nodded genially. "Representative, did you vote for the legislation either time it came before the House?" Paul spoke into the microphone.

"No, I didn't."

"Could you please explain to the general assembly and all the people here today why it is now, when you know someone who has been terribly hurt, you are suddenly for the bill?" Douglas Kinser pressed gleefully. Paul smiled and leaned forward into the mike, keeping his eyes on Representative Kinser.

"Because before, the legislation covered the dog's own property and it was too broad." The two men continued to sportively duel at the podiums, and occasionally Mr. Kinser would look over, giving me a positive glance. He was conveying he would vote for the bill, but his role was to embarrass the minority leader.

I couldn't stand to listen much longer to the two men banter back and forth. I was now beyond smiling back at anyone; my expression grim, I continued waiting, sitting in the chair. Representative Kinser was sitting down. From the other side of the room, came another man holding a copy of the legislation in his hands. Dale Grubb was from rural western Indiana. He worked at Grubb Grain when the legislature was not in session. Dale sat in the very last row of desks in the chamber close to his friend Jim Bottorff, also from a rural district. Jim Bottorff was a member of the Natural Resources Committee. With a few exceptions, it was a group held together by country good old boys who were watchful about the rights of hunters.

On the affluent north side of Indianapolis you would often see license plates showing an eagle flying towards the sun, framed in a light blue sky. The extra funds paid for these plates went to the Department of Natural Resources whose committee at the state house often was more concerned with blowing the great bird out of the sky.

Perhaps Representative Grubb thought he was making his mark in the chamber. Here was the opportunity to bully the other side's leader who sat right up in front. As he started to speak, the narrow eyes became mere slits as the papers in his hand were waved. "This law interferes with my rights and might get in the way of my huntin' dogs," he glared at Paul. "I'm not votin' for your bill," he snarled. Representative Grubb was not a great speechmaker but was definitely in good-ol'-boy form. Paul was nodding and smiling at him anyway. The man from Grubb Grain was striding across the front of the chamber still waving the legislation in his hand. High theatrics—he seemed outraged.

"Don't worry, Caress," Velda was whispering behind me. "If he even read the legislation, he doesn't understand what it says."

A big man with a florid complexion came to the podium. He was voting for the law. His wife had been attacked by a pit bull. He was confirming that the law had been written so the owner was held responsible only if the owner recklessly, knowingly, or intentionally failed to restrain the dog. I watched heads nod as he walked back to his seat.

Paul waited by the podium; no one else came forward. The Speaker, still expressionless, turned toward the microphone and called for the vote. Chairs moved across the carpet, and one hundred men and women leaned forward to press aye or nay on their individual desks. Paul sat down in his chair and quickly leaned forward to vote as the lights started to appear by the names listed on the front wall of the chamber. Velda's hand came down on my leg as we watched the green lights appear.

"Congratulations Caress!" she squealed. I wobbled to my feet, and nodded to the legislators, before walking out of the chamber.

Velda was pulling on my arm. "Yes! Yes!" she said, her

eyes twinkling. "A landslide, Caress!" Still stunned that this hurdle was over, I didn't move and turned my head to see Paul walking into the little hall. Beaming, he handed me a white paper.

"I thought you might like to have this," he said, for it showed the record of the vote. Only four members had voted no. Paul, the quiet, careful lawyer and politician of few emotions was genuinely happy. "It will be another month before it gets to the Senate," he said.

"What Democrat will you ask to sponsor the legislation in the Senate?" Velda asked.

"I don't know yet," he answered.

"What about Senator Hellmann?" she asked. He had helped to ban greyhound racing in the state and was the Senate's minority leader. Paul had returned to being the unreadable politician and was quietly listening. Velda noticed the lack of response. "Well, I don't know if he would be all that great this year," she chuckled. "He is known as Senator Whizzer around the state house." Senator Hellmann had been arrested for publicly urinating in a parking lot late at night, unable to make it to any open facility before nature took over. Paul grinned as Velda turned to return to the judge's chambers. "Great job" she called to him over her shoulder. "Caress, come upstairs after the cameras are gone."

The Speaker's voice was coming across through the chamber. "I've got to go back now, Caress," Paul said.

"Do you want to be on the news?" I asked as the television reporters came through the grand oak doors and toward us.

"No, I need to go back and vote."

"Thank you, Paul," I said, giving him a hug as he left.

Camera lights came on and a microphone appeared. "Why is this legislation so important to you?" the reporter began, the lights very bright in my eyes. I was feeling extremely tired.

"Because children are the greatest victims of these attacks

and children have no voice once they are attacked; they are simply forgotten." My voice was dropping.

"Do you expect the legislation to make it through this legislative session?"

"I'll do everything I can to see that it does."

"Congratulations for getting it this far," he said as the bright lights suddenly snapped off. They realized how very drained my voice sounded.

The news media remained very kind and sympathetic to me, which was a blessing, I thought as I climbed the grand staircase up to Velda's office. It was close to six in the evening, and most employees had left for the day. Velda had been busy in the last half hour, notifying friends to notify friends that the dog bill had made it through the House of Representatives.

"Caress, I have a television warmed up to watch the news."

"I don't think I can stand to watch," I told her.

"But you won a big victory down there today."

"Look at these idiots who didn't vote for this bill," I said, feeling absolutely disgusted.

"Remember, you can't take it personally, Caress."

"I'm taking this real personally, Velda; these people are assholes—partisan assholes."

"Well," she nodded, leaning back in the swivel chair, "you know there are assholes here at the state house." She laughed, "I never thought you'd say anything like asshole, and here you are, one asshole, after another."

She made me smile, just like always. "I'm not going to say it any more."

"You're gonna ruin your sweet little lady reputation." She was still laughing. I felt drained and definitely not sweet.

Outside the tall window panes the early evening was rapidly turning from dark dusk into early winter blackness. "Pat," I said out loud, remembering he would be looking for me.

"I've got to go," I said as Velda also bolted in surprise out of her chair. We both raced out of the judge's chambers and into the deserted halls of the state house, past Gene's executive desk to the edge of the landing whose stairs descended to the third floor. There was Pat wandering the lower floor, and we watched him for a moment from the ivory tower.

"I'll call you tomorrow," I told her, stepping down onto the first stair and grabbing the bannister.

"Caress," she called again before I took another step. I turned to look back at her. "Just remember, all that asshole business is safe with me."

"I will, Velda," I answered. Though we had known each other for only a few weeks, she was someone I would have trusted with my life.

Walking toward Pat, I almost touched him before he turned around. He looked tired and worried not having found me. "It passed," I simply told him as he took my hand and we left the state house, walking out into the February night.

* * *

There would be a break in politics at the state house. Paul had said it would be a month before the bills changed and the dog bill would be sent to the Senate. There was nothing to be done at the state house for the moment so the timing for the trial was, in Velda's words, "perfect." I dreaded the trial, now only a few days away. Since the attack my friends in the press, lobbyists, those who stopped me on the street, would talk to me about finally having justice. The thought of the man never entered my mind; only the wish that the ruined animals that attacked me be destroyed. Justice for the man belonged to God Who had sent me on my mission.

The deputy prosecutor called; the court date was still set for next Tuesday. I was sorry Sandy Rowland from H.S.U.S. would be in Michigan for another trial. She had sent me a copy of *Sporting Dog Journal,* a dogfighting publication. The man involved in my attack had ordered his dogs from breeders who advertised in this magazine. Though the man was not charged with dogfighting, Sandy's testimony that the dogs had been purchased from two nationally known dogfighters would have raised eyebrows.

Sandy had educated the prosecutor as to why the dogs had so many different names. Her words came back to me. "If the animals are fought it makes them harder to track—these people fear exposure. I've told you before, everything about your attack indicates animals that are trained fighters. It's just a disaster that Animal Control over there couldn't have helped your prosecutor more. When a sheriff is more help to a prosecutor than Animal Control, it really says volumes, negative volumes."

I knew what Sandy was saying, for we had lost opportunities to collect evidence. The prosecutor also understood this fact. I suspected other dogs than the two collected by Animal Control had actually attacked me. The dogs pictured and described in the paper and magazines were black. The two dogs that had attacked me were brown. But I had no proof and over and over again the message came through to me to stay on mission—to let the color of the dogs go and concentrate on the legislation.

* * *

The day of the trial arrived and Pat wrapped the bandages around my leg as he did every morning. He remained much better at wrapping the leg than I. There was a certain talent in keeping the bandage from coming loose and slipping during the day. Pat had finished with my leg and sat looking at me. Without a death in the family, this was one of the very few times I could remember his not leaving the house in early morning for work.

"You know I love you very much," he said to me now in the quiet, early morning darkness. He had been to the pretrial hearings, and thinking of the man bothered him. For the last two months he had taken care of my leg, and sometimes I would notice him looking at the long red scars and indented skin that covered the missing muscle tissue. He grieved and was angry at the man who coveted his vicious dogs. He kept his anger to himself because I could not stand any bitter emotion, and to me the man was very distant.

Benjamin and Matthew were beginning to stir as alarm clocks started to ring and a radio blasted out rock music. The dogs trotted into our bedroom, ready to be let out to the backyard. Chuck wagged his tail and ran around the bedroom. He was the only one in the family who had a morning personality, and elderly Boomer eyed her fellow canine with weariness. "Come on dogs, let's go outside," Pat said as he clapped his hands and both dogs followed him expectantly, knowing the routine. Gray light was beginning to erase the darkness outside the windows as Matthew, still half asleep but dressed for school, shuffled into the bedroom.

"Are you sure this guy won't go to jail?" he asked me.

"No," I told him, "though I'm hoping the dogs will be put down and he'll get fined."

Matthew looked so young, standing and looking at me with his navy blue school pants and collared shirt. His hair was sticking straight out at the sides. He hadn't made it into the bathroom for the daily hair combing ritual. He was frowning and looking at the bandages. "Why do you have to wear that?" his head nodded downward towards the bandage around my leg.

"It's important for me to try and get people's attention right now."

"You don't need it though," he cried half angrily. His shoulders sloped downward and his arms hung at his side.

"It makes my leg feel better," I told him quietly, "the pressure helps the scars." His expression was glum and depressed. "Matthew, did you ever stop to think that maybe there were some things more important than how you feel?" He looked up at me.

"I just don't want you in the newspapers anymore. I don't

want everyone asking me about you at school. I just want it to end." His shoulders drooped even lower.

"You want me back like before?"

"Yes," he said, as the soft hazel eyes reminded me how very sensitive he was and that it was hard being fifteen.

"I'm never going to be quite like I was before ever again, buster," I said gently to him. "Maybe I will be better than before all of this. I do know that there are some things worth a little sacrifice and this is one of them." Telling him what I believed to be the truth, I added, "There probably will be something in the paper and on television." I looked back at Matthew, feeling for his misery. "I know you're unhappy and I'm sorry you're unhappy, but this will end."

He remained standing and staring at me, mouth down-turned. "Matthew, you had better go comb your hair because you look like a rooster." He left for the bathroom mirror, since the only thing worse than your mother on television would be looking like a rooster at school while everyone asked you questions about her.

* * *

People walked rapidly through the revolving doors of the City-County Building. Men and women were moving quickly across the main floor, joining us as we headed for the elevators. I wondered how long we would be in the courtroom as the floors quickly passed and the little steel box that held us opened on to the fourteenth floor.

Bright camera lights were in my eyes as the doors opened. The press studied court dockets and they were waiting for me. I recognized several of the cameramen and waved to them before passing into Municipal Courtroom, Number Eight.

The deputy prosecutor was waiting in the courtroom. Greg Ullrich was someone I had been talking to for months but had never actually met. "Well, I know who you are," Greg said with a smile as I came through the door.

"The defense lawyer is here and inside the court," Greg

informed me as City Prosecutor Mark Mertz came into the hallway.

"We've been reading all about you," he said pleasantly as he shook my hand. "Would you like to sit down?" he asked as I glanced around the courtroom that reflected the rest of the City-County Building—no frills, functional, and slightly seedy. Velda would sometimes refer to the City-County Building as a poor relation next to her dignified state house.

"Riff-raff hangs around that place, Caress," she would say to me with a sniff. "I always feel like I need a bath whenever I leave that building." I was thinking she was right, there was no ambiance here, as I noticed the well-used, molded plastic seats. The jury box was over against one wall. Since this was not to be a jury trial, members of the media were seated in the jury box, waiting for the judge.

The man's lawyer had left the courtroom hurriedly. Greg Ullrich walked towards where we were seated. "Caress, the lawyer had the times mixed up when the trial was to start. He's gone to call his client to tell him to get down here fast. The judge gave him an hour," he said, leaning over the molded seats. "It's too bad you have to wait. If you want, there is a cafeteria on another floor."

I had no interest in food but felt my brain going numb at the thought of waiting. At this point, after weeks of conversations, Greg was a friend. He knew Velda, her judge, and had spoken several times to Sandy Rowland. He also knew Indianapolis Animal Control had been no help in the case. The man we were now waiting for had only been charged with harboring a non-immunized dog. In the state of Indiana it had the potential of a jail sentence and a one thousand dollar fine. It was not the felony charge that would have been leveled against a dogfighter.

I began to feel nervous about seeing the man in the courtroom. This was a scenario I hadn't thought much about but now felt great empathy with men and women who came to court after suffering any kind of violence. Minute by minute, the hour passed slowly. The press continued to sit in their seats in the jury box, occasionally glancing over at me.

Suddenly the side door from the hall opened and the man and his lawyer walked into the courtroom. The man was even bigger than I remembered—tall and powerfully built. His lawyer carried a grocery sack in one hand. They both looked straight ahead as they passed, heading for the table reserved for the defense.

"All stand for the Honorable Taylor Baker," said a voice at the front of the courtroom as the judge entered. The black-robed judge mounted the stairs to his enclosed dais. There is an immediate perception of power and authority that impresses people as a judge enters a courtroom. The courtroom and the judge that dominates have strong parallels to a church with a pulpit and a minister in a black robe. The name of God is invoked to each person who testifies and most of those in the room hope for truth and a verdict that will serve the innocent. A stroller's clicking, rolling wheels turning on wet pavement, raw November weather came running through my mind.

Greg Ullrich and the man's lawyer approached the judge. The man walked with them towards the bench as the judge leaned back in his chair looking directly at Greg. "You've reached an agreement with the defendant?" he inquired.

"Yes, we have, Your Honor," Greg answered. The judge eyed the man.

"Do you understand the complaints filed against you?" he asked.

"Some," the man slowly answered.

"The prosecutor has just stated that he has an agreement with you to dismiss some of the charges. However, you will plead guilty to the charge the State of Indiana has filed against you of Harboring A Non-Immunized Dog, a Class B Misdemeanor. Do you understand that charge?"

"Yes, sir," he answered.

"It is alleged that you did knowingly harbor a dog that is

a pit bull over the age of six months and not immunized against rabies, which caused bodily injury, that is severe lacerations to Caress Garten by biting Caress Garten. Do you understand?" the judge asked again.

"Yes, sir," the man repeated staring straight ahead. The judge went back and forth on legal procedure, grilling the prosecutor about forms used to file the charges. The judge glanced over at the press. I thought he must be wary. Recently a high profile case involving a dog and the death of a policeman had been overturned on a legal technicality. The judge was obviously not going to have this happen to him in this courtroom.

I was lost in their legal wranglings until I heard the words from the judge, "Are you pleading guilty?"

The man answered, "Yes." There were more questions from the judge as I sat listening in the molded plastic chair. My mind was tired, an hour had passed, and the trial was just starting.

Greg Ullrich looked at some notes on a nearby table then said, "State calls Officer Taylor." A sheriff's deputy walked past me to the witness chair. "Were you working in the position of sheriff's deputy on November 5, 1992?" Greg asked.

"Yes, sir, I was," said the officer.

"Were you the investigating officer of a woman who was attacked by a pit bull and injured?"

"Yes, sir, I was," he repeated.

"What did you do to investigate the case?"

"Well," he began, "at approximately 11:00 P.M. on November 5th, I made contact with a man at his residence. He stated that his dogs had been involved in an incident where a female had been attacked. He informed me that he wanted to make everything right and that he had contacted the sheriff to turn the dogs in to us."

"So you went to the house?"

"Yes, sir, I did," he answered.

"What was the conversation?"

"Well, he was very cooperative with me when I got there. At first I noticed two dogs were there, those were the dogs he was going to turn in, but he had three dogs in the home. I asked him to turn in the three dogs because we didn't know which dogs were involved in the attack. I also asked if the dogs had been immunized, and he said one of the dogs had been immunized in Texas, but he wasn't sure if it had expired. The other dog in the attack had not been immunized." The sheriff glanced over at the man.

The prosecutor continued. "Is that man in the court-room?"

"Yes, sir, he is."

"Where is he sitting?"

"Right over there in the black suit," as the sheriff nodded toward the man. The defense had no questions.

"I call Caress Garten," said the prosecutor as I found myself moving, then sitting in the witness box. I stated my name.

"Do you remember November 5, 1992?" Greg Ullrich asked.

"Yes," I answered.

"And on that date were you in the vicinity of East Fall Creek Parkway?"

"Yes," I responded again.

"About three in the afternoon, two pit bulls attacked you, is that correct?"

"That is correct." I told him.

"Could you tell us about the injuries you received at that time?" My eyes focused on the prosecutor.

"When I arrived at the hospital I was given three units of blood, I had three surgeries, two on my leg a week apart because they couldn't close the leg, and one on my head. My hand was injured; I had —"

A voice yelled out across the room. "Your Honor, I would like to ask a question," interjected the man's attorney.

"You may," answered the judge. The lawyer looked at me.

"Have you been sworn in?" I turned cold. I had never

thought anyone would question my honesty.

"No," I answered. A feeling of repulsion went through me although there was no time to dwell on that thought. I was sworn in.

"My injury to my leg is—I have a *misshapen* leg," I continued. "My doctor told me last week that when he first saw me, all of the muscles from my leg were ripped away from the bone, and that he could take his hand and run it up along the bone inside the leg."

"All these injuries were the result of what the dogs did to you at that location at that time?"

"Yes," I said. The prosecutor announced he had no more questions. I stared hollowly at the defense attorney as he approached.

"Ms. Garten, can you describe to the court what type of dress you were wearing at the time?"

"I ... what type of dress ...?" I was confused; what did he want to know?

"Outer clothing," he prodded.

"I was wearing pink cotton slacks, moccasins, I had on a light sweatshirt and a light wool short coat."

"Did the coat have any fur on it?" He asked.

"The coat was ripped and torn, is that what you mean as —"

"No, Ms. Garten, I mean fur shelling on the outside of the coat?"

"No ... no," I answered.

"Did you have any type of fur clothing?"

"No," I repeated.

"Shoes or anything?" he pressed. Resentment started to build for this man who defended the owner of vicious dogs—the one who had trained them to hang on, tearing their victims.

"No," I answered firmly. "Leather moccasins, cotton slacks, wool coat."

Pink slacks, I had pointed out the color pink, remembering the red blood soaking into them and the brightness.

"When the dog first approached, what occurred?" asked the judge.

"I watched the dogs running in and out of trees as they approached," telling the story once again. "I smiled at them and held out my hand for them to sniff. They circled me and crouched low to the ground very suddenly, then attacked. I ... I was totally taken off guard ... if I had acted ... if I had run, acted in an aggressive manner they ... they would have ... I would be dead."

Did you see any leashes?"

"Not that I recall," I answered.

The judge went into my injuries, the surgeries, point by point of the attack. Question by question. When did I slip? Did one dog ever let go of my leg? How far away was the man? Which dog injured my head? I desperately wanted the judge to understand more than the answers to his questions. I wanted him to understand about dogfighting, my mission, the children.

The judge finished questioning me, and for the moment the prosecutor and defense were finished. I sat down.

The judge called the man and his lawyer forward, and for a long while I listened, sometimes confused, as to the structure of the law, the references to Indiana Code and City Ordinances. Hours had passed. A member of the press turned and caught my eye. Her mouth formed the words about an interview. I nodded my head yes.

"Your Honor, I also have written material," I heard Greg Ullrich say to the judge, "about controls and dogs in general." He was presenting material from the Humane Society of the United States, dealing with vicious dogs who attacked without provocation.

The defense attorney quickly added that he also had written material he might wish to submit, "because it pertains to the disposition of the dogs."

A sinking feeling went through me, seated in the back of

the courtroom. The man was going to fight for the return of his dogs. "They're worth money to him, Caress," Sandy Rowland's words came back to me.

"Your material relates to the dogs?" questioned the judge.

"Yes, Your Honor," replied Greg, "as far as what is to be done with the dogs. I would like the city prosecutor to deal with the disposition of the dogs, Your Honor. The City Ordinance provides for forfeiture, and Mr. Mertz is familiar with this ordinance."

"First I would like Mrs. Garten to speak to sentencing." I watched the defense lawyer and the man. How much could I tell before they stopped me?

"Your Honor, I ... am very concerned about these dogs. In some way they have been conditioned, making them vicious. I believe they cannot, no matter who owns them, be rehabilitated. I fear other people will be hurt, so I would ask you order these dogs be humanely put down. There have been many people who have come forward who have had very close calls with these dogs. One a cyclist, who was forced to place the bicycle between himself and the dogs." The defense attorney jumped up.

"We would object. She didn't observe the incident."

"Keep your comments to this incident," counseled the judge. I hadn't gotten very far telling the other stories so I must make my point with this judge.

"These just weren't dogs that took a bite and left. They were very strong. I was not strong enough to have gotten myself out of the situation. With every ounce in me I want to tell this court how powerful, how vicious, how unrelenting, they were and that they are killers."

I wanted to tell this judge the story about these dogs being asked to pull men on bicycles to build their upper torsos and the reason for the multiple names of the dogs. "Remember he's not being charged as a dogfighter, Caress," whispered Sandy Rowland's voice to me.

"Your Honor, we would request the dogs be forfeited to

the City and destroyed. Ownership by another person would not be satisfactory given the nature of the attack," the city prosecutor spoke up.

I decided to try and make one more point. "Your Honor, I am worried about this man owning dogs. I would like him placed on probation from owning any dogs—out of safety's sake for his neighbors and others," I quickly added before the prosecutor returned me to my seat.

The defense attorney called the man to testify, asking first, "Sir, what do you do for a living?"

"I drive a truck and haul. I'm also a part-time security guard," he answered.

"Are you married?"

"Yes," he replied.

"Children?"

"I have four children," he said.

"Do you go to church, sir?"

"Yes, I do," he replied.

"Do you recall the day of November 5th, 1992?"

"Yes, sir, I do."

"You own how many dogs?"

"At that time I owned four or five dogs."

I thought to myself, Only three months had passed and the man couldn't give a clear answer as to how many dogs he owned.

"How many dogs did you have on your premises that day?" the defense lawyer questioned.

"Three," the man answered. "Turbo, he's the oldest dog. Then there's Thunder—he has two or three different names because the owner would not transport the name out of him." I wondered if the judge was confused by this statement or questioned if the man was telling the whole truth. "Then there's Hook, he's the younger dog."

The defense lawyer then asked, "Now you say you owned other dogs?"

"I've owned other dogs before," he answered.

"Why do you have three dogs?" The man's lawyer asked.

"I love animals," he replied.

"Have you ever had any incidents with these dogs before with the general public that you can recall?"

"No, sir, I haven't," the man answered, staring straight at his attorney.

I remembered the conversation with the man's neighbor who had stood screaming on top of his car for his wife to bring his gun.

"You let your children go around these dogs?" asked the man's attorney.

"Yes, I have a son seven years old, and he feeds the older dogs, the dogs that I have sometimes."

What older dogs that he had *sometimes?* I wondered.

"Sir, are you aware of the reputation or at least public allegations that have been made against dogs or this breed?"

"Yes, I'm aware of the reputation," said the man in the witness box.

"Before this incident, you have been successful in maintaining their security?"

"Yes," he answered.

"Have your dogs ever chased anyone?"

"No, sir, I haven't had no report of my dogs chasing anyone." The defense attorney spun around and looked at the press, then back at the man.

"Your dogs ever been loose, let loose, or gotten loose into the community that you know of before this incident?"

"No, sir."

The defense attorney walked back to the table and picked up an envelope. "I would like to submit as evidence Exhibit One and Exhibit Two. Could you please tell the court what these are?"

"This here's my daughter and son standing with Turbo."

They had produced the pictures of the loving family with the pets. Sandy Rowland had told me owners of dogs that could fight usually claimed they were family pets.

"Sir," the defense attorney began again, "tell us about what you were doing with your dogs prior to the incident involving Ms. Garten."

The man shuffled in his seat. "I had took or broughtn' two dogs with me, one dog just a puppy, and one grown dog, both on leashes. The puppy had an attitude, wanting to play with the older dog. He caused them both to be tangled up in the leashes, and for me to untangle them I had to unhook the leashes. Then there was this squirrel that runs in their sight, and they takes off after him."

The defense attorney walked to a table and pulled a thirty-foot leather leash out of a paper bag. "Is this the leash you were using on November 5th?"

"Yes, sir, it was."

"When the dogs ran away from you, what did you do?"

"I chased them," he answered.

"How far away were you from the dogs when you first saw Ms. Garten?"

"A long way."

"Did you see the incident that preceded the attack."

"I couldn't really focus on what happened."

"But you went to her assistance?"

"Yes, I did."

"You ever let your dogs out without being leashed?"

"No, sir."

"Do you believe that if the Court sees fit to not destroy the dogs you would be able to maintain the dogs in a manner that can assure the Court that there would not be a repeat of this incident?"

The man answered confidently, "Yes, sir."

The judge looked at the man. "Now, are you saying to the Court that Zebb and Turbo are the same dog?"

"Thunder and Zebb are the same dog," corrected the man.

"Why do they have so many names?" the judge asked, shifting his hand under his chin.

"Well," the man began rambling, "the owner, he does

not take his dogs out of ownership—and then you have a call name."

"What do you mean call name?" asked the judge.

"Whatever name that I wanted to call him beside ownership," the man answered.

The judge hesitated before responding with "Okay."

I sat in the back of the room remembering that the dog's original name would be important for bloodlines, breeding. A new owner could change the name for security to make the dog hard for law enforcement to trace. "Call name" was a term commonly used in dogfighting circles. I wondered if the judge had any idea what he was hearing?

The prosecution began with Greg Ullrich asking for clarification. "Now, what are the names of the dogs that were with you the day of the attack?"

"Thunder and Hook," answered the man.

"Which dog is also called Zebb?" Greg asked.

"Thunder, he's also got a name Zebb."

"So, Turbo's at home the day of the attack."

"Yes, at home," the man answered.

"The vaccination papers from Texas, which dog are they for?"

"That's for Thunder."

"Thunder was shipped to you from Texas?"

"Yes. The papers the judge has—they came with him."

"Where were they sent from in Texas?"

"I couldn't really say," the man answered.

"How did these dogs arrive, did you pick them up or did you order them shipped to you?" The man hesitated.

"Uh, ordered them."

"They're shipped to you?"

"Yes, sometimes different dogs be in different state dog shows or something." The man shifted in his chair. "You might pick them up at a dog show, or auction or something." I thought of a pit bull dog show with chagrin. Who would hold a pit bull auction? A mixed breed, what would they be worth unless these dogs had something else to offer?

"So Zebb-Thunder had his vaccination?"

"Yes," the man answered.

"The other dog, Hook is what you're calling him, doesn't have a vaccination because you say you're not sure of his age? Whether he was old enough to be vaccinated?" the prosecutor asked.

"That's right."

"Do you know where you got Hook? Was he shipped to you, or did you buy him at an auction?"

"Hook—I think he came out of North Carolina." The prosecutor stood still and looked at the man.

"Turbo, the dog at home who you say was not involved in the attack, was vaccinated after the attack on Mrs. Garten?"

"Yes," said the man. Prosecutor Ullrich had proved two dogs were not immunized at the time of the attack. My brain was so tired I was having trouble keeping up with the myriad of names thrown out by the man. I had to remember he had not been charged with dogfighting.

Mark Mertz, the city prosecutor, took over from Greg Ullrich. "What did you do back on November the fifth to get the dogs off Mrs. Garten?"

"The one dog that I got off her, I used a stick," he replied.

"How big a stick?"

"A small stick," he answered.

"Would it be about an eight or nine inch long stick?"

"Yes."

"How big around? The size of a hammer handle?" the city prosecutor added. The man eyed the prosecutor.

"Yes," he answered.

"Was it a hammer handle?"

"Yes."

"What did you do with that stick?"

"Far as what?" the man questioned.

"To get the dog off," the prosecutor pressed. "Put it

between his teeth and opened his mouth using a prying motion?"

"Yes," he said.

"You weren't able to get the dog off with a command or otherwise any training that the dog had?"

"No."

The city prosecutor had the hammer handle in his hand and lifted it up. The sheriff had found the handle on the path the evening of the attack.

I knew, sitting silently in the courtroom, that in the language of dogfighting, this was the parting stick.

"You also testified that you were always successful in maintaining the security of your dogs, keeping them away from people and so forth; were you referring to these three dogs or were you speaking of all the dogs you owned?"

"Repeat that again," the man muttered.

"The question is have you always been successful in maintaining the security of these dogs?"

"Yes, I have."

"Is this true with all the dogs you've owned?"

"Yes."

"You've never been cited for allowing a dog to run loose?" The man moved in his chair, hesitating.

"No," he said.

"You've never been in Court Twelve before on that charge?" The man froze.

"I can't recall the charge that I have had, what it was for."

"Have you ever been fined for an animal violation?"

"Yes," he finally answered.

The city prosecutor smiled, tossing his pencil on the table. He had caught the man in a lie. "No further questions, Your Honor," he said.

Greg Ullrich responded, "Nothing else for the State, Your Honor, only to point out Mrs. Garten's testimony as to sentencing. The city prosecutor will speak finally as to the request of the disposition of the dogs." Mark Mertz stood and asked the judge to accept the man's admission of guilt on owning a non-immunized dog and impose fines and court costs. He also wanted the dogs forfeited and destroyed by the City.

I was listening in a tired haze, only hearing his final words "the attack was unprovoked, it was sudden, it was perhaps the most serious attack that I've had occasion to bring to court in eight years. These are vicious dogs exhibiting vicious behavior without being provoked and both dogs were involved."

The judge was asking the man's attorney for a final summation before he ruled. The defense attorney walked toward the judge and I knew what was coming, for the man didn't care about the fine; *he wanted his dogs back. I wanted them dead.*

"Your Honor," he began, *"McPherson Buick* was a case that I'd like to use today with regard to the Court's pending decision as to how to handle these dogs. Now, you know if an automobile was being carelessly driven by this man and had injured someone, he could be sued, but the car wouldn't be committed to a dump for destruction. This is because the car was just an extension of the man driving that car. The same situation applies here in this case. My client attempted to explain his dogs were loose from the leash, and no matter what he might say, his explanation was not going to be good enough, certainly not to Ms. Garten. We want you to accept the guilty plea, Your Honor, because we feel the problem does belong with my client, not with the dogs. This man wants to take the responsibility and pay this fine; he also wants to apologize to Ms. Garten. But the blame for all of this should not be carried over to his pets. He has tried to demonstrate that these dogs are family pets. This is a family man, a religious man, he has children, he loves his dogs. Perhaps some alternative sentence and penalty would be appropriate. Placing this man on probation and returning the dogs to him. This man could go to a program that would ensure proper training. If these dogs aren't given back, there's nothing to stop him from buying more dogs just like these or maybe worse. We would also ask the minimum penalties for this man financially and that he be given an adequate time to pay."

The judge watched the attorney take his seat. "I think in the case of *McPherson Buick,* the liability was tracked back to the manufacturer where one might consider an innocent purchaser had obtained a vehicle that, at least in that case, was contended to have some defect. The analogy is not clearly applicable. An animal is a living being."

"Your Honor."

"Yes, Mr. Mertz."

"Certainly the court ordering what the law allows would not prevent this man from going out and buying more dogs, but it certainly would prevent these two dogs from ever engaging in another unprovoked attack on an innocent person. We stand by our request," ended the city prosecutor. *Amen,* I thought.

The judge left the courtroom to review the statutes. Now early afternoon, the trial had gone on for hours. The reporter for a television station approached me again, bending down, beginning to ask her questions. Some others in the press had gone into the hall to tell their cameramen to be ready. We were just waiting for the judge.

I was beyond watching a clock anymore, and shortly the doors opened and the judge entered. "I have reviewed the city ordinance violation of section 6-7, A Vicious Dog To Be Confined, and state statute regarding harboring a non-immunized dog. The section that does cover termination of ownership seems to be a lot clearer in language when it comes to dogs dealing with fighting contests." The judge paused for what seemed an eternity. "The Court, however, does find the City established a preponderance of evidence of a violation of the City ordinance that the defendant did permit two vicious animals to go unconfined on Fall Creek, on November

5th. The Court imposes a fine of one thousand dollars, and the dogs forfeited to the City. With respect to Harboring A Non-Immunized dog, another fine of one thousand dollars and one hundred and eighty days in jail, suspended on condition of two hundred and eighty hours of community service." The judge stopped and looked over at the man who owned the dogs. "Sir, you have another dog of the pit bull variety, correct?"

"Yes, sir," he answered. The judge then ordered the family pet, Turbo, to always be properly licensed and immunized, to wear a muzzle in public and be always on a leash as a condition of the probation. Turbo was also to go to dog obedience school.

Velda would later chortle at all the little French poodles leaping into their owners' arms when Turbo came into doggie obedience school. "Kind of like trying to retrain Charlie Manson," I whispered to Pat.

Finally the trial was over.

My arms felt so heavy as Pat helped me on with my coat. We walked up to Greg Ullrich, the deputy prosecutor. He was smiling, and so I smiled. "Thank you, Greg," I said to him. I felt totally drained as Pat opened the door for me towards the large outer hall where the television cameras' bright lights were waiting.

"How do you feel about what happened today?" a local news anchor asked me.

"I'm happy with the outcome. According to the law it is the best we can hope for." From somewhere a great calm was coming over me and I smiled at the news reporter.

"Do you feel the dogs were killers?" I looked at the reporter from the evening paper, repeating what I had said in court.

"I feel if I had run or acted in an aggressive manner, they would have ... I feel I would be dead." A local television reporter stood next to me, holding a microphone.

"What did he do after you were attacked?" he asked me

with intensity. I watched his eyes. This question wasn't going to make the news. The reporter's body quivered when he asked me again slowly pronouncing each word. "What did he do after you were attacked?"

The answer made people furious, and it amazed me how intensely, how personally involved people felt.

"He left me," I said quietly to him.

"He left you," he said passionately. I could see this film being clipped from his report as quickly as it was screened, and obviously the newsman didn't care. He was angry and wanted to let it out.

"You know, I don't think about it and I was all right," I said to him. "Remember it's a bigger issue than me, and it's what happens at the state house that's really important." My coat was beginning to feel as if it were lined with steel as I started to walk toward the elevators. The reporters followed.

The elevator door opened and I smiled at the cameras as the doors shut. "Good job, Buster," Pat told me as the elevator dropped floor by floor, doors opening into a stream of people in the busy lobby. "I'll go get the car." Pat walked away in the crowd. The sock on my foot was starting to slip again and stopping, I pulled it up, leaning exhaustedly against a wall of polished granite. I watched for Pat from behind the glass-paneled front of the building. A young woman carrying a drink in her hand came towards me. In her early thirties, she looked like hundreds of other women who daily did her best for one of the many city departments.

Stopping a few feet away, she said quietly, "I just wanted to tell you that all of us on my floor have been praying for you."

It was the strangers that touched and humbled me with their caring. They always appeared with perfect timing when I seemed to need their support the most. I watched her walk away, the messenger, bringing and leaving with me continued assurance, continued love.

NINE

Wolf's Territory

It was now the end of February. Hook and Thunder had been given lethal injections and died an hour after Judge Baker's decision had been made. The bold black newspaper type read; "Execution Swift for Two Pit Bulls."

"Why do they have headlines like that?" Velda said with disgust in her voice. The dog lover, she didn't like the word "execution" applied to an animal. She knew the dogs that attacked me were a paradox: vicious due to breeding and training, yet innocent because they depended on man. They had been a living aberration of what most people loved and recognized in a dog. I continued to wonder if the right vicious dogs had been euthanized.

"All bite victims want the dog put down," I remembered Belinda telling me. She was right, and I empathized completely with people's terrible and haunting fears of anyone else being hurt by the same animal. I knew the man had a partner and I wondered if others connected with the underground and illegal world of sporting dogs were following this story.

"Damn little socialite," laughed Velda, rocking back in her chair enclosed behind the panels. She stopped rocking suddenly, sitting forward, turning serious. "Caress, are you ever afraid?"

"Of what?" I asked her.

"Of dogfighters?" she replied. "They're a dangerous group of people."

"Velda, can you imagine if they tried to hurt me? I've gotten so much press, now people in Florida are writing." I envisioned my demise, murdered by dogfighters, then Belinda, Jackie, and Linda, my armed friends, blowing the dogfighters away. "They wouldn't want to cross all of you."

"You're probably right," she smiled. I had been away from the state house for a few weeks, and now it was time for me to come back down and be "seen" again. The bills were ready to change sides at the state house. Legislation that had passed the House of Representatives would now go to the Senate and vice versa. Once the bills changed over, there would be just a few weeks for the dog bill to pass the Senate. Velda had informed me the time was shorter on the second side.

The local papers were filled with news of partisan fighting in the House of Representatives, beginning only a week after the dog bill was passed. "It was great timing, Caress, that we got that bill out of there when we did," Velda said with relief.

House Bill 1001 was the number given to the state budget, and a bitter war of words and strategies had erupted between Paul Mannweiler and Speaker Mike Phillips. Paul, and many others in the minority party, had offered amendments to the budget, wanting individual legislator's votes recorded as they were on all other bills. The Speaker had ruled individual votes did not have to be recorded, and now there was war between the two men.

Having broken ranks on the budget issue, Mark Kruzan, the one member of the majority party I knew we could count on to talk to the Speaker, had become a pariah in the Speaker's eyes. Paul and Mike Phillips' politely strained relationship had now deteriorated to open mutual disgust or worse.

I felt we had crossed a shaky bridge over a deep ravine, and as I stepped safely on the other side the bridge had collapsed.

In Velda's little enclosed enclave the two of us studied the situation being belted out on the floor directly below the ivory tower.

"Did you know Speaker Phillips likes to hunt birds?" she confided.

"He does?" I said, knowing this was a definite negative from Velda.

"Yep, not out in the wilderness, but in hunting preserves where birds raised in captivity are let loose for people with guns to just blow them out of the sky. There was some legislation passed here a few years ago banning hunting preserves in Indiana, but only ones that provided exotic animals to kill. You know, lions and cougars that had been raised in captivity. That was fine with the Speaker because he doesn't hunt exotics, just birds. So, you see, that bill couldn't be introduced to include the poor birds raised in captivity, because the Speaker enjoys that part. He has lots of power and you always have to consider him whenever you want any legislation."

There was always a trace of sad regret in her voice over the creatures she loved. She simply could not understand why anyone wanted to shoot any innocent animal.

There was a stack of court cases on her desk that she now lifted onto her lap. "These belong in the judge's office. Do you want to look inside? I don't think he'd mind."

I was curious. This was the ominous room directly on the other side of the law clerks' office. Velda was now moving at full speed, carrying the briefs through the first doorway as I followed her.

"I'm going to look in the judge's office," I said furtively to Joe the law clerk, who smiled knowingly. He often looked up toward the outer office when the judge would come pouncing out of his private chamber. Walking into the inner sanctum, I momentarily stopped breathing. A massive elk's head peered down from the most prominent wall. Another wall held the head of a handsome antelope. Deer's antlers lined another wall. Pictures of the judge with fish he had caught and birds he had shot. Pictures of him saddled up on a horse in a winter storm.

With the exception of the massive executive desk, the furnishings in the room could have fit comfortably into a heated log cabin. A well-used sofa held a coverlet, old lamps sat on rustic tables, their light spreading a warm glow throughout the room. A large cupboard had been placed against another wall that held a foldaway bed. The judge spent some nights in the state house rather than make the long trek back up to northern Indiana.

However, it was the overall effect of the room that made me speechless, for Velda, who had given her adult life to the protection of all wild creatures, had worked for twenty years for a hunter!

"He's a very bright man, Caress, who likes to kill animals." Velda stood by a mallard duck who was now eternally suspended in lifeless flight, attached to the wall by a thin wire. She had one hand on her hip and looked mildly disgusted. "I've said to him, 'big-man-shot-the-little-duck.' He really did feel bad when they brought the elk's head past my desk," nodding toward the wall where a pair of big brown glass eyes stared into space. "It about made my knees buckle."

A smile appeared in the corners of her mouth. Velda did see humor in her darkest moments. "The judge told me he'd preserved this animal forever at it's zenith, at the very peak of its male maturity. You know what I told him?"

"What was that?" I answered, half smiling.

"I said, 'You know, men are at their peak at about nineteen, and it's just a real shame somebody couldn't have preserved you.'"

"What did he say?"

"Nothing, it's just that he's part of the old school, you

know, when men were men and went out in the woods and bonded." She shook her head. "I hope someday he'll get beyond all of this and finish evolving."

I glanced over at one wall, interested in looking at the judge's plaques, the ones without the remains of animals. I studied the orderly desk.

Velda watched me make a slow tour of the room. "He writes very well, Caress, and I really do love him a lot," she said, her voice trailing off as she began turning off the lights. I didn't say a word as she silently guided me through the door.

There was no reason for me to stay and sit with Velda who had plenty of work to finish, so I descended the flights of stairs, listening to the voices reverberate throughout the halls. The car was parked on Ohio Street just north of the main parking lot. The meter had run out, but I had missed the ever-vigilant squad of city police that ticketed cars every few hours. I wondered where my friend in his bib overalls had gone with his old rowboat attached to a trailer. He had been at the state house for weeks, just standing next to the rowboat with a roughly painted sign stuck on the back of the trailer. "State House thieves—get rid of the boat taxes." He had been kind to me, always depositing his extra change in the meter where my car was parked.

"Don't you worry about anything," he would say as he patted his baggy pockets filled with coins. He felt less confidence about my success in the state house. "Nobody but the big interests have any influence in there," he would tell me, nodding toward the building.

"I don't have any big interests behind me," I would tell him gently. He had been gone from the parking spot for several days. Probably felt like he had made his point, I thought, although I missed his guarding my car and his big smile.

The heat came on quickly against the dampness, and the car became a sheltered cocoon for me against the raw, last day in February. Ed was on my mind as I drove the familiar route, returning home. The road, built along stretches of Fall Creek, came close to the water and its grassy banks would wind near the highway. The great bird was like a spirit that would occasionally flicker across my thoughts; a special bird, who befriended humans. I quietly muttered a prayer. "Please, Father, never let Ed end up on an office wall." He was too much a part of the heavens and belonged solely to the blue sky. We mortals were allowed only glimpses of his soaring beauty, and it crossed my mind that perhaps the great blue heron's wings had been designed to resemble those of angels.

The afternoon was ending as I drove up the long driveway and rounded the curve in the bend that passed the now giant white pine. I remembered when the tree was not so very tall, and a stepladder could almost reach the top branches. Trees measured time most gracefully, I thought, maturing into majesty not bothered with choices or missions, just quietly bending with the storms and the seasons.

A short, low ring began in the car as I entered the garage. "Wouldn't you know I'd call even though you just left," Velda chuckled. "I ran into Valerie, Teresa's secretary, in the hall. Senator Garton has assigned the bill. Corrections, Criminal and Civil Procedures—it's okay."

"Is this the Senate version of the House Committee we just left?" I asked.

"I think so, Caress, at least it's not Natural Resources,"—home of Velda's hated hunters.

"What committee did Paul hope the bill would go to?"

"Judiciary," I said quietly.

"It would have made sense for it to go to Judiciary, but I guess Senator Garton didn't see it that way," she said while flipping the pages of the legislative handbook, reading the names on the Judiciary Committee. The chairman was a good friend of Paul's and Teresa was on the committee. "My senator is on Judiciary too. He would have been helpful."

"Who's that?" I asked her.

"Luke Kenley, and I can legally talk to him," she laughed, "even if I do work for the court of appeals."

She was still thumbing through the handbook. "Senator Landske is the chair of the committee we've been assigned to, and I don't know her," Velda muttered as if she had been thrown a fastball. "The other committee would have been easier," she said, thinking out loud as she concentrated on the names of the other members. "But, Caress," she cooed, "you are a hard little lady for anybody to turn down."

I smiled to myself; assurance had always been provided for me. God worked beautifully with those who were open to goodness, even those who did not see His presence.

"We may not have gotten the perfect committee, but we're gonna do just fine. Senators are being swamped with bills and information that have started to come over from the House side. We've got to start strategizing. It's going to be different in the House of Lords. Remember, these senators have never seen this legislation before—it's never gotten out of a committee on the Senate side."

"This is the year, Velda," I told her.

"You're right," she answered. "Does Teresa know you, Caress?"

"Yes, she does," I said.

"That's good, that's very good," she repeated. "Can you come back down tomorrow?"

"I'd planned on coming."

"Then I'll set up a time for us to meet with Teresa," she told me with some sense of urgency before hanging up the phone.

Senator Teresa Lubbers represented the north side of Indianapolis, and her senatorial district included Paul's House district. Teresa had auburn-colored hair, and my friend John Hammond called her "Red." She was one of those women who, though not particularly tall, had a definite presence and stature about her. She was a new state senator who had won election despite the fact she had not been the chosen candidate of the county Republican Party machine. I liked Teresa, a bright woman and very genuine. She had been an aide to Senator Richard Lugar, and was well known to the team helping me. It was Teresa for whom the legislation had been originally designed.

I was very well aware that all the women around me had been involved in the political process for a long time, but one thing remained remarkable to me. None of them ever questioned that I would make the final decision. I recalled again while drafting the bill the many silent pauses as the women around the table waited for my response. A gifted group had been provided to support and help me, and now it was Teresa's time to carry the legislation.

Only one thing worried me and it wasn't Teresa's intelligence, perseverance, or just plain spunk—it was her newness at the state house. I thought of Paul who knew all the moves and the players in the grand old building, the many people who owed him favors. And there was his considerable power. Teresa was a novice, and no one owed her anything. It had been left up to me to choose the senator and I had chosen Teresa, but I was worried. Teresa was worried too.

Paul had asked two Democrats in the Senate to place their names on the bill along with Teresa. Senator Morrie Doll, who was a respected former prosecutor from Knox county in southwest Indiana, and Senator Katie Wolf, a diminutive woman with white hair, who had been a court clerk. She was married to a farmer in a northern Indiana county.

"Wouldn't you know Paul would pick someone with the last name of Wolf," Velda had laughed. "It's so appropriate." I had never met either senator, and they had signed on to the bill as a favor to Paul rather than any personal commitment to the issue. Paul had not taken Velda's suggestion of Robert "Whizzer" Hellmann, the minority leader of the Senate. I remembered Paul's silence when the name was mentioned after the vote on the bill in the House. Even though Senator Hellmann was considered a good lawyer, Paul had chosen Senator Doll to legally defend the bill. Perhaps Senator Hellmann and the Speaker, who was now being referred to as the "fat man" by some House Republicans, were friends?

My foot dragged across the carpeting inside the house. At the end of the day my energy left me, and going up the stairs, I lifted my leg slowly. The nerve endings were still sensitive to the touch. People grieved over losing a leg, an arm, a breast, for humans want to remain whole and beautiful. Women would still hold my face and examine the slight scars that came down from my forehead. Still terrible to many who knew me was the thought that I might have been facially disfigured.

In a recent Humane Society publication there was a picture of a child. Sandy Rowland had shown it to the press in Indianapolis, but they had not published the picture. Only a little boy of three or four when he had been mauled, now he was close to seven or eight, probably sitting in a second grade class, examining and listening to the children around him. The baseball cap he wore partially covered the light wisps of hair that fell around the side of his face. A long, jagged, red scar ran down his cheek, and from his lower lip another deep scar ran toward the side of his head toward a missing ear. His eyebrow was gone, his nose and left eye disfigured. Deep scars and indentations where the dogs had torn hunks of skin and muscle covered the top of his forehead into his scalp. The other side of his face showed an uncommonly handsome little boy. A clear, dark eye gazed out from the picture. The gaze was that of a little soul who had lost his childhood. Without words his eyes said that he lived in a different world from most children. A world that had lost its magical illusions and carefree laughter. Was he chosen to play in games or was he anyone's special friend? I would study the scar down his cheek. It looked very similar to the long scar on my leg. I knew when he laughed the act of smiling would be stiff and painful. But he did have courage, for his unblinking gaze looked you straight in the eye. He was, as children are so naturally, a lesson in acceptance and grace. He was much braver than I and my inspiration for being at the state house. Perhaps the reason my face had been spared was because people could more easily respond to someone who was considered pretty. Prettiness to display ugliness: a paradox, but completely understandable to me. God always did have His reasons. My leg would always be stiff like the little boy's face, and both legs would never be a perfect match again. My doctor promised me I would "have pretty legs again," but he was a mere human and could never make them perfect. The leg was slowly becoming like a piece of concrete, but I had made my decision. No physical therapy yet. There was no time.

The upstairs bedroom was darker than even the late winter dusk outside. Instinctively, I walked toward a window that faced the front of the house. Hidden behind the curtain was a single little electric candle that stood like a solitary tin soldier in the window. I could not bear to put the little fixture away in the attic after Christmas. I plugged the candle in the light socket, and a soft golden glow spread through the room. My eyes fixed on the little candle, the only one I had not put away.

My safe haven between battles was ending. "You've got to step out on faith sometimes, Caress," Sarah would say. Her words were stored up in my memory to replay while I thought of the coming days and weeks.

There was the meeting tomorrow with Teresa. John Hammond came to mind, for he would have wise suggestions for me to share with the new senator. I reached for the bedroom's phone. John answered the call, talking against a noisy background of children.

"Caress, have Teresa ask for an early hearing next week. We want to get this bill heard, not backed up in some bottleneck of bills dying a slow death. Ideally, it won't be amended because it could all come apart and be held up in conference committee. The senator heading the committee needs to be approached *quickly.*"

I heard a clatter of dishes hit the floor. I hadn't called at the best of times. "Caress, I'm going to have to go—tell 'Red' I said hello."

I closed my eyes that evening with the little tin soldier on guard—a light against the darkness, welcoming in March.

* * *

In the morning the second hand of the kitchen clock struck nine. What did the senators really understand about the bill? Could I learn anything more for the meeting later today? Dialing the House switchboard, I wanted to know if there were many calls coming in from around the state, pro or con, about the dog bill. The House telephone center was manned by women who must have worked in the political trenches since Benjamin Harrison in the last century. However, they were important messengers to legislators from the voters back home.

The phone was ringing. "House switchboard. How may I help you?" a voice with permanent laryngitis answered.

"Good morning, I've called about the vicious dog bill. Have you gotten many calls in support of the bill?" adding hesitantly, "maybe, *against* the bill?"

Dead silence came over the phone as the operator inhaled and exhaled a long drag of an early morning cigarette.

"That's Mannweiler's bill isn't it?"

"Yes, it is," I replied sweetly. "Are you hearing much about the bill?"

The deep voice, a combination of back woods and southern Indiana drawl, answered, "Yae-us," followed by, "that's that bill where those dogs chewed up that woman, right?"

"Yes," I answered slowly. "This is the *chewee.*" There was a long silence; I could envision the cigarette being held suspended between two gnarled fingers as a surprised open mouth let a spiral of smoke escape between the parted teeth.

The drawl began again, "Waall, yes, we've had calls," she said. "Most all positive, but those messages have gone to the House side and that bill's already been sent over."

"How many messages have been sent to senators?" I asked.

"Waall, not as many as gone to the House, but ya know those senators got their calls too early, they'll forgit everything by the time they vote." I remembered that very comment being made to a caller when Velda introduced me months ago to the ladies of the switchboard. "Yep,—timing was off," she said with certainty.

Velda's voice ran through my head: *"Timing is everything,* Caress."

"If folks really feel strongly, they'll take the time and get through, make it personal with their senator."

I feared those who were against the bill would be more likely to make it personal with their senator.

"Well, thank you for your time."

"No problem, ma'am," as the nicotine coated voice from rural Indiana hung up the phone. The switchboard brigade seemed to know the score.

The state house had begun another day with bills continuing to flow from the Senate to the House and vice versa. Senator Robert Garton, as a leader, was particularly busy. He was in many ways a charming man, an eloquent speaker who loved standing before a crowd repeating the poem *Ain't God Good to Indiana.* However, the president pro tem of the Indiana Senate also had a distant side, sometimes becoming aloof with his fellow senators.

The head of the majority party in the Indiana Senate, he could simply kill a bill by never assigning it to a committee or assign the legislation to a senator, who as chairman of a committee, had no intention of giving a hearing to that bill.

This is what had happened to the vicious dog bill in past years in the Indiana Senate.

Had Senator Garton thought much about where he assigned the dog bill? The luxury was gone of having a seasoned politician and good friend available while the legislation worked through his chamber. I missed that security and now felt I walked on a narrow path with a deep chasm by each side in the Indiana Senate. On the other hand, there was the interesting point that Senator Garton and I did share the same last name, and that at the very least seemed lucky to me.

Early every morning I listened to one of the Presbyterian minister's sermons. He seemed to be able to encourage and reassure me, even though he didn't know I existed. I would occasionally play the sermon on Gideon that had so connected me to the minister. The story of the man who needed assurance and more assurance. This was also me, and every day.

* * *

The assurance from the tapes I played took me step by step into the state house the first day of March. The entranceway was wet with melting slush that dropped from the shoes of the many people that were entering the building.

"Where did you park that car?" the voice said as I stood in pools of dirty melted snow inside the door. Rick of the Capitol Police leaned over the desk to my right.

"Oh, I parked it up the street at our business."

"Don't you do that," he told me. "You park in this lot," he said, pointing out to the legislators' parking lot. The Capitol Police considered me one of their own.

"Somebody will get mad at me if I do that," I told him.

"Nobody's gonna get mad at you. We won't let 'em," he said with a grin.

"I'm chicken."

"Naww, you're no chicken," he said back to me with a wide grin that spread over perfect white teeth. "You feeling all right?" he called after me, always looking at the bandaged foot.

"I feel better every day," I said, smiling, before walking toward the heavy balustrade that marked the beginning of the stairs to the third floor.

There was a sense of frenzy in the state house. The bills had completed changing from one chamber to another. The grand stairway was unusually busy as legislators and lobbyists made their way up to the next floor. Today they weren't waiting on the elevators; there didn't seem to be the time.

I was going to see Paul and ask for any advice he might give before seeing Teresa. His office was again a busy terminal packed with people who wanted to see him before the session began.

Legislators stood huddled together in little groups outside Paul's office. Cathy sat behind her desk in the outer office, smiling at me as I entered. "Well, are you leaving us for the Senate?"

"Yes, but I'm still going to visit. I wanted to ask Paul if he had any advice for the other side of the hall."

"There he is," she said quickly as Paul headed for his office door at a fast trot.

"I'm going to meet with Teresa, Paul, is there anything you would want to say to her?"

He paused and looked solemnly at me, saying two words quietly but firmly, *"No amendments."*

He was deadly serious. Any changes and it's over was the message. The Speaker would kill the bill in conference committee. I felt a heavy weight on my shoulders.

Hurrying through the regular traffic in the halls, nodding to lobbyists, and waving to members of the House, I came close to knocking over Velda who was looking for me on the Senate side. "Velda do you think anybody over here will even know who I am?" I said breathlessly as we hurried along.

"If they read anything or watch television they're gonna know who you are," she answered.

"I just feel like it's a new field of people and it's been a long time since that press conference in January."

"It's their business to know who you are, Caress, and they will remember," she said firmly as we made our way through the clogged halls toward a guarded door.

The Senate doorman on the fourth floor stood wearing his navy blue blazer and gray slacks. His hands were held behind his back and he rocked back and forth against the marble wall. Mr. Leroy Hoke was a retired mortician who now filled his time during the legislative session guarding the Republican wing of the Senate offices at the state house.

A large man with a big frame, he seemed sure of his position outside the Senate chambers. Mr. Hoke had twinkling blue eyes that smiled out from a big, jowled face. Much like the hawks circling high above the winter farm fields, his eyes never blinked. They continually scanned the crowd that stood huddled together talking in small groups; then they returned to watch me.

A large brass plate was nailed above the door. "Senate Chambers" it read, and below a smaller black plaque stated "Legislators and Staff Only, Main Entrance on the Third Floor."

The fourth floor corridor directly outside the Senate chambers currently held only lobbyists having quiet meetings with a few senators returning from lunch. The Senate gallery was open to the general public on this floor, but only a handful of people had arrived as there was still some time before the afternoon session began.

"She's the only one that has any right to be here." The big voice boomeranged off the marble walls as he glared out at the round-eyed, paid lobbyists who now stood silent. Mr. Hoke's large hand engulfed the brass doorknob behind him. "I'm glad to see you made it over here," he said genuinely while making a courtesan bow. "Would you like to go inside?"

"I do have a meeting with Senator Lubbers," I said.

"Anytime you want to visit, just let me know." Mr. Hoke

opened the door with a grand sweeping gesture. I had become for him the princess of the state house. Inside we stood in a small area with a receptionist's desk whose occupant had left for the moment. Velda was already climbing a little stairway that wound up two short flights. She wasn't waiting around for any self-appointed authority figure to tell us what to do.

"Come on," she said insistently as I stood staring at the empty desk. "And don't ever tell me again nobody is going to know who you are over here."

I followed her up the creaking stairs past nooks and crannies until she suddenly stopped in front of a single door with names of senators placed to one side. Senator Lubbers' name was listed, and we walked through the entrance. Desks were close together with a few partitions giving a little privacy.

One senator had isolated himself by surrounding his desk with partitions, completely blocking himself from view. The creation reminded me of the indoor forts I had made on rainy days as a child. Wreaths of cigar smoke came from inside the cubicle. The smoke, rising in the air, made a slight haze over the small, enclosed area that was wedged into the corner.

Senator Meeks from the northern part of the state was at work although hidden from view.

An aisle just wide enough to squeeze through wove directly to Senator Lubber's desk located inches from the path. Valerie, her secretary, sat a few feet away. There was room to squeeze two chairs behind her desk, but no privacy. Teresa was talking on the phone, the desk covered with stacks of legislation and notes. Pictures of her little girls were placed on nearby bookshelves. She hung up the phone. "I'm sorry to keep you waiting," she said with a smile. Teresa always looked like she stepped from a bandbox with her auburn hair held neatly back with a black velvet headband. She was a woman whose appearance struck a pleasant ground between professional and pretty.

"Teresa, this is my friend Velda, who works in the court of appeals."

"I stopped Valerie in the hall yesterday," Velda bubbled, sitting forward. "She probably wondered who that woman was chasing her down the hall. I saw Senator Garton assigned the bill."

"Yes," Teresa answered, "and I've gone ahead and asked the chairman of the committee we were assigned to for a hearing. We've missed the first week of hearings," she added. "They meet tomorrow and we're not on the schedule." Teresa was solemn. A precious week where hearings would be conducted had eluded us, slipping by quickly. This was a blow. I vaguely wondered what it took to have your legislation be one of the very first to be heard in the Senate. Maybe the chairman was personally interested in these first bills, or perhaps an influential senator or lobbyist representing a large group of voters back home had gotten the first slots.

"What do you think of information packets about this legislation going to everyone? You know, magazine articles, a letter from Caress," Velda asked Teresa.

"We're swamped with paper," Teresa nodded toward her desk and the stacks of legislation sent over from the House for the Senate to mull its way through. "I think we should forget sending a lot of reading out to all the senators."

"Okay, we'll just concentrate on this committee," Velda decided.

I felt myself mentally drifting, tired, exhausted, hoping this was the right decision. Why wouldn't everyone want to read about this issue? Children, the safety of their lives was at stake. The little boy at home with his torn smile danced through my memory.

I glanced around at the different desks, men and women were reading, talking, thinking. They had never seen this legislation and might never see it if we didn't get a hearing. I was present to personally promote the issue, but the legislation had never been debated in the Senate as it had been for several years in the House. The ugly pull of depression was grabbing me along with the physical strain. I watched Teresa's expression; she cared and she was on top of the situation. Hopefully, the hearing would come next week.

"John Hammond says hello," I told her, thinking of the "Red" comment.

"Oh, do you see John?" she asked.

"John has been my personal guide book to every legislator I've seen here," I said, smiling at her. The phone was ringing and Teresa shook her head towards Valerie that she couldn't talk to the caller.

"While you work on the chairman of our committee we'll direct Caress towards meeting the senators." Velda was thinking about immediate action. "Let's have her go find the two minority senators and thank them for sponsoring the bill over here."

"They'll be on the other side," Teresa nodded down the little corridor that ran by her desk. "I think that would be good," she stated. Velda looked at me.

"We might as well try to find them now; I know what Senator Wolf looks like. Can you believe that name?" Velda's eyes sparkled while rising to leave. "Wolves really aren't interested in people, you know, they're too shy; they're not like politicians. This human Wolf is a nice lady."

I felt reassured, for the new Senator Lubbers had listened intently; she would try very hard not to lose this bill.

"They're gonna 'luv' you over here," Velda said, smiling over her shoulder as we had started to make our way through a maze of bends and passages.

"They will?"

"Yep, did you see them all sitting up at their desks as we passed by, looking over their glasses?"

"No, I really didn't," I answered, watching the bandaged leg flop out of the loose shoe.

"Get your shoe on 'cause this next group of politicians just can't wait to meet you. You know, Linda is so worried about your shoes," she said as I hurried to keep up with her.

"She is, why?"

"She wonders what you will do with all the shoes for your left foot you can't use. What size do you wear?"

"Seven and a half medium."

"Well, maybe there's some amputee who would like seven and a half medium pumps for the left foot. I'll bet you've got some nice ones too." It was gallows humor, but she could make me laugh and keep me going.

We finally reached the minority party's wing of the rabbit burrow and searched for Senator Wolf. Heading down a flight of stairs, Velda abruptly stopped. A petite, neatly groomed, white-headed lady stood against the wall. "Senator Wolf," Velda crooned, "I want you to meet my friend Caress Garten. She's the lady who was attacked by the pit bulls, Paul Mannweiler's legislation that is just reaching the Senate." Senator Wolf smiled up at me, still standing on the top stair, taking a concerned, grandmotherly look at my leg.

"Oh, yes, terrible thing," she said softly.

"Thank you, Senator, for sponsoring the bill."

"Why, you're welcome, dear," she answered, nodding sympathetically. "Does the leg hurt you?"

"No, doing fine, just trying to keep my shoes on in the slush outside." The senator smiled as if we were standing on the steps of a country church, Sunday morning services having ended.

The senator didn't have questions or many words for us. Her demeanor explained to me why Paul had asked her to be a sponsor. The seemingly gentle Senator Wolf would be well liked by members of both parties. "We just wanted to find you and say hello. You'll be hearing more from us," Velda smiled at her.

I noticed the diminutive senator, whose back was pressed against the wall, had both little feet standing on one stair. Katie Wolf continued to smile as we passed. The senator was really not unlike her namesake in the animal kingdom, for it seemed possible, at least in this first brief meeting, that she too possessed a quiet, even shy personality whose sharp eyes assessed correctly the nuances of newcomers into her territory.

We were once again on the third floor and still inside the Senate offices. A small sign stood outside Senator Hellmann's office, "Minority Leader," it read. I wondered if his chambers were similar to Paul's on the other side of the building. I hoped he would support the bill. Senator Morrie Doll, the other minority sponsor whom Paul had asked, was nowhere to be found.

"Well, I guess we'll have to meet him another day. Do you know him?" I asked Velda.

"No, I've never met him. You'll just have to get out that little handbook and find him from his picture."

We were beginning to get questioning looks from some of the secretaries and staffers who were passing us in the little outer corridor. "I still feel like I'm not too well known over in these parts."

"Just act like you know what you're doing. Remember, I told you I didn't want to hear again that no one knows who you are after that doorkeeper's bowing to you."

"I *do* know what doorkeeper to come to over here," I said as Velda escorted me out of the enclosed area, where our Senator Wolf roamed, back to the busy outer hall.

* * *

The following few days were a blur of greeting state house employees and lobbyists, now all friends, in the halls outside the Senate. I had still not spotted Senator Doll at the state house.

Jim Trulock, the lobbyist for the United Auto Workers, would say emotionally, shaking his head. "It's hard to get a law, Caress." He knew previous dog bills hadn't gotten very far in the Senate.

"Tell me if you get a hearing, Caress, and I'll come testify for you," Elmer Borders from the state police called as he passed me, wearing his ever-present raincoat. I thought of

Lieutenant Columbo and wondered if everyone in law enforcement owned the same wardrobe.

Susan Williams and Randy Shambaugh, two Indianapolis City-County Council members, rested on one of the wooden benches outside the Senate. "Who sponsored your bill over here?" Susan asked.

"Morrie Doll and Katie Wolf," I told her.

"Morrie Doll is a very good lawyer, Caress, and he's well respected in his caucus." I need to find him, I thought to myself. "How are you doing?"

"Fine, just trying to locate senators."

"So are we," she nodded over at Randy with a tired half smile.

The halls were busier. The Senate was ready to begin its afternoon session. Looking through the plate glass window, I saw Teresa enter and take her seat in one of the large leather chairs placed in front of each desk. My well-used handbook provided seating charts for both chambers, and quickly flipping the pages, I tried to match senators with their pictures on the glossy pages.

Ed Smith was the doorkeeper who stood where the Democrats entered the chamber. He watched me peering through the glass. "Can I help you find anyone?" he asked.

"Oh, I just need to talk to each one of them, but now they're all too busy."

"Not too busy for you," he said kindly.

"Who's that senator?" I asked curiously of a big man with a large, square face. His large hands thumped the desk where he sat looking over legislation, shifting uncomfortably in his suit.

"That's Senator Robert Meeks, he's a Republican. Notice all the senior citizens in the halls? He's sponsoring the grandparents' law," Ed noted pleasantly. "With only three weeks left in the session, people supporting it are all over this place. They've sent in hundreds of notes to the senators." I felt depressed. This was an emotional issue for grandparents' visitation rights. The senators were certainly not getting hundreds of notes from me on the dog bill.

I recalled this was the same senator who barricaded himself behind the portable office panels. He looked like he would enjoy a cigar, I thought, recalling the smoke above the little enclosure.

"I hope they remember why I'm here," I said to him, feeling the other bill's competition for time and attention.

"Why, they will—you're someone people recognize."

The chairman of the committee the dog bill had been assigned to was Senator Sue Landske who represented a district just outside Lake County in the far northwest section of the state. I was trying to find the face that matched the smiling picture in the handbook from the senators that were in the chamber. Standing alone by the plate glass window, I leafed through my picture gallery—a hand touched my arm. Velda stood holding a sheet of paper. There was a blank expression on her face. "Caress, the committee hearings for next week are out and we're not listed," she said simply. Velda was not upset but she wasn't happy either; there was an ever so slight glimmer of concern. "We need to find Teresa Lubbers and ask her again about the chairman. Now, don't be upset," she said in a low voice. There had to be a way to get the chairman's attention, I thought frantically. "You're upset aren't you?" Velda said a little more anxiously, following me quickly down the hall and up the marble stairs toward the Senate offices. I just turned and looked at her as we rapidly climbed the stairs, "You *are* upset," she said, hurrying to keep up with me.

The senators had gone into recess and Mr. Hoke was on guard. He saw me coming, and the door swung open as we sailed past the startled receptionist who couldn't react in time to stop us.

Teresa was standing in the little aisle beside her desk. She walked quickly towards us. "I know," she said as we met halfway to her desk. "I've stopped her several times, asking for a hearing," she said, pacing a couple of steps back toward her desk then towards the two of us again. "I've said this is the legislation I care most about." Teresa's shoulders dropped momentarily; exasperation filled her voice. "The last time, she threw her arms up in the air and said, 'Maybe in a month.'"

We all were quiet. We didn't have a month. We didn't have a hearing scheduled for next week, and now there were only two weeks left, two opportunities, to keep the bill alive.

My worst fears were coming true and I felt Teresa had the same fears—a freshman senator to whom no one owed a favor. "Teresa," I said quietly, looking towards her. "Do you want me to ask Paul to call this senator?"

"Yes," she said clearly, standing still in the little aisle. Another politician's ego wouldn't have let them say "Yes," but Teresa cared about the bill and she cared about me and she was too secure in her own abilities to worry how a hearing was granted.

"I'll call him tonight," I said flatly.

I always hated to call Paul at home, feeling it was his chance to be with his family and forget the state house. He answered me with one sentence. "Well, Caress, I'm not supposed to interfere on the Senate side," he paused, "but, I'll do it."

A man of few words, he never discussed when or how he would ask the senator. I watched the clock tick on the bedside table. Everything reminded me there wasn't much time. I had wanted to grill him: "When will you call her? Will you tell me when you have?" and then add, *"We don't have much longer."* Paul had said he would call, and now I had to trust him.

Promises had been made to me and they had always been fulfilled. I listened to one of the Presbyterian minister's sermons. His voice always calmed me. The last few weeks had been a time of death for the ruined dogs and of narrow escape before the House had gone to war. Time was now the enemy. That evening I remembered something that Velda once told me. Wolves sing at night—communicating with one another in the darkness. I needed our lone Senator Wolf, Teresa, and Senator Doll to lift their own voices calling for support of the bill. There were few days remaining this year at the state house and into the dead of night the senators debated. Confident of my task, I now had to wait and watch the promise unfold.

TEN

Hunters Are Coming

The following Monday at noon the doors of the state house were opened for me by the Capitol Police. "You're going to have your hands full today just getting upstairs," a policeman told me. My protectors all looked concerned as they watched me from behind the security counter of the state house. The ground floor resembled an old Hollywood film, mobs of people herded together like cattle, forming a human wedge. These people were pumped with angry energy—frustrated workers with a cause. The United Auto Workers were protesting at the state house, and thousands of men and women decked out in black silk U.A.W. jackets and worn jeans were noisily pushing their way to the third floor, filling the stairways and elevators. "Let me go with you to the stairs," the policeman offered as he started to clear a path through the sea of humanity. "Where are you going?" he shouted over the noise as people squeezed to one side. A big man stumbled, shoving me forward. A yellow air horn boomed.

"Up to the fourth floor," I yelled.

"It shouldn't be as crowded up there," he shouted. Perhaps my friend thought I wouldn't be trampled to death in the ivory tower, sparing him from having to scrape up my remains. He nodded as we reached the stairs and raised one hand as a good luck send-off.

A moving river of people were ascending the steps and then rounding the corner on each floor like a great flowing current. More air horns were echoing through the long halls, sound ricocheting off the marble walls, spiraling upward, circling the rotunda. There would be no lobbying the halls today—no one could hear. This was the U.A.W.'s day at the state house. The mob spewed me out as my foot landed on the first stair leading to the fourth floor. Gene, the bailiff, stood at the top of the landing looking down, a big grin on his face. "Well, you really picked a day to come down here," he laughed as I came up the stairs.

"Is something going on?" I yelled back, coming closer as a barrage of air horns went off. One hand on each hip, the black face beamed as he slapped his leg, shaking the holsters and the silver badge.

"Didn't you know this rally was today?" he chuckled.

"No, my paper is lying at the bottom of my hill, and I think I ran over it coming out of the driveway."

Velda was on the phone. Dropping my heavy coat on one of the depression era chairs, my arms ached. Tired, and the day had just started. Velda's voice was speaking quickly, and her desk was piled high with legal briefs. Waving to me, she uttered a quick "gotta go now" as the receiver went down.

"Caress, I'm swamped with work. The judge wants these memos retyped by late afternoon. Isn't the noise disgusting?" she said, crossing and uncrossing her legs covered in blue tights. "It's stupid, just irritates everyone. It's also what people do who don't have any power," she said bluntly. Her eyes twinkled. "You know a lot more about how things work down here than those people."

"I *do?*"

"You do," she said as the phone rang once again. She quickly scribbled a note while talking to the caller and crammed it in my hand. "GO GET A HEARING," it read in large, scrawled letters. She was very busy and there would be no coffee break time to guide me in the halls today. Suddenly, I felt six years old, insecure, and unsure.

The Presbyterian minister's words from a sermon came to me, "A Pilgrim is one who sees a glimmer in the distance and makes for it; she may or may not reach her goal but she's one who's on her way." Velda couldn't come with me, but there was no doubt of my pilgrimage, and today a dire part of that journey consisted of either getting, or confirming, a hearing.

"Going back down?" Gene asked me, coughing into his hand.

"To get a hearing," I heard myself say.

"I know you'll do that," the graveled voice answered assuredly.

The peaceful fourth floor was heaven compared to the fray below. The return to the third floor was similar to suddenly stepping into a hurricane. The noise was deafening. Off the last step I was again in the thick of humanity filling the entire floor and packing the corridors of both the Senate and House so tightly there wasn't room to move. Inching forward, shoulder to shoulder, I moved closer to the Senate.

How wonderful to be a bird. The graceful blue heron flew into my memory, transporting me over the heads of the crowd, placing me down close to the Senate doors. He was freedom—this was claustrophobia.

Ed Smith looked up from his work. He seemed pleasantly composed, in spite of the surly mob. He moved quickly, handing off messages to pages. "You're here today?" he yelled in order to be heard above the noise.

"I'm looking for a senator," I shouted back. He handed a small pad of paper over to me.

"Write a note. I'll send it right in." Ed ignored the others around him.

The top line requested the name of the legislator. "Senator

Landske," I printed, adding, "I would like to speak with you about the vicious dog legislation."

I wondered if I should say I was Paul Mannweiler's friend. "They'll know who you are—try it on your own," Velda would say if she were with me in the mob. Signing my name, I handed the note to Ed's waiting hand and he disappeared inside the Senate chamber.

He returned almost immediately, crestfallen and apologetic. "Caress, no one will take the message." Not understanding, I stared blankly at the doorman. "Senator Landske is a Republican, and this is the Democrat's entrance. They won't pass the message."

"They won't?" I said, looking at him in disbelief. "How long before they go into session?" I asked frantically. Did I have time to push to the other end of the hall, through the crowd, to reach the Republican entrance? Ed glanced at his watch.

"You have about twenty minutes."

With a quick push away from the table and a struggle out from between two men, I started toward the Republican door.

Inching along the wall, the mob pressed me against the Senate's plate glass window like a suction cup. Today, the protestors out in the hall were the ones in the fish bowl. The senators were moving comfortably around in the chamber and seemed oblivious to the noise and people. I struggled for room to open the little legislative handbook to the section of pictures. "Senator Sue Landske (R)" printed in black type. Light brown hair framed the face of a pleasant-looking woman smiling toward the camera. Looking into the chamber at the chatting senators, I searched for Senator Landske.

The palm of a hand thumped the window beside me. A thin-lipped man wearing a cap covered in greasy smudges stood staring at the few senators that had looked our way. Another arm covered in the material of a tailored suit touched my shoulder. "Who are you looking for?" Jim Trulock, the man whose day I had stumbled into at the state house, was yelling in my ear. The U.A.W.'s lobbyist was a tall man whose dark hair had started to recede. He was a genuine man whose face reflected his kindness. His eyes never blinked or strayed when he spoke to you, and he bent forward to better hear me.

"I'm trying to find Senator Landske," I told him.

"She doesn't look like her picture," he half yelled.

"I have to find her. She's the chairman of the committee the dog bill was assigned to."

"Caress, they assigned too many bills to that committee. Lobbyists have been sending in notes to her all morning, and she's not coming out." My stomach turned as Jim's eyebrows came closer together in a frown.

"Would it help if I talked to Senator Garton?"

"Yeah, sure. If you can get a hold of Garton, it would help. It would have to help."

Immediately I was off through the crowd, shoving Jim's U.A.W. members aside, moving toward the doors of the Republican Senate offices on the third floor. My other option was to push through the crowd to the House side and try to locate Paul. First, I would try and find the head of the Senate before he went into session, then I would have at least stated my case if Paul hadn't reached Senator Landske.

I now had only fifteen minutes before the senators started into the afternoon session. I *had* to have a hearing.

The oak door to the Senate offices inched open as several horn blowers were moved out of the way to make room for me to step into the waiting area. The narrow chamber was packed with men and women talking on cellular phones, the trademark of the state house lobbyist. Few noticed as I came in the door.

The receptionist was casually dismissing callers. "No, he's getting ready to go to session, can you hold? No, I'm sorry, he's already in the chamber and cannot be reached. I'll give him your message." She scribbled down something on a note pad and looked up as I walked toward her desk, her eyes moving toward the bandaged leg.

"I would like to speak to Senator Garton." She eyed me warily.

"There are a lot of people who want to speak to Senator Garton who are already waiting."

She waved her pencil like a scepter between her fingers, wishing me away.

"Would you send a note to Senator Landske for me?"

The receptionist looked uninterested and answered, "She's already in the chamber." The familiar line was then added. "I heard she's not coming out. You can leave your name, and I'll call you if Senator Garton can meet with you." The conversation was over. I sat down in a newly vacated place on a side bench. A small man in a brown suit was leaving in frustration, his cellular phone still attached to his ear. Other lobbyists were resigned to wait. A black-rimmed schoolroom clock hung from the wall. The second hand was going around, ticking off the seconds. I now had ten minutes to talk to Senator Garton.

A little entrance way to my left was labeled "President Pro Tempore." These people around me were going to rot waiting. You've got to move, I thought as my legs stood up and were walking me toward the receptionist who saw me coming at a clip. Her mouth opened. "I told you I'd call when the sen—You can't go back there!" she yelled as I took a left back down a little corridor to the senator's office.

A young girl sat at the desk near his office; her eyes became saucers as I placed my hands on her desk. "I'm *Mrs. Garten and I want to see the senator.*"

"Are you really Mrs. Garton?" she barely whispered.

"I've been Mrs. Garten for twenty-two years and I– WANT–TO–SEE–HIM–NOW!" I demanded as the slight frame became electrified, propelling her to her feet.

A door slowly opened to my right, and a man whose hand held a pipe to his mouth stepped out into the hall.

Blue eyes sparkling, dimples flashing, Robert Garton stood looking at me. Quietly his hand took the pipe out of his mouth and a half smile appeared. "You're Karen aren't you?" The senator appraised me, trying to take in the fact that a second wife stood before him.

"Yes, I'm Karen," I told him, deciding not to explain he had the wrong name. Being his wife was enough.

"You're Paul Mannweiler's friend," he said almost to himself.

"Senator, I need a hearing for the vicious dog bill."

"Where did I assign that bill?" he asked, still holding the pipe with smoke curling softly upward.

"You assigned it to Sue Landske's Corrections Criminal and Civil Procedures, and she was given too many bills," I informed the man who had made the assignments. "This is one of the few Republican bills that made it out of the House. Now I *need help over here getting it through.*"

The senator began smiling at me again as he placed the pipe back in his mouth. A bell had sounded announcing the Senate session would begin shortly. A man walked out of another office. "Bob, it's good to see you." The man extended his hand. The senator turned as he returned the handshake.

"Well, hello, good to see you."

I had lost the senator's undivided attention as the Senate bell sounded again. This was a man who had a thousand details on his mind. There were lots of people reminding him of their own special detail.

Senator Garton looked back at me over his shoulder and nodded. I wanted something in blood or at least concrete, but he had nodded and the eyes were sparkling. I thanked him.

A few steps away from the senator's office a silver-haired man with a cellular phone walked with me past the other benched lobbyists. "His wife has blond hair ya' know," he told me.

"She does?"

"Yep," he said, laughing, glancing at my dark brown hair, "She does."

There was a new boldness about me as I flew out the door in a race to find Paul Mannweiler in the House chamber on the other side of the building. Had he spoken to Senator Landske?

The crowd was thick in the halls and a chant had started: "Jobs now! Jobs now! Jobs now!" Snow and dirt had melted from the many heavy shoes that had tracked slush up to the third floor, making the marble floors filthy and wet. Water soaked through the white sock on my left foot that was mopping the floor as I moved shoulder to shoulder through the crowd. Pressing into two women from U.A.W. Muncie whose thin faces were framed by wisps of hair, my foot brushed up against a pair of bright red cowboy boots. "Didn't mean to step on your foot ma'am," she said kindly, almost speaking in my ear. Looking directly in my eyes she seemed to be searching, trying to figure out why she thought she knew me. The other woman patted my back and made a little space to her side for me to get through.

"Good luck!" she said in a loud voice through a mouth that sadly had lost a front tooth.

"I need all the help I can get," I yelled back over my shoulder towards the two of them as the shoving match continued toward the side oak doors that led to Paul's office.

House doorman Uncle Todd Eggers watched me push through the crowd. He opened the door when I ran past him, smiling at his flushed cheeks and curly white hair. The big doors shut behind me. By the relative silence and the single voice over the loud speaker, I knew the House afternoon session had already begun. I was too late to see Paul. The voice on the loudspeaker was a female. "It takes a lot of guts to be Miss Indiana" were the words that a pretty young woman in a magenta suit and rhinestone crown was telling the hushed chamber. I had reached the entrance closest to the front of the chamber and Paul's desk. This was as near as I could come without actually going in to get him.

Paul was gently rocking back and forth in his chair as Miss Indiana stood next to him. His head was turned away from the entrance, showing only a half profile of his face. My hands waved back and forth from the little entrance; no one saw me—all eyes were on Miss Indiana.

The pages had vanished, probably out delivering messages, and Cathy hadn't been at her desk when I ran by Paul's outer office. I needed to know if we had a hearing. Paul could tell me if he had spoken to Senator Landske, but I would have to make a spectacle of myself and disrupt a sincere Miss Indiana if I went in to the chamber. I had been spinning my wheels, fighting the crowd, missing on timing, just missing, without any new knowledge of a hearing.

There was one more chance, a long chance, to try again to reach Senator Landske. I glanced at the House clock and wondered if the afternoon Senate session had begun.

The wet sock was clammy and sagging around my foot as I hobbled back up the little corridor, bolting back through the heavy oak doors into the mob. The blaring noise level continued to surprise me every time I left a location where you could hear others speak without screaming. There was a slight parting in the crowd as I pushed my way back through to the Senate side. Many of the protestors I had passed not long ago saw me coming; they were still stuck in the same places I had left them a few minutes earlier. "You're back again?" said the woman with the flashy cowboy boots who stepped backwards, pushing into another body to make a little room so I could pass. Curiously she watched me. "You here for the Union?" she yelled.

"I'm here for children," I yelled back.

"Well, I'm for them too," she belted out as I continued using my shoulders and arms to move the best of the U.A.W. out of my way to reach the other side.

The Senate side of the state house was still tightly packed.

This time I was going to ask Teresa to step out of the Senate. Perhaps she would personally take my note in to Senator Landske. I struggled to make my way toward the Republican end of the hall to write my note. I wasn't going to make that mistake ever again.

Suddenly I felt two arms come down around both shoulders, stopping me in my tracks. Jim Trulock had grabbed me and was yelling, "Caress, there's Landske!" His hands propelled me through the crowd towards a professional-looking, white-haired woman surrounded by lobbyists. "Put in a good word for the U.A.W.," Jim yelled as the force of his final shove pushed me within touching distance of the senator.

There she was. It seemed impossible. The elusive and all-important Senator Landske was a few feet in front of me. Lobbyists were trying to talk to her while clinging to their cellular phones. She seemed to be listening patiently but suddenly was stepping backwards to the Senate entrance a few feet away. There was no room for me to work my way in between the lobbyists who had beaten me to the senator. I stood directly behind Senator Landske; she was going to have to mow me down to get back into the chamber. She was turning, the lobbyists were still talking to her; my hand impulsively touched her shoulder. Surprised, she turned completely around to see who was behind her.

"Senator Landske, I'm Caress Garten, Paul Mannweiler's friend and I need to know—I mean—I need a hearing for the vicious dog bill." If blood were sweat, I was now sweating blood.

She calmly looked down at my leg and then back at my face. "Paul Mannweiler called me this morning," she said simply and smiled pleasantly amidst the clamor, "and you *will* get your hearing."

The senator was finished in the hall; not turning around again, she re-entered the Senate. Jim was standing beside me, eyes wide, wanting to know the verdict. "We have a hearing," I said to him.

"Well, congratulations, Caress!" he boomed with an enormous grin. He was relieved, and there were no words to describe my burden that had been, at least momentarily, lifted. He placed one hand on my shoulder, "Are you all right?"

I watched my friend in his blue suit as speeches for the union were beginning on the main floor directly under the rotunda. All of the third floor doormen seemed to shift on their feet in semi-disgust, the noise irritating to them. These men were indeed the hawks of the state house, watching the participants, knowing who was effective, and whose chance for survival was greatest. Ordinarily, my chances would not have been good. A political novice—many factors had to bend my way.

The ancient Gideon stood invisibly in the hall. "Assurance and more assurance, just like me," he mocked.

"I'm fine, relieved—you've had a big turnout, Jim."

"It's been great," he said, as he ran a hand spontaneously through the thinning dark hair. Gently touching my shoulder, he turned to tend his flock.

I needed to find Velda. She had sent me off like the Spartan Mother. "Go get a hearing." I couldn't return without one—but now, *we had a hearing*, I thought, joyously climbing the first gritty marble stair back up to the ivory tower.

I stepped onto the green carpeting, feeling I really was the State House Princess. Velda spun around in the swivel chair and smiled as one finger was held up for me to wait. "I've got to go, someone is waiting for me," she told the caller, hanging up the phone. Turning back to me she sat on the edge of the chair.

"We have a hearing," I said breathlessly to her.

"Yes-s-s!" she squealed, turning back to the phone, punching in buttons. "I knew you could do it. How DID you do it?" she asked as the phone dialed.

"Paul called her," I said.

"Bless his little heart," she said, grinning. "It took you a long time down there," she added.

"You wouldn't believe it," I began as Velda started speaking into the phone.

"Belinda, we have a hearing." She had called Fort Wayne. "Next Monday, 'cause there's just one more week after that for these committees. Yep, I sent Caress down to kick some butt with about a thousand union guys in the halls." She turned and winked. "Sure she'll be ready—knock 'em dead again."

"Ask Belinda if she'll be packin'," I said.

"Caress wants to know if you'll be packin'?" She nodded her head back at me. "She's bringing plenty of ammo too." Belinda, the policewoman, could duel it out if she had to with about half of the members of the Indiana Senate who were always armed. "Be ready," said Velda over the phone. "I'm gonna have to call you back with the time. I don't know where this committee meets either. Paul Mannweiler asked this senator for a hearing. You bet it's a good thing." She laughed into the receiver. "He treats Caress like she's his sister." This was true, I thought to myself. "Does he have any sisters?" Velda asked, carrying on two conversations at once.

"No, I think just brothers."

"Well, you're the new sister—sister."

"I don't know if anyone from H.S.U.S. can be there," she said over the phone. "You may have to be ready for all kinds of questions from this group. They've never seen the legislation before in the Senate. It's never even gotten a hearing, but we're on a roll now, I feel it."

I knew what a conversation was like with Belinda at the shelter in Fort Wayne: dogs barking in the background, staff talking to her as she spoke on the phone; a gifted woman, her effectiveness was nationally known. Her own home number was unlisted and few people knew where she lived in that city. She worked with the Allen County prosecutor in trying drug dealers who used dogs to guard their crack houses. Belinda and her husband, also a police officer, had adopted two abandoned Rottweilers who now sat, stopped, and barked at her command. They were a deterrence to the occasional criminal who found his way to Belinda's house.

They were all miracles, these gifted women who had banded together to help me.

"Now we've gotta attack that committee," Velda said. I nodded. *No time* flashed through my brain. I felt like the soldier with the commander-in-chief telling me the battle plan for one of the final offensives. It was do or die. "They'll all get the material. You'll hand deliver each packet to each member. I'll help you find them in the halls." Velda had become the hunter.

The little legislative handbook that had become an extension of my hand was rolled tightly inside my left fist. Peeling back the pages, I read off the committee members' names. "Landske, Chair."

Velda shook her head, "Nope."

"Bray."

Velda nodded, "Smart lawyer, was in the House—from southern Indiana somewhere. Next?"

"Harrison."

"Don't know him, but he's been here forever."

"Meeks."

"Don't know him," she said again.

"Johnson."

"Linda knows him and he's smart."

"They're not all smart?" I asked innocently.

"Wel-l-l, some more than others," she answered out of the corner of her mouth. The names Paul, Doll, Bowser, Breaux, and Randolph were all followed with Velda's head continually shaking back and forth. "No, I don't know them. Not too many animal people," she said softly. "It doesn't make any difference," she then said cheerfully. "You'll just find 'em and they'll fall all over themselves."

I had my doubts about the hurt little lady business with this bunch.

That evening, John Hammond agreed as we went over each name. "Dick Bray is the son of six-term Congressman William Bray, who for years was the ranking member of the Armed Services Committee. He's a very bright man, a former prosecutor and he must be satisfied on all fronts," John said emphatically over the phone. "Senator Meeks is a former state trooper, very involved this year in the fight against local control of firearms." The same Senator Meeks was also involved with the grandparents who walked the halls. Two well-publicized pieces of legislation.

"Make sure Morrie Doll will speak up in the committee and on the floor," added John—the elusive Senator Doll whom I hadn't been able to find in the halls or at his desk. He probably didn't know that much about the issue, which was discouraging.

"Anita Bowser is a college professor at Purdue, and Lonnie Randolph, newly elected, is an attorney from northern Indiana. Anita is one of the most liberal members in the Senate."

Senator Meeks crossed my mind as being on the opposite end of the political spectrum from Senator Bowser.

"Caress, make sure you have the same good, credible people speaking again and press the point the bill passed the House ninety-four to four. Will Paul be there?"

"I hope he'll be there, but I don't know; it's the Senate."

John finished with words I had heard before. "Try and stop any amendments—have Paul talk to Senator Bray."

Velda phoned an hour later with instructions. Teresa had been informed we had a hearing, and Velda expected me to begin hunting down senators the next day, delivering packets, and being most charming.

* * *

The following morning I was ready. Velda escaped the judge's outer office on her official coffee break. We both carefully held several packets to be delivered to committee members. As the elevator doors opened onto the third floor, Velda grabbed my arm. A big man in a navy blue suit stood staring at us before stepping onto the elevator. The massive Senator Meeks filled the remaining space left in the elevator, and I understood immediately that the two of us were going wherever Senator Meeks was going. I felt Velda's hand nudge my arm.

"Senator Meeks," I said softly as the old elevator rattled back and forth.

"Is that for me?" he asked as the large, square face looked down unenthusiastically while he extended a thick, fleshy hand forward for the packet.

"I hope you'll read this." The senator nodded with a slight grunt. He wasn't in a good mood, and his demeanor was intimidating, unusual in my meetings with legislators.

"I'm Caress Garten, Senator. This information is for your committee meeting next week." Senator Meeks continued to look disinterested. The doors creaked open and the senator stepped out into the painted concrete hall of the state house basement.

We both watched him walk down the hall as the doors closed. "He seemed pretty surly," I commented as we rattled back up to the third floor.

"Maybe he'll come around," Velda said, as she too sensed the senator was not ecstatic over our bill.

"He's a former state trooper; I thought he'd be a shoo-in," I told her, having read his biography in the legislative handbook. It was a naive assumption that because the State Troopers Association was for the legislation all state troopers active or retired would be for the bill. Perhaps Elmer could work on him, and I made a mental note to ask for his help.

Now I was worried about both Senator Meeks and Senator Bray. Velda handed me more packets to deliver on my own in the Senate chambers. It was never as easy without Velda, but she did have a job and the coffee break was about over. The far south end of the fourth floor held additional Senate office spaces. These secluded Senate chambers didn't have a guard posted outside. They were off the beaten track for most of the general public up on the fourth floor. Names posted on the outside of the entrance told me Senators Breaux, Bowser, and Randolph had offices inside. Three committee members who were Democrats. I headed toward a dark wooden entrance where the offices of about twenty state senators were located. The offices consisted of three old rooms cramped with office dividers between the desks. "May I help you?" asked a young black woman who looked up from her desk. The desks around her were empty. I had not arrived at an opportune time.

"I'm looking for Senators Bowser, Breaux, or Randolph."

"Well, the only one here is Senator Breaux," she said with her arms around a stack of bills waiting to be distributed. "Her desk is over there around the corner." Senator Billie Breaux was a teacher in the Indianapolis Public School system. She taught at school #27 where I had volunteered as room mother and where Donald, with the big blue eyes, had been a second grader. Senator Breaux remembered me and smiled as she looked up from her desk, putting down the papers she had been reading.

"Sit down," she said, motioning me toward the single chair by her desk. The silence around us was odd after the constant noise in the halls.

"Senator Breaux," I began quietly. "I'm here for the vicious dog legislation."

"I know you are," she said softly. "How are you doing?"

"Well, I'll be doing a lot better if this law is passed," I said, placing the packet on her desk.

"I've been getting letters about your law."

"You have?" I said, still amazed that the public followed what I was doing.

"Yes—and they're all against you." My eyes dropped to the handwritten letters scattered on her desk. "But—I'm for you." I watched the placid expression on her face for just a moment as my body relaxed. "Will you be testifying?" she asked.

"Next week. I'm just trying to meet the committee members now. I know you're busy —" I began as a memory floated in front of me. "Beware of the Dog" the little store-bought sign had read posted on the rusting gate across from School #27.

"I think of school #27 and my little friends," I said, balancing on the edge of the chair.

"We thank you for coming," she said simply.

"Thank you for your support," I said in a hushed tone as Donald waved to me once again, boarding his bus.

Velda was in the shack running off opinions on the copier when she decided to check the bill room on the main floor. She wanted a copy of the dog bill that had been reprinted when it passed out of the House and entered the Senate. Velda was a familiar pro in the old room and quickly opened the correct drawer, pulling out House Bill 1218.

"Yes, it's a bill that is now entering the Senate," she heard the bill room assistant remark over the telephone. "Well, they'll have a hearing, then if it passes committee it'll be passed on to the full Senate." Velda could distinctly hear an angry voice on the other end of the phone line. "We don't have anything to do with bills other than copy them here. No, I don't know what she's trying to do. I know she was hurt—yes, she has gotten a lot of press." Velda waited, her ears perked up, sensing we had an enemy on the line.

"No, I never see the senator," the assistant continued. "Well, you'll have to watch the papers and see if they get a hearing." The voice coming over the line was shrill. "Well, then call Mannweiler's office," the assistant answered. "No, I couldn't do that, we just make copies here. Yes, of course, just come on down." There was a click. The bill room assistant heaved a quick sigh as her cheeks blew air toward Velda.

"Call about 'vicious dog'?" Velda asked, using the name the press had coined.

"Someone real mad over 'vicious dog,'" the assistant answered. "I hope that woman doesn't pounce down here today. Sometimes these people think because we answer the phone we're responsible," she expounded while handing copies of the bill to Velda.

"Thanks," Velda said, hurrying back to the judge's chambers.

The Senate was ready to go into session as I passed the chamber after leaving Senator Breaux. Members were filing in slowly, taking their seats. As usual in early afternoon, the halls were fairly busy. My arms were still filled with packets, having delivered only two.

"Well, bring lots of buses and pack the halls," the emphatic voice was telling two women who were listening intensely.

The voice belonged to Senator Doll. He continued talking with the women as I stopped. This might be my only chance to come in contact with this man, I thought to myself. Senator Doll *did* look like his picture in the handbook. Whoever these constituents were, they were hanging on to his every word. The senator continued repeating "to fill the halls" with demonstrators.

I wondered if the senator really believed what he was saying since Velda had impressed upon me the lack of effectiveness the horn blowers really had in the halls. Senator Doll turned towards me as his eyes peered curiously through framed glasses.

"I'm Caress Garten, Senator. Thank you for sponsoring the vicious dog legislation." Handing him a packet, it was unclear if he knew what I was talking about. He looked down at the information. Trying to keep his attention for a moment, my eyes focused upon his face. "I know if the law is passed it will save lives." He was trying to place me.

"I hope so," he said slowly, studiously. Paul must have asked him to sponsor the bill in return for some favor at one time or another. The senator did not have a very good feel for the legislation and seemed to be very busy with other issues.

"Thank you, Senator, for your support," I said to him as the Senate chamber was being gaveled to order. He seemed amiable, thoughtful, as he watched me turn and walk down the hall. I hope he looks at that stuff, I thought to myself, worried that an important sponsor was not up to speed.

I made my way around the corner, walking toward Paul's office. The Corrections and Criminal Code Committee was starting to make me nervous. I now sensed what it was like to introduce a new law in the Senate that had never been debated or read before. If the real fight had been in the House, I now had my worries about the ultra conservative Republican Senate.

Mr. Eggers opened the doors. Cathy looked up as she saw me standing at the entranceway. "Come in and sit down. How's it going?"

"I'm worried," I said, over the endless House speeches coming through the wall speakers.

"What's going on?"

"Do you know Senator Meeks?" I asked. Cathy nodded her head. "I've got a bad feeling about him not voting for our law."

"Well, Bob," Cathy said, as if a friend had disappointed her. "I wonder what's wrong with him? He's usually pretty good."

"Cathy, I want you to tell Paul this is no piece of cake with the senators. There's also Senator Bray—he's supposedly a stickler."

"I know Dick real well; in fact, I'm having lunch with him tomorrow," she said, beaming. "Caress, you know what? In all my years here I have never lobbied for anything but

I'm going to for you. We'll get Senator Bray's questions answered before the hearing."

I could almost hear John Hammond laughing in the background. "What do you need me for?" he'd say. I'd forget about Senator Bray's packet and let Cathy convince him on her own.

"Tell Paul I need him at this hearing."

"When is it?" She picked up a pencil.

"Next Monday morning, March 22nd."

"He'll be there, Caress; he's not going to let you down now." I listened to the voices in the background droning on, one bill after another, several going down to defeat. So many ways for a bill to be killed. This would be the end for some, others would be resurrected in conference committee, if it pleased the Speaker. There would be no resurrection for my bill should it be killed. This couldn't happen. I must have faith, I did have faith, there would be success.

I stepped out into the main hall, wondering what to do next.

"Will you have scars?" asked a man standing next to Mr. Eggers' folding chair as the great doors closed behind me. A businessman looked at my bandaged leg.

"Yes, I'll have scars." I tried smiling at him as he shook his head.

"Do you have trouble walking?" he added impulsively, wanting to know more about me.

"I have trouble putting my heel down completely," I told him, suddenly feeling slightly wilted. The businessman in his pin-striped suit looked horrified, like so many who had a personal terror for what I had been through.

"Well, I wish you the best," he said genuinely.

Another stranger who wanted to connect with me, I thought, walking across the smooth marble floor toward the stairs leading up to the ivory tower and Teresa's Senate office. Fatigue was occurring more frequently—a creeping weariness. I wasn't going to stop, but I was tired. The jagged long scars on my leg were closed but remained bright red and tender to the touch. The leg was concave on one side. The bandage was no longer needed, but it was still effective at the state house. I was wearing the bandage until I was finished. Who knew how much longer.

I heard Sarah's voice, "He hasn't brought you this far to let you down now, it's going to happen." Often winter can seem never-ending, then finally, the first green shoots appear through the earth. I was in the last days of a wet, dreary, Indiana winter, and God was walking with me into spring. Now, He might have to carry me the rest of the way.

I continued at a slow pace, looking at the several packets still to be delivered to committee members. Mr. Hoke watched me come toward him from outside the main Senate office door. He had already opened the door, ready once again to make a bow. "You don't have to do that for me," I told him gently.

"Why, that's what I'm here to do," he replied. "You know the senators have caucused—both sides fighting over the budget," he told me with a smile and a wince. "You going up to see Senator Lubbers?"

"Yes, if I can," hoping Teresa could tell me new information about the senators on our committee.

"Of course you can," he said as he simultaneously called inside the door. "This lady is going on up to see Senator Lubbers." A secretary watched wide-eyed as I went on up the narrow, carpeted stairs unchallenged.

The Republicans, at least, were no longer in their caucus. Every senator was at work in his or her office space. Many had phones to their ears. It was the end of the session and the pressure was on. They were all consumed with work, writing rapidly, talking on the phone, conducting and arranging hurried meetings.

No cigar smoke drifted up from behind Senator Meeks enclosed little fortress.

I wonder where he is? I thought to myself. A nearby voice

caught my attention. "Well, I've been a state trooper, so I understand that position," a senator was explaining to the caller. Another former state trooper, I noted and filed the information away. His last name was Adams, and he briefly looked at me as I put my head down and walked past his desk.

Maybe Senator Adams would speak for the bill on behalf of the state troopers?

Valerie was on the phone as the secretaries were also on overdrive. "No, she isn't available right now," she was saying. "Well, I'm sorry, ma'am," she paused. "No, she's committed to the bill in the Senate. Yes, ma'am, she will get this message, and she has received your other messages." Valerie spoke politely, glancing toward Teresa who watched as the conversation continued. Teresa motioned me into a seat and pointed toward Valerie who was hanging up the phone.

"We have a woman who is calling here every few hours—upset. She's about ready to drive Valerie nuts. It's over the bill," Teresa added calmly. "I don't know everything she wants, but we're sure not going to change anything."

I suddenly felt ill, actually having heard part of the conversation.

"Passing out packets?" Teresa asked with a smile, trying to get my mind off the caller.

"I'm trying to find everyone. Should we be worried about this woman?"

"So far, all she's been doing is calling here and ranting," answered Valerie. "We haven't actually seen her, though it sounds like someone fixated that you're out to get her." *Out to get her,* my brain repeated, wondering if this woman was attached to a bad dog.

"How could anyone logically be against this law?"

"I haven't spoken to her yet," said Teresa. "I'm trying to avoid her like the plague."

The phone rang again. Teresa picked up the phone and began to jot notes. She was obviously very busy, and there was nothing she could do about this new caller. Teresa was trying her best for the bill, so standing up silently, I mouthed good-bye. There were senators to hunt.

The narrow hall soon led me by a pleasant-looking man with broad shoulders and sandy hair who was working at his desk. The familiar phone was propped under his chin as he wrote with one hand and shuffled through papers with the other. He was Allen Paul, another committee member. A quizzical expression crossed his face as he noticed me with my arms full of packets. Senator Paul continued his conversation, sensing I wasn't moving.

He represented Richmond, Indiana, a mid-sized city, and the home of many hunters who enjoyed shooting game in nearby rural areas. I remembered the name of a big game hunter who lived there, a local businessman who had spent thousands of dollars hunting animals in Africa. These animals now stood silent throughout his home. Heads of buffalo hung from the walls. Gazelles stood vacantly, staring into space on silent hoofs placed eerily on brown living room carpeting. I wondered if Senator Paul knew this flamboyant constituent. I hadn't mentioned to Velda the story of Richmond's big game hunter.

He hung up the phone and was all business. "How can I help you today?" he said bluntly.

"Senator, I'm Caress Garten and I'll be testifying in Senator Landske's committee next week."

"Vicious dog bill," he answered efficiently. He knew. "I've already had some phone calls and letters opposing the legislation, and I haven't decided my vote," he said, looking at me directly.

"I hope you will vote for the bill," I said as my voice picked up some steam while I placed a packet down on his desk.

"They're afraid of losing personal freedom with their animals," he said as if stating his own opposition.

"I don't want people to lose any freedom. The law is designed for prevention, simply trying to protect the innocent from irresponsible people who own dangerous dogs."

Senator Paul watched me noncommittally. "I'll read your

material," he said to me with a definite tone in his voice that he now had work to do.

"Thank you," I said, moving on around the corridor. I would have to think who we knew in Richmond to call this senator and ask him for his support.

A bell rang calling the senators back onto the Senate floor. Mid-afternoon and not much accomplished. There weren't going to be many more days or opportunities to talk to the committee members before the hearing.

The packets in my arms appeared to be growing instead of diminishing. I was not being overwhelmed with support on the Senate side. God had never promised me this would be easy, only that I would be successful.

Anxiety over the hearing and a dull, creeping weariness made me aware that long spaces of silent blankness were now occasionally coming over me. The pressure of my coming testimony loomed. I reasoned if my story was a repeat of the one in front of Jesse's committee, it might not be as effective. There was the story of Brandon Spradley, the little six-year-old, who had been attacked by two pit bulls while waiting for his school bus. I looked at the old newspaper picture showing Brandon's heavily bandaged head. His big brown eyes and sweet smile looked out at me. Perhaps the committee should hear Brandon's story as well as mine.

Spring vacation was also approaching—only two weeks away—and the trip seldom crossed my mind. When the occasional question from Benjamin or Matthew would arise, only then would I think briefly about going.

The trip was planned last October in what seemed another lifetime. Over the last months it had appeared certain the bill would have passed both chambers and gone to the governor's desk by now. But the process was longer and more difficult than I had expected. Long-time state house watchers had told me flatly that bills hurry up only to slow down, and that is exactly what had happened.

My family, would they mind going without me? The long

red scar stood out, tender to the touch; my legs didn't match anymore. How would the water and waves feel on the tender tissue? These thoughts were momentary, for my limited ability to focus and concentrate labored only to deliver the legislation.

* * *

The remaining days and nights before the Senate hearing ran quickly together. It was the end of the week and the following Monday would bring our do or die committee meeting. My taped sermons spoke with certainty of the Great and Good God that watches over us as He watches even the sparrow. I dreamed of Ed, the great blue heron. He floated through marble halls looking for me, a sharp-eyed messenger from heaven, watching and disappearing as he sailed high in the blue glass rotunda.

I had told my doctor the Senate hearing was coming the next week. "You'll tell them," he said confidently, for the doctor remembered my descriptions of the hearing in the House.

"You don't understand what I'm up against," I said. "Almost everyone in Indianapolis is for the law, but there's a whole state out there that's mostly farm land and rural—they look at things differently."

I remembered Representative Grubb standing up in the House, dark hair falling across his eyes. "I'm not gonna vote for your bill, might get in the way of my huntin' dogs."

The power of hunters on rural legislators was real, if they were motivated against the bill. Some were against the dog bill, and one by one they were calling their legislators.

The surgeon couldn't see the tired soul. He was the one who dealt in muscle and flesh. He was only a mortal doctor, and whatever he was to gain through me I would never know. There was a message for him in my mission even if he saw only bits and pieces and merely heard faint whispers.

Early Monday morning before leaving for the 9:00 hearing. I called the doctor's office. There was a foreboding about the next few hours. I thought it was connected with my fading strength, but there was something else. *"Hunters were coming."* For some reason, beyond explanation, I knew this was true. "He's supposed to say a prayer," I told the receptionist who answered the phone. "Tell him I think hunters are coming."

"I'll make sure he gets the message," the voice assured me.

The doctor would pray, I knew he would. "It's faith, Caress," Sarah's voice came to me.

The state house was frantic as the session was approaching its final weeks. There was a real sense of dwindling time for everyone connected with a bill that had a remote chance of passing. Some legislation would affect millions of people; other bills were simple addenda to existing laws.

The dog bill would save children: Children I would never meet, children waiting to be born, children who now toddled toward their mother's arms. If not their lives, then the quality of their lives, saving their eyes, their smiles, their ability to run and play. This was the weight but also the promise that rested with me.

Cathy stood behind her desk, guarding Paul's office door. "You're to go on down, and he'll be there as soon as he finishes this meeting. It shouldn't last too much longer," she told me.

I smiled, for Cathy would not let Paul's meeting go on past time. "Have you been getting phone calls from someone, a woman, who is really against the bill?" I asked.

"Yes, very unhappy and very demanding." Cathy grimaced. "She never wanted to speak to Paul or to have him call her. 'Make sure he gets this message. DON'T FORGET!' Then she'd slam the phone down."

"What didn't she like about the bill?"

"The gist is that she thought it was unnecessary. She was unreasonable though, Caress. I know it won't bother him."

I smiled again at Cathy. "Good luck, Caress," she said, returning the smile. "I'll be thinking about you."

The phone caller bothered me. Who was she calling? How knowledgeable was she about the state house? Had she called the members of the committee?

Velda and Belinda Lewis waited for me in the hall.

"You packin' today?" I asked, looking at Belinda.

"Always. Are you ready?"

"I hope so," I said, beginning to feel the pressure.

Our hearing was scheduled in a medium-sized, makeshift room. It was painted old building tepid yellow. Rows of plastic chairs filled the room, nearly touching the two plain folding tables that had been placed together for the senators.

Velda marched towards the front, entering a row close to the senators' seats. Belinda sat next to me and glanced around. The utilitarian room was the very antithesis of the distinguished chamber where the House testimony had taken place. No grand chandelier or massive doors leading into a stately room; only the purpose of the hearing was the same, and equally important. American law could be made in a sallow-colored basement room as well as historic chambers.

Belinda turned in her seat again, scanning the people entering the room as well as those already seated. "There's no one here from the DNR," she whispered towards Velda. Anxiously, she watched for anyone connected with the Indiana Department of Natural Resources who just might be in attendance.

She was a woman who had power in a traditionally male dominated arena. In the city of Fort Wayne, Belinda, as head of Animal Control, had fought animal trapping along the three rivers that flowed into the city. The traps had been placed close together and occasionally in the backyards of people who lived along the rivers. The city council had given her the authority to remove the traps for public safety, particularly the safety of children playing along the riverbanks. The DNR claimed she had no jurisdiction over the rivers and their banks. Believing that the jurisdiction belonged to the DNR, eighty angry hunters and trappers appeared at the council hearing in coonskin caps and fur vests. They insisted their constitutional right to hunt and trap was being violated. Belinda had won the debate and the traps were removed. However, for some, she became the enemy. Along the quiet tree-lined street, men in pickup trucks would watch her house. Later, they filed criminal complaints that she abused her children. Belinda and her husband had no children of their own, but neighbor children frequently played in their yard. This group of radical hunters and trappers traditionally had the support of the Department of Natural Resources. Belinda was looking for any of these men who, having found out she supported the dog bill, would come to try and ruin her credibility.

For the moment, none of the coonskin brigade knew she had entered the state house.

People filtered into the room, sitting down, opening brief-cases. Velda sat next to me, swinging her crossed leg up and down. "You know, you really are somebody you can dress up and take places." She looked at my blue linen dress and bandaged leg. "You're gonna wow 'em."

One by one the senators filed into the room, eyeing lobbyists and legislators who would speak. There was a movement beside me as Velda moved to the next chair. Paul sat down between the two of us. "Where's Teresa?" he asked me, placing a file of papers on his lap.

"She's in another committee meeting but she'll be here," I answered. Velda leaned towards me, voice low.

"The Associated Press reporter is in the front row and so is the reporter from the *Louisville Courier Journal.*" People in the southern part of Indiana who lived in the towns nestled along the Ohio River read the Kentucky newspaper. I thought of a distant cousin in the southern part of the state. She would have to write a letter to her state senator.

Belinda whispered in my ear. "I was talking to a man from the Health Department. He's going to testify for the bill but he had a question. We don't want any questions—

just straight positives. Did you see your friend from the state police?"

I turned around and there was Elmer, sitting a few rows back, wearing the familiar raincoat. He gave me a wave and nod. Valerie, Teresa's secretary, was sitting directly behind me. "I wouldn't miss this, Caress," she whispered excitedly. "Teresa's on her way."

Senator Landske entered the room and was asking for the "Request to Speak" forms. Senator Doll could not be present today as there was another committee meeting he had chosen to attend. This was a blow. He was the ranking Democrat on the committee, and his support could be very important. My initial feeling about the senator was proving correct, for today there was another issue that was more important to him.

Some of these senators that were appearing around the table were unknown to me. I had spoken to six of the ten committee members. Senator Meeks sat at the end of the table, leaning over his papers, his massive frame far too large for the hard little plastic chair. The senator appeared uncomfortable in a coat and tie. He seemed more suited to rolled up sleeves and an unbuttoned shirt around the thick neck. His expression never changed when he occasionally turned and the large, square face assessed those sitting in the room. I noticed he made no hint of recognition towards me. A *bad* sign, I thought.

On the other side of the narrow room, a young woman walked down the aisle and picked up a "Request to Speak" form. She had spoken against the language in the bill when I had testified in the House. I remembered she owned German shepherds and had also been at the House subcommittee meeting.

Paul had become very still as he watched the lawyer-lobbyist take a seat near the front. There's a rule of conduct among lobbyists and politicians that if you're going to testify against legislation you inform the sponsor. Paul had thought the language disagreement had been resolved. "What's she doing here?" whispered Velda.

"I don't know," he whispered back.

Senator Landske began. "I call the meeting to order and Senator Soards has asked that his legislation be moved forward."

The senator was handling a piece of legislation referred to as the corpse bill. The corpse bill made it a felony in the state to have sex with a deceased individual, or as it was more politely worded "performing certain acts that would outrage a reasonable person."

I groaned inwardly, for the dog bill had been previously listed near the top of the agenda. Now the wait to testify would be longer as Brandon's story began to repeat in my mind. I felt strained, for there were children to be saved and we were spending time regulating necrophiliacs. Paul was expressionless, calm, waiting.

Teresa had arrived, slipping into a seat next to Valerie. She patted my back and smiled. "I'm here. We're ready." Additional anxiety began to creep over me. I didn't have the strength in late March that had been with me the first of January. My eyes traveled downward, staring at the Ace bandage wrapped tightly around my leg. The white sock that covered the ball of my foot rested on the floor. The hearing had just begun and I was beginning to fade.

"Are we ready for the vote?" Senator Landske's voice broke my thoughts. Ayes followed and the corpse bill passed out of committee.

Senator Landske next called a bill dealing with computers and storing information. Senator Meeks was carrying the bill in the Senate, and the legislation had passed the House with little objection. The senator began to explain the main points of the bill. I studied the other senators around the table. Senator Bowser, the professor, was listening intently. She was seated next to Senator Lonnie Randolph, a freshman senator, a lawyer from East Chicago, and a board member for the local NAACP.

"Is there anyone who would like to speak for the bill?" Senator Landske questioned. There was silence.

"Is there anyone who would like to speak against the bill?" A man in the back of the room quickly gave his name and occupation. He launched into a lengthy description of the dangers to privacy the legislation proposed.

"Where were you on the House side?" Senator Meeks asked as the heavy, jowled face turned red. "I was asked to carry the legislation and did so because it passed the House almost unanimously." The senator was not having a good day.

"I didn't become aware of the bill 'till yesterday," the man answered.

Senator Meeks was irritated. The committee was agreeing with the new stranger. The debate droned on for an hour and a half until it became apparent the computer bill wasn't going any further this session.

The hearing was still crowded with bills to be heard. Paul remained almost motionless in the chair next to me as I thought of the many people waiting to see him upstairs. The dog bill slipped further down the agenda. Senator Landske knew Paul was there along with Teresa, both patiently waiting—surely our time would come.

I watched Senator Meeks, who had assumed everything was secure with his legislation when the unexpected had happened. Someone appeared whose point made sense to the committee and that killed everything. Surely that wouldn't happen to our bill. So many people had looked at the legislation from every angle.

"You have only to step out": That was the message. Yet today, I felt like doubting Thomas. I sensed something, for I had called and left the message for the doctor. This was my mission and there had always been assurance. I was in a battle with myself, fighting for faith in the real world of secular politics.

The senators' voices blended with whispering behind me. "Is that the voice on the phone?"

The corner of my eye caught Teresa bending toward Valerie who answered slowly and very quietly, "That's the voice." My ears strained, hearing another voice two rows behind me. There were furious whispers coming from someone who wanted to be heard, yet couldn't stand and scream to the room.

"She doesn't have to wear that bandage," the voice spat. "She could have sued him. She didn't have to try to change the law." I glanced at Paul who seemed unaware of the conversation. This was the caller who had vented her emotions on anyone who would answer a phone in the state house. *She was the hunter and I was the hunted.* I felt her eyes penetrating the back of my head.

The bandaged leg had been effective. Lawyers and politicians at the state house visibly paled when the leg was discussed, and none of them wanted to actually see the long scars or misshapen leg.

Belinda and Velda had noticed two men sit directly across from us on the other side of the little aisle. A worried expression crossed Belinda's face as a barely audible sigh let out whatever air she had stored away in her lungs. "Department of Natural Recourses," she said quietly. The good old boys had arrived.

It was now eleven in the morning as I watched the second hand pass the tiny black notches on the watch Paul wore on his wrist. We had been waiting for two hours. Teresa had left the room to vote on a bill for the Education Committee. Hopefully, she would be back soon because Senator Landske would look for her to introduce the bill.

The woman behind me continued to rant in a raspy, emotional voice. She was sitting next to Elmer Borders who was expressionless, listening, as his seatmate demanded his attention.

Senator Landske looked quickly at her agenda and placing

the paper down on the table, she crisply called "House Bill 1218." Members of the press looked up and turned toward Paul. They had been waiting for the dog bill. The chairman looked expectantly around the room. "Senator Lubbers." Teresa was waiting in the back of the room. She had decided to return, not voting with the other committee.

"Thank you, Senator. This is a bill that passed the House ninety-four to four and is needed due to a void in the law. Representative Mannweiler is here as the chief sponsor of the legislation." Teresa momentarily appraised each senator. Dressed entirely in white, the new senator was in command as she introduced the bill. The auburn hair fell neatly around her face as she presented her own political style.

"There are several individuals here to testify for the bill, and Representative Mannweiler will answer any legal questions connected with the legislation."

Teresa stood in the center aisle, then slowly walked toward the committee. There was a sense of expectancy in the room. Paul was motionless, and on my other side Belinda sat quietly. Now it was up to those testifying and in particular—me. Senator Landske looked at her stack of papers with names of people to testify. "Is there anyone who would like to speak in favor of the bill?" A chair scraped against the floor as Belinda stood and walked to the front of the room.

"Belinda Lewis, Director of the Department of Animal Control in Fort Wayne, President of the Association of Animal Control Officers in the state of Indiana. We support this bill and feel it is needed to address irresponsible owners."

Belinda smiled confidently. Tenacious was the word for her, I thought, staring down at my blue linen dress which had started to crease.

I held Brandon's picture in my hand; the little boy's bandages covered most of his head. The very long wait had drained me. Everything depended on the bill getting out of this committee. Paul, who never seemed to move, still quietly waited beside me as the third hour of the hearing began. I wondered if he heard the woman behind us who continued to harp. Belinda's voice floated in and out of my thoughts. It was a good thing Paul was here, my brain told me quietly, for this committee was hard to read. My legs felt numb. My arms heavy by my side. I would do this, I had to do this, I had come so far.

Belinda had finished her testimony and was sitting down beside me. Elmer Borders came to the front of the room.

"The state police strongly back this legislation and the exemption of police dogs while acting in the line of duty."

Elmer was making his points, gesturing with his hands, slightly bending toward the table. I still held out hope that Senator Meeks might be swayed by the state police. Senator Randolph twitched in his seat next to a thoughtful Senator Bowser.

"The state police have worked with dogs for years and they have been trustworthy. These dogs have been invaluable." He continued to use the words "reliable," "supportive," "needed," trying to move the committee. Elmer finished his testimony. His gray raincoat flapped open as he walked back down the aisle.

Brandon's little black face peered at me from the newspaper article that lay in my lap. "Does he have scars?" I had asked his mother.

"Yes, Brandon has scars," she had told me. Scars that covered his head and scars that still frightened his soul.

"Mrs. Garten," Senator Landske was saying as her eyes came right to me. My body stood and the bandaged leg hobbled towards the side of the room near the front. I leaned against the yellow wall. Where were the words? Maybe I should just repeat the testimony from the House. No, I would tell Brandon's story.

"My name is Caress Garten and I am a resident of Indianapolis." The committee seemed to be listening impassively. "I am married, a mother." Those who had waited so long, watched, eyes penetrating me. My voice continued the litany of introduction "... active in the community." I felt they must be so bored with my story. My voice quivered. I was wilting. The story was told again with a shaking voice. "There was so much blood that flew. They would have killed the infant in the stroller." My hand came up holding Brandon's picture. I glanced over at Velda and saw her looking down; her hands were clinched, the crossed legs seemed frozen. I could almost hear her: "Caress, get a grip." Paul remained motionless having turned into some kind of living statue. He showed no emotion.

"Brandon was waiting in the darkness for a school bus when two pit bulls appeared and pulled him down, ripping off an ear and tearing his head open." It was so odd to hear my voice shaking.

A senator looked down at the floor. Steven Johnson was a young articulate man, a leader whom I thought was politically ambitious. He was very uncomfortable watching me struggle. Uneasily, the dark-haired senator avoided my eyes. "He will never be the same," I said to the senators, placing Brandon's picture down on the table. Senator Breaux looked at the clipping, she was a teacher in the same school system where Brandon had been attacked. I hoped she remembered the story. The other senators remained passive. There had been too much emotion in my voice, too much blood and guts, I thought. Like a living corpse, I sat back down in my chair.

"Thank you Mrs. Garten," Senator Landske was saying. I felt only blankness. It was March 22, 1993, almost five months since my attack. A pleading prayer came instinctively inside me to hang on as all my physical and emotional reserves had been used up over months of anxiety and exhaustion. It was almost noon when Paul stood and stepped by my seat and walked to the head of the table.

He smiled at the senators on his way to the front of the room. He was almost casual. "This is a very simple bill that deals with vicious dogs and their owners, not a cocker spaniel that nips at your heels. There are twenty-six states that have similar laws. Indiana needs the law to address cases like the ones you have heard. Morrie Doll is helping to carry the legislation on the Senate side." The Democrats present needed to know the absent committee member was for the bill.

"Who's against the bill?" asked a low voice from the end of the table. Senator Meeks didn't look enthusiastic as he held one side of his head with an arm resting on the table. He only looked at Paul while he asked the question.

"The Farm Bureau had been opposed to the legislation in the past but now has no problem with the bill. There is no threat to the farmer's dog on his property." Senator Meeks shifted his big body in the chair.

"Hasn't this bill been seen before in committee?"

Paul, still smiling pleasantly at the senator, answered, "It's never had a hearing on the Senate side."

"It seems to me that if Indiana has a law that protects cattle from vicious dogs, we should do as much for people," a voice interrupted from the center of the table. Senator Bray, the former prosecutor, the stickler "who must be satisfied," had spoken. Cathy must have been convincing when they went to lunch.

"Doesn't a farmer have the right to shoot a dog attacking cattle?"

"Yes, a farmer has that right," answered Paul. Senator Bray was now lending his support. Other senators around the table seemed ambivalent about the discussion. The majority of the Republican senators on the committee were from rural areas traditionally against any kind of restriction on an animal. Senator Joe B. Harrison was silent in the questioning. He was from Attica, a small town in the rural westernmost part of the state. Senator Harrison was the majority floor leader in the Senate and had to be loyal to leadership, so maybe Paul's presence would make a difference with his vote.

Senator Paul was also quiet. Perhaps he had received more negative calls on the bill?

"What happens if your dog leaves your property and bites someone in another yard?" Senator Meeks was asking, after he abruptly pushed his chair away from the confines of the table.

Paul smiled patiently, looking at the massive senator. He didn't answer, but his eyes twinkled and his mouth turned downward and with mock hurt he said, "Bob,—I *always* vote for your bills."

Instantly the blasé senators dissolved with laughter. Even Senator Meeks offered a half smile. Paul was good. He wasn't angry and not close to threatening—just charming, that was his style. However, there was a message. I want this legislation, and there's a bill you're sponsoring coming to the House.

Senator Meeks resembled someone bested in chess at the last moment. "Are there any more questions for Representative Mannweiler?" asked Senator Landske. Some senators shook their heads no while others remained motionless. Paul sat down having called upon his friendships and his power.

In the front row, the lobbyist-lawyer Linda Valentine showed no emotion. She had an authoritative presence and was attractive with her dark brown hair and long legs. I remembered her legs along with her concerns during Jesse Villalpando's House committee hearing. A real-life drama had unfolded where people had stood silently, grimly, staring at me then back at Linda. Today she appeared business-like and solemn, stating her name.

"I've come to give my support for this bill. The language has been changed, and I now have no objections to its passage. I wanted to come and support Caress."

No one around me had moved or glanced at the other. Belinda and Paul had frozen. Velda made no sound. Unseen and unspoken relief came with her words.

"I would like to ask Mrs. Garten some questions," came

a senator's voice from the far end of the front table. Lonnie Randolph had been silent through the hearing. He was still learning the ways of the state house.

His voice, calling my name, surprised me. My legs were wobbly walking over to the side of the room. "Mrs. Garten," he hesitated, "how do you feel about the use of dogs by the government?" The senator spoke calmly, politely, sitting very erect. Resting against the wall for a moment, I understood what was going to happen. I remembered Lonnie Randolph was active in the NAACP. This was part of the information printed next to his picture in the legislative handbook.

Immediately my brain flashed through old black and white film footage, civil rights marches, the use of police dogs on protestors. I had never witnessed abuse by the police with a dog, but this senator from East Chicago had, and he was getting ready to challenge the exemption of police dogs. He waited for my answer. The support of the state troopers must be maintained for the passage of the bill. There could be no amendment; how *many times* had Paul told that to me. He would have no power if the bill were eventually sent to conference committee. Speaker Phillips would *kill* his legislation.

I had never liked the use of a dog to control or corner people. Dogs could not reason on the same level as people, only do what they were told. Their masters were responsible for their actions. Why did I have to be so exhausted? There wasn't a good answer for me to give. I couldn't agree with the senator, for there must not be an amendment, and not wanting to alienate him, there couldn't be a real challenge to his thinking. "I don't have an opinion, Senator" was my reply to his studied look. It was the equivalent to taking the Fifth Amendment. He nodded his head and looked at the other senators as I returned to sink slowly down into the hard chair next to Paul.

"What happens if a policeman should lose control of a dog? Or a police dog should attack an innocent person?" he asked. Senator Meeks, the former state trooper, sat looking at Lonnie Randolph, lower lip jutting out.

"That's just not going to happen with these dogs," he said abruptly. "They're too well trained." Ironically, Senator Meeks didn't want to discuss the matter, considering it a waste of time.

"I think the matter deserves further discussion," Senator Randolph insisted, leaning over the table towards the unresponsive Senator Meeks who didn't flinch. Senator Randolph sat back in his chair and said the unspeakable to the chairman: "Senator Landske, I would like to propose an amendment."

I saw Velda stop breathing and mouth the word "NO."

"I propose that this clause exempting government dogs in the line of duty be removed from the legislation."

Senator Landske repeated "Senator Randolph has proposed an amendment to remove Section three: 'That the owner of a dog is exempt if the dog commits an act described in section three during the period that the dog is owned by: 1. the United States; 2. an agency of the United States; or 3. a governmental entity, and the dog is engaged in assisting the owner or the owner's agent in the performance of law enforcement or military duties.'"

"Is there further discussion?"

There was movement on my left as I watched a woman quickly stride to the front of the room. She tightly grasped a copy of the legislation that was covered with markings from a red pen. I hadn't seen the face before; only heard her voice. She was angry and unfamiliar with the protocol of committee hearings. The discussion at the front of the room had moved at a fast pace. Aware that a vote was going to take place, she had come forward quickly, afraid her chance to testify on the bill was over. "I would like to say something," she said adamantly. Senator Landske looked calmly toward the voice. The woman was primly dressed in navy blue, a blazer, and skirt. Somewhere in her fifties, of medium height, she was memorable due to the contrasting color of her hair. Originally dyed dark brown, a third of her hair, growing from the crown of her head, was totally white.

"May we finish our voting on the amendment first?" asked Senator Landske, who had been interrupted.

"If there are no further discussions, may I have your vote." The challenger stood still, waiting and staring forward.

Senator Landske looked at Lonnie Randolph. "Yes," he said to his amendment.

Senator Anita Bowser who sat next to him added her "Yes." My breathing stopped.

Richard Bray answered, "No."

Senator Billie Breaux, who I feared might agree with Senator Randolph, answered, "No."

Senator Steven Johnson, "No."

Senator Allen Paul, "No."

Senators Meeks and Harrison, the two most conservative members of the committee answered, "No."

Last to vote, Chairman Landske added her "No." The amendment had been defeated. Months of work and anticipation could have been gone in moments.

Senator Landske nodded to the waiting woman in the front. Unable to further control her anger she began, "I want to speak about —"

"Could you please state your name and position?" interrupted Senator Landske. Members of the press looked over at the woman who was now glaring at the senator.

"I'm just a private citizen who wants to make some comments. This legislation is —"

"Please state your name," Senator Landske interrupted again.

"I'm just a private citizen who would like to make some comments. This bill is a —"

"You *must* state your name," the senator said firmly.

"I don't want to state my name, I'm just a private citizen."

"Then you may not speak." The senator had heard enough

and started to return her attention to the committee. The bill held in the woman's hand was now crumpled and clenched in a fist. Her anger was now fury.

"I thought a private citizen could come down to the state house and make their comments," she spat. Senator Landske looked up from the table. The would-be spoiler was not ready to leave.

"A private citizen may always come and give their opinion, but you *must* state your name."

The senator had finished with the florid-faced woman.

"WELL, SO MUCH FOR THAT!" she yelled, hesitating, glaring at the room, before bolting down the aisle and out the door.

No senator had heard her challenges to the legislation or was aware of her hatred of me. Senator Meeks wasn't given any ammunition to back his objections to a law he considered too restrictive. The waiting press did not hear her protests for *she could not speak.*

The hunter had arrived and was prevented from the kill. The doctor, who cared for the leg, had been praying. I felt the prayers preventing the hunter from her prey. The only person who had ever challenged the appearance of my injuries could not speak. *She had been silenced three times.*

"Are we ready for the vote on the bill?" asked Senator Landske, looking around the room for anyone else to testify. No one stood.

Belinda cautiously glanced over at the men slouched in their chairs from the Department of Natural Recourses. They stared with disinterest at the chairman.

"They must be here for another bill," she whispered in a barely audible voice.

Seeing no one come forward, the senator proceeded. I listened to my heart pound as this committee, with very divided political persuasions and personalities, voted.

"Senator Randolph," called Senator Landske.

The senator who certainly would vote "No" uttered,

"Yes." Then rapidly the names were called:

"Senator Bowser,"

"Yes."

"Senator Bray,"

"Yes."

"Senator Breaux,"

"Yes."

"Senator Johnson,"

"Yes."

"Senator Meeks …" There was a pause. He then spoke in a low voice.

"What did he say?" Paul exclaimed in an excited whisper as he sprang to the edge of his seat. He leaned forward looking around wide-eyed, first at me, then at Velda who turned towards him.

"He said, 'Yes,'" she whispered back, "but he's not going to vote for it on the Senate floor."

There was a deep breath as Paul leaned back from the edge of his seat.

Senator Harrison had nodded "Yes."

"Senator Paul," called Senator Landske.

"Yes," he answered.

The chairman glanced around the table before adding, "I vote *Yes*," as she looked toward me with a smile.

Three members of the press left their seats to see my expression as Teresa patted me on the back. Velda was standing, pulling me up from the chair. Belinda walked behind me as I moved in a haze toward the door. The buzz of the room was all around me.

"How do you feel about the vote?" Asked a reporter from the *Louisville Courier Journal.*

"I'm very pleased," I heard myself say. We stepped into the hall where three more reporters took notes. The reporter from the Associated Press scribbled down my words: "The vote was unanimous and sends a message to the full Senate."

Paul slipped out the door into the hall, a big smile on his

face as the everyday mask that hid his feelings dropped. He was in a hurry to get back to his office. Relieved, he knew we had dodged several bullets to receive the committee's total, if grudging, support.

Velda believed in timing and luck, but there was more at work in the old basement room of the state house.

Prayers had been answered—the bill had escaped—and the hunter's snare was empty.

ELEVEN

Hangin' On

Lonnie Randolph walked through the open rotunda and up the first flight of marble stairs. His shoes hit the stairs evenly one step after another, quickly rounding a corner as he climbed the second grand staircase to the fourth floor. He took the stairs impatiently, briskly walking towards the entrance that listed his name, then down the winding corridor that creaked beneath his polished shoes. Senator Randolph was the best-dressed member of the conservative Indiana Senate.

Velda had quietly commented to me, "He sure is a flashy dresser." He lived up to that reputation this morning: His cream-colored suit contrasted with the usual navy blue favored by most of the men on the Senate side. Lonnie had reached the end of the hall and entered the series of rooms where Senators Breaux and Bowser also had their office space. He smiled at the receptionist and moved toward his chair, pulling it out from behind a nondescript desk bearing a bright red sticker. The sticker featured a gun with a heavy line through it encircled in red. This lack of support for guns placed him at odds with most of the other Indiana State Senators.

The date was Tuesday, March 23rd, and the *Indianapolis Star* reported in the morning edition that the vicious dog bill had moved through committee the previous day. The story stated that "a bill making owners of vicious dogs criminally liable sailed unchanged through a Senate committee Monday. Under the dog bill, owners could face criminal penalties in unprovoked attacks." Senator Randolph had read the paper. Sitting down at his desk, he noticed a light blue envelope and opened the seal.

"Caress, you have to thank these people for their votes," Velda had told me after yesterday's hearing. She always had a strategy. "If plan A doesn't work you have to go to plan B." Plan A had worked but it was built on matchsticks. The votes yesterday in the basement committee room had come for a variety of reasons instead of firm support. The attentive press was unaware of the different factors leading to the morning paper's heading "Sail through."

"You have to get these notes out to them quickly—and it's best if you hand deliver them. Let them know the hurt little lady really appreciates that vote. They'll all love the attention." A smile had appeared on my face, for Velda was very savvy. "Not too many people say thanks," she said with firm assurance, green eyes glimmering in the soft glow of the ivory tower's brass chandeliers.

I returned to the state house early the next day on her orders to get those notes out. Senator Randolph was a worry. He hadn't arrived when I placed the envelope on his empty desk.

He now read the note: "Dear Senator Randolph, I want to thank you so much for your vote on Monday for the passage of House Bill 1218, Vicious Dog. I feel very deeply that if passed, it will save others, particularly children, from being mauled. Thank you for listening to me. I truly believe I spoke for many too young to say a word. Wishing you the greatest success in all your good works. Sincerely ..."

The memory of my voice trembling only a few hours

earlier was painful, and I wondered if Senator Randolph had been uncomfortable. Senator Meeks was not at his desk either. No curling smoke rose from behind the office panels. Picking up a pen, I printed "Senator Meeks" on the outside of the envelope, then hesitated a moment, thinking the effort was probably a waste of time.

It was quiet in the Senate offices this morning. Members of the Senate and House were staying late, voting on bills for final passage. This session of the legislature was entering its last days.

We were to leave Saturday morning for Grenada, far south in the Caribbean Sea. School spring vacation would begin on Friday. So little time, and so far this morning I had already missed two senators just trying to pass out notes. I headed back to Velda's office, passing Gene who was reading the morning paper. "Well, good morning," he beamed. "See you're down here early; see also your bill passed out of that committee."

"I'm delivering thank you notes this morning—Velda's idea." Gene chuckled under his breath.

"After those notes are dropped off, you're always a guest of mine and the court of appeals."

"I know I've got a friend here, Gene."

"You sure do. I think about you and those dogs—did I ever tell you I had a pit bull once?"

"No, sir, you didn't," I said, watching Gene's face become serious.

"She was a good old dog but somebody stole her. 'Bout half year later that dog came home and had a big scar on her back—somebody fought her. Had to put her down—she wasn't the same. Once they've been fought, they're not the same. Made me mad."

"Gene, do you know the man whose dogs got me?"

"Yeah, I know who he is, lots of people know who he is—that man has lots of dogs." Gene folded his arms as the

deep, gravel-laden voice lowered. "He has a partner that works
with him."

"How do you know?" I asked.

"I've met people who know him." Gene brushed the side
of his head with his hand. "I'll keep my ears open 'bout him
and his dogs."

Pit bulls leaping, encased in a gray drab day, flashed before
me. Dead black eyes came close to my own, seen between
fingers covered in blood.

"She's here early this morning," came a voice from behind
me. Velda, her hands full of papers, had been working in the
shack. "What have you been up to?" she asked.

"I've been to see Senator Randolph and Senator Meeks,
neither one were there, though. I left those thank you notes."

"Boy, you tell her to do something and this little lady's
got it done," she laughed, looking over at Gene.

"We former Junior League presidents can whip out a
thank you note faster than lightning," I said.

Velda chortled. "You goin' back to see either senator?"
she asked, a quizzical look crossing her face.

"I thought I would see Senator Randolph."

"That a girl," she said; a smile came brightly across her
face. "You learn fast. Chances are Meeks *is* a lost cause. Mind
if I come with you—just to listen? You know I can't get
involved or actually lobby," she reminded me again.

"You've been around lawyers too long," I told her.

"Well, I have to be careful," she replied. "The branches
of government must remain separate." Velda always made
her calculated innocence abundantly clear to me.

"I would love for you to come with me," I told her, grateful
for support, and she thrived on dueling with the system and
winning. The wheels were turning in Velda's brain.

"I'll take a coffee break and we'll go now. I think we
should try Lonnie before any meetings get started and before
the Senate session." She turned and placed her armful of

copies back inside the shack, immediately appearing again. "Let's go find Lonnie."

The halls were sparsely populated this morning. Only a few lobbyists were standing in alcoves, talking on their cellular phones. The protest days, filling the halls with signs and horns, were over for this session. Time was short, the pressure on, not only for the dog bill, but every bill left standing.

"What will you say to the senator, Caress? Something like, well, Lonnie, I think you're a real great dresser—and I need your vote—and please don't do anything like try and put an amendment on this bill."

"Yeah, I'll say exactly that and ask for his autograph too—you're good you know."

"What do ya mean?" she asked, slowing down. "Am I walking too fast, Caress?" she asked, glancing down at the wrapped leg.

"No, you're not going too fast; my leg's so stiff I can't even feel it below the kneecap, so it doesn't bother me. What I meant by 'good' is that you just won't let me get too serious."

"That's good?" she asked.

"That's very good," I told her as we entered the carpeted corridor that led back to Lonnie's office.

"We're here to see Senator Randolph," I told the secretary inside the door.

"Just have a seat by his desk," she answered.

"It looks like the senators are busy with meetings this morning," added Velda, who was good at making small, leading remarks, gleaning information whenever possible.

"Yes, the black caucus met this morning." The secretary seemed slightly interested in us, coolly looking down at my leg.

"Well, we won't take too much of his time," Velda said, putting on her most cordial smile.

Two chairs were wedged tightly into the little office space alongside the senator's desk. "You go in first," I told her, as I looked over my shoulder, noticing a woman watching me from a nearby desk. Senator Rose Ann Antich, a TV personality and psychic, stared unblinkingly at me. "I'm Caress Garten," I said to her.

"I *know*—" she responded quietly.

I turned my head toward Velda who seemed not to notice the senator's fascination as Lonnie Randolph came quickly down the small aisle and around the side of his desk.

"I read your note," he said, smiling pleasantly, quickly sitting himself down.

I tried to hide any anxiety, he was so important to convince.

"Thank you, Senator. I wanted you to know how imperative it is for prevention to have this law." Senator Randolph smiled politely. He seemed amiable as I studied him for any sign of disagreement.

"The law is important for children," I reminded him again, "and the issue is totally bipartisan."

I didn't want to bring up the dreaded word—*amendment.*

Today an amendment seemed the furthest thing from Lonnie Randolph's mind as he enjoyed the conversation, leaning back in his chair. I watched his face for expression, trying to decide if I should ask him specifically not to attempt what I most feared. Velda was giving him every ounce of her attention.

"Thank you for voting for the bill and moving it out of committee," I told him, personally repeating the contents of the note.

"That was a terrible thing that happened to you," he added.

"Well, I hope some good can come from it, and I seem to be the perfect person to have been attacked."

"She has been pretty perfect," Velda added, slightly bouncing up and down in her chair, hands folded in her lap.

"We just wanted you to know this law is needed 'cause Indiana doesn't have anything on the books. I work up in the court of appeals and follow animal legislation. Caress lets me come with her sometimes when she visits with a legislator 'cause she knows I'm interested." Velda smiled her pert and bubbly smile at the senator. The senator was seeing Velda as the innocent ingenue, just along for the ride. I glanced down at my lap to clamp a smile. She was such a fox, understanding the law better than most lawyers.

"I don't have any problem with the basic law, but I wish some changes could have been made," he said intently. Velda nodded her head.

"I see you don't like guns," she said, remarking on the red sticker plastered on the side of his desk. "I don't either," she added, shaking her head.

"Most of the Indiana Senate comes armed every day to the state house," laughed Lonnie.

"There's a lot of good old boys down here visiting the big city," Velda quipped. Lonnie and Velda laughed while Senator Antich continued to stare wide-eyed, watching over the meeting from her desk.

"I would so appreciate your vote when the bill comes up for passage, Senator." I spoke up not wanting to get further off track with the subject of guns.

Lonnie nodded amicably, "How is your leg?"

"Stiff, and the scars are still tender, but I can walk pretty well."

"She sure can—keeps up with me," Velda said with a laugh.

My plea had been personally given. It was the moment to go and not take any more of his time. "Thank you for listening, Senator," I said.

Velda quickly added, "Nice to meet you."

Standing, I noticed the name plaque on the cubicle closest to the window. The name was printed in bold letters, "Senator Alexa." I had not met or seen the senator but remembered his picture from the now well-worn legislative handbook. *Another* senator I had not spoken to.

Senator Randolph stood as we left, thanking us for

coming to see him. I proceeded toward the door with Velda behind me, followed by the eyes of Senator Rose Ann Antich.

"He seemed supportive," I said, walking down the hall.

"I thought so too," she agreed before becoming silent, mulling over the conversation.

"He didn't say anything to make us worry," I said stopping, wanting assurance.

"No," answered Velda. "He was very nice to the little hurt lady." We had reached the marble floors of the fourth floor, and the activity in the state house had picked up with pages and legislators leaving their morning meetings. A calm came over me as we walked back toward the court of appeals. Maybe it was only exhaustion, but the two of us seemed alone, invisible, while others hurried to begin the day's official business.

"Just a few more days and you'll be off on spring vacation," Velda said happily. At home the suitcases had been brought down from the attic.

"When do you think the bill will get to the floor for a vote?"

"Soon, it has to be soon; first, second reading, then the final vote."

"I'm thinking of not going, Velda." I mustered up the words that had been somewhere in the back of my mind for weeks. My legs stopped moving as I touched the railing that circled the stairs close to the shack.

"Just have to hang on don't you?" Velda mused, quietly looking at me. "You remind me of my husband Joe. When he was a little boy growing up along the Mississippi he used to go down to the riverbanks with his big brother. They both used to swing way out on the river on those monkey vines that hang from trees. One day one of their friends was watchin' Joe being swung way out on the river where the current was strong. 'Why do you swing your little brother so far out he could drop into the river and drown?' 'Well,' his brother answered, 'I'm just teachin' him that sometimes in life you just gotta' hang on.' That's what you're doin', Caress, hangin' on," she ended, her mouth firmly set, green eyes wide, unblinking, understanding.

She remained thoughtful for a moment, looking at me while visions of long-ago little boys swinging far out into a great river floated before my eyes.

"This afternoon they'll list the bills on second and third readings for tomorrow," she said, breaking the spell. "Maybe we'll make second reading tomorrow and a final vote on Friday. When would you leave?"

"Early Saturday morning."

"That's cuttin' it close, but it might work. Can you change the tickets?"

"No," I said, reflecting for a moment on that possibility. "The hotel and flight have been booked since October."

"Well, maybe you can join them in a few days," she added hopefully.

"Maybe, Grenada—it's just so far away, almost to South America."

"You would have to be going somewhere halfway around the world," she said, bemused.

I looked over at the rows of portraits of the judges of the court of appeals—long-ago men with horned-rimmed glasses and full beards. Just getting to the state house over rutted dirt roads by horse drawn carriage would have been difficult. They wouldn't have dreamed of going to a place called Grenada or of two uppity women trying to change the law.

"Did you get the rest of those notes out?" Velda was snapping back to political reality.

"I'm going to take the rest around before I leave the state house today." Almost by habit I muttered, "Is this going to work, Velda?" She was used to the question now.

"It's going to work, Caress," she always answered sincerely. My prayers told me it would work—to continue— just continue.

The news at noon was on the car radio as I drove home, having finished delivering notes. The lead story was coming from the state house. The state was facing a crisis with only two weeks left in the 108th General Assembly. Governor Evan Bayh was late in presenting his budget and was now predicting massive layoffs with catastrophic effects if it wasn't passed. The House had passed the budget; now the governor was in a battle with Senator Garton and the Republican Senate. Whispers of a special session were starting to be heard at the state house. I hoped everyone there thought the dog bill was something positive to unite around compared to the growing ugliness of the budget battle.

Daffodils were blooming after the drabness of winter. My favorite flower, they seemed to always brave the last of the spitting snows. Blades of green grass were appearing in the yard as the car wound around the long driveway.

Inside the house Geneva was ironing. She placed shirts and shorts in piles. "It's about time for you all to be going," she said cheerfully. "I'm glad you can leave, and I'll be here to feed Boomer and Chuck. I know Benjamin and Matthew will be happy, you all together."

Geneva cared about me, as I cared for her. She had been with me through a difficult pregnancy, sick children, family deaths, and now the dog business. Geneva had helped the household function while I lay in the hospital. With a discerning ear she had screened visitors' calls.

"I don't think I'm going to go with them, Geneva, or at least leave with them."

"Whaaat, you're not?" she said wide-eyed, looking up from the folded clothes.

"No, I just can't, until it's right to leave. I don't think God would have a very good opinion of me if I quit to go on vacation."

"You have to do what the Lord is telling you," Geneva spoke with confidence, "and I'll be here to help you because you always try to do what's right."

"I've been trying, Geneva, just pray I can get through this and with success."

"You know I will," she said as I took an armful of clothes upstairs to be packed. The shoe I had been wearing for months was stretched from the bandage and flopped up and down as I went up the stairs. I walked on the ball of my foot stair by stair, grateful the days of the upstairs and downstairs walker were gone. The window at the top of the landing looked over the front yard. Would the hawks living at the top of the tall trees produce a chick to circle the house and soar by the windows?

The radio was on when I reached the bedroom; a familiar voice was speaking.

"There's slick Willy and then there's slick Evan. You can't wait until the end of the session to present a budget and expect it to go sailing through without question."

Paul's voice continued with more negative comments about the governor. *What was he doing?* The governor was needed to sign the dog bill—*Paul's* bill. It was Cathy who connected the phone call while I waited for the interview to end. "I've been listening to you," I told the radio star dismally.

"Did-you-hear-that?" Paul said.

"Yes, and I'll bet I wasn't the only one to hear that 'slick Willy, slick Evan' comment. Paul, what if he won't sign the bill?"

There was a slight guffaw—*"Ohhh, I-don't-think-so,"* he answered. "He'll sign it, Caress. If it gets through, that's one he's going to have to sign."

"I hope you're right," I paused, before adding, "I'll be coming tomorrow for second reading. I'm worried Lonnie Randolph might try to put an amendment on the bill."

"Teresa has to fight it, Caress. Have you spoken to him since the committee meeting?"

"This morning—he made no mention of an amendment."

"Well, he has to inform Teresa if he's going to try for one." There was a slight sigh. "It's not Evan Bayh, it's Mike

Phillips who has the power to hold that bill hostage or kill it in conference committee. The order will go down with whomever he appoints to vote, and it will be done to get me. That's the reality with an amendment—let me know," he said, as the phone call ended.

With a short call to Teresa's office, Valerie assured me there was no indication that Senator Randolph was preparing an amendment. She would let me know if they heard differently.

It was an uneasy calm, this waiting. Like the brown mouse hidden in the Indiana corn field, waiting beneath the stubble of withered stalks, ears tense, eyes darting, body low to the ground, searching for his kernel of corn forgotten in the damp ruts of dark earth. His moment of safety would come when the skies cleared of hawks that watched for him. He would eat or be eaten—a game of sorts. The mouse played a game of judgment and intuition much like a politician. As with the mouse and the hawk, the state house would eventually produce a winner and a loser.

* * *

Work at the state house had continued busily, frantically, into the late afternoon. Velda had stayed cloistered in the judge's chambers, trying to catch up on work. Her calendar hung from the office partitions. The picture of the month featured kittens playing with yarn. These felines were displayed directly over the smiling Elvis and alongside pictures of the winding Ohio River in fall. The animal work was taking a back seat this afternoon to the judge's memos piled on her desk. Joe, the young clerk in the inner office, stuck his head around the office partitions. "How's the legislation going?" he asked.

"We're moving," Velda said.

"Where's Caress?" he asked, pushing the wire-rimmed glasses on the bridge of his nose back toward his eyes. "I thought she would be down here campaigning for sure."

"She's gone on home for today, and, Joe, I'm worried about her—she won't be able to handle it if this bill doesn't pass. I think it will — but you never know."

"I hope it passes for her," he said. "You have to feel like it should—after everything."

"You would hope so," she pondered. "She feels that this all happened for a reason. I don't know 'bout that, but she wants to make something good come from somethin' terrible. I am not religious you know," she said, shrugging her shoulders. "I got tired of people telling me when I was little that we're all born sinners. Never understood that or appreciated people trying to convert me. Caress believes she was chosen for this, believes it deeply. Blood flying, teeth sunk in to her. I asked her why God would do this and hurt her?"

"What does she say?" Joe asked, watching Velda rock in her chair.

" 'I never thought about it hurting me' is what she says— and that she knew so soon afterwards what she was to do down here. She's always believed, since I first saw her, all she had to do was come down and she could change the law and it would save lives, lives of children."

"Never talks about her leg or how she's doing?" Joe asked.

"Naw, my friend Linda worries 'bout that all the time. 'How will she ever buy shoes?' Afraid she'll have to wear one shoe for the rest of her life. You know, I've never seen a bill go through the state house like this—just like you read about in the government books," she added with a wry smile. "That would really be somethin' if it goes on and happens wouldn't it?"

"Everyone's constantly talking to her; I don't know how she stands it. How much longer do you think this will go on?" he asked.

"We'll know one way or another if it's gonna escape going to conference committee within the next few days." The phone rang, and Joe lifted the palm of his hand up to say a silent good-bye as Velda picked up the receiver.

"Hi, it's Cathy from Paul Mannweiler's office. I've just gotten this call from Fort Wayne, from Belinda Lewis. She says the bill isn't right, and the prosecutor in Fort Wayne won't be able to use the law. I guess there's an example of a case where a woman was held using a pit bull."

Velda was sitting straight in her chair. "The bill never covered attacks on the dog's own property, Cathy. It holds dog owners accountable off the dog's property. I can't believe she didn't realize that."

"I know we don't want an amendment of any kind," said Cathy. Paul wasn't in the office and didn't take the call, but I thought someone needs to call her."

"Do you know who else she's called?" asked Velda, flipping through the desk Rolodex for Belinda's Humane Society number in northern Indiana.

"No, but I would guess Teresa."

Velda's voice went up a notch. "This isn't the time for change."

Cathy half laughed. "No, definitely not, too close to the end."

Velda punched in the phone number to Fort Wayne. "Pick up, pick up," she muttered. This was the problem working with other people, she thought; very good people, experts even, but they didn't understand politics. This was exactly the kind of thing that could snowball into something else if she couldn't quiet the issue. The prosecutor in Fort Wayne could start calling people, saying the bill was useless for him in prosecuting criminals who used animals as weapons on their own property. This could motivate an amendment, or cause other people to come out of the woodwork at the last minute to defeat the bill. Then there was Caress who was new to the state house and had worked all these months—she could *not* deal with this— *"Belinda!"* Velda half screamed into the phone, "this is walkin' on eggshell time; you don't go calling now and say the bill isn't right—it's too late."

"I was worried about the prosecutor up here who thinks he's going to get a law that will help him prosecute a few cases. What am I going to tell him?"

Velda said calmly, "You're going to be quiet, then when the bill passes say, 'Wel-l-l-l—I'm sorry, guess we'll have to get that part for you next year.' Then we'll see what we can do. Belinda, we never had anything about attacks on the dog's property in the bill. The risk is greater than you think calling around the state house when people are canning legislation left and right. Called anybody else?"

"Senator Lubbers," she said.

"Anybody else, anybody in Fort Wayne?"

"No."

"Well, you make sure you don't, or we just might end up getting *nothing* this year!" Velda yelled.

"Okay, I've dropped it."

"Good," said Velda standing by the desk, glaring at the grinning Elvis. "I've gotta go find Teresa."

"Okay, okay, I'M SORRY, good-bye."

Velda propelled herself around the office dividers and outside the doors of the judge's chambers. She took the stairs running, then propelled herself into the mob of lobbyists and senators who had ventured out into the hall. Velda hurriedly wrote a note at the message desk, slipping it to a page. "Teresa—need to talk to you about our bill—urgent." Velda glanced down the hall. Senator Randolph looked up from a conversation, smiling broadly, raising his hand in a brief wave. Velda was waving back as Teresa entered the hall. "Did you get a call from Fort Wayne?" asked Velda.

"A note. I really don't know what to do about —"

"Well, we don't do anything about the prosecutor in Fort Wayne," said Velda.

"Right, since we don't want an amendment," uttered Teresa.

"You haven't heard anything from our senator down the hall have you?" questioned Velda, rolling her eyes in the direction where Lonnie was speaking.

"No, nothing," Teresa answered.

"I think we're okay," Velda sighed in relief as the wildfire seemed to have been stomped out in time.

* * *

The packing had begun for Grenada. It was Thursday evening, March 25. Velda had called late on Tuesday telling me we weren't on the list for second reading the next day. Then a call Wednesday night; the dog bill hadn't made Thursday's list either. I had lost hope of leaving with everyone on Saturday.

"I will never understand why you have to do this," Matthew told me. "I have never understood it, never. Now, you can't leave with us." He stood in his room packing his suitcase. "Do you have to dress up for dinner at this place?" he asked unhappily.

"Yes, you do, it's English, and at night you have to wear a blazer and a tie. You always have a good time, even dressed up, don't you?"

"Please come and be with us, Mom?" he asked as I helped him fold the navy blue blazer in the suitcase.

"I'm going to come, in just a few days, I promise."

The travel agent had made my ticket switch for next Tuesday. There was a warning that if I wanted to cancel the flights and hotel, it would have to be done no later than six in the evening that day. The flight was at seven. Reaching the island wasn't easy: first a commercial flight to Atlanta, then another to Miami to spend the night before one last plane trip almost to South America. Tuesday was the last day it would be practical to leave before the vacation ended and the family would come home early Saturday.

"Remember to put that sunscreen on your ears, on top of your feet, everywhere," I said to Matthew, who never got tired of running in and out of the waves.

"What will you do while we're gone?" he asked.

"Try to follow the bill until the final vote—and the final vote has to be soon." I whispered the last few words almost to myself.

"Just gotta hang on don't you?" I heard Velda say.

"I will miss you so, Matthew," I said suddenly to him, "and I love you so." There was a fragility about me momentarily, and he sensed my exhaustion.

"Mom, we'll be okay," he said, bending over, putting his cheek on my shoulder. He reminded me of the long-ago three-year-old who would show me his love by nestling close. Maybe someday he would understand and remember this time with his mother.

"There's a phone call for you, Mom," called Benjamin from downstairs. Maybe it was Velda with news, putting an end to this limbo of waiting. Picking up the phone, I heard Velda happily chirp.

"It's scheduled for second reading tomorrow, and there's no sign of an amendment—just checked with Valerie in Teresa's office."

"Finally, some movement," I said, relieved. "I'll be down there by noon."

"Got to have you sitting in the gallery, Caress, so they can see you—saw our favorite state senator," Velda added nonchalantly.

"Lonnie?" I asked.

"Waved right at me and gave me a big smile, looked dressed to kill."

I could picture Velda trotting past the Senate wing, just happening to see Lonnie Randolph. "I hope he's not going to say anything tomorrow," I said dubiously.

"Lonnie's too busy thinking about other things—looking good—sounding good."

"Probably so," I laughed.

"Family still going on Saturday?" she asked.

"Bags are being packed as we speak," I said, noticing Matthew's red suitcase had been zipped up and placed by his door.

"It's just a shame they couldn't have scheduled that bill a few days earlier. I'm glad you're going on Tuesday. Will that leg stop you from doing much?" she asked.

"Oh, I never think about what I can or can't do, Velda; too much else to concentrate on right now." A momentary flash of the concave leg and a bathing suit ran through my mind.

"Well, you do have your plate full. One thing at a time, that's always best. I'll see ya down here tomorrow."

That evening and the next morning were busy at home, but the state house was never far from my thoughts. In politics, I had learned to never count on anything until it was completed. There was a nagging feeling that something wasn't right. "He has not brought you this far to forget you now," were Sarah's words. I gave my own prayer throughout the night. "You have brought me through every crisis. You gave me knowledge that I *would not die—understanding* that the law should change, and through every step, seen and unseen, You provided the way. I will not fear defeat—for You are near."

I listened to one of the Presbyterian minister's sermons, making the bed, getting dressed. His voice was comforting, and through those tapes he had grown to be a dear friend.

It was ten o'clock in the morning. I couldn't stand the waiting anymore, and there was that intuition that continued to bother me. Phone in my hand, I called Teresa's office where Valerie answered. "It's Caress, Valerie, what do you know?" She hesitated.

"Caress, Senator Randolph will try and place an amendment on the bill this afternoon. Senator Lubbers is preparing right now to fight. He notified us this morning."

Valerie had said the words that I had somehow known,

and I responded, "I'm on my way. Tell Teresa I know." With the click of the phone I calmly uttered the words, "You knew this," and then, "remember the promise."

The state house was glowing, warm golden-colored light filled the busy halls as the afternoon session was close to starting. A state trooper stood against the wall in front of the Senate chamber. He was in full uniform, standing erect, watching the crowd. His badge glistened along with the gold braid on his uniform, black leather holster and gun resting ominously on his hip.

I had never seen a uniformed state trooper at the state house and wondered if he was here today in some connection with the bill. I headed for him through the crowd. Elmer Borders was watching from the other end of the hall. He had hurried to the Senate after hearing of Lonnie's proposed amendment and worried as he walked toward me.

The officer was watching the crowd in the hall. My arm touched his arm with one thought on my mind. "Are you here today for the vicious dog law?" I asked him.

"No, ma'am," he said politely. "I'm here to guard the Senate."

"Well, I'm here for the vicious dog law. There's a senator who's going to try and place an amendment on the bill today, and if he does, all the dogs that work with police will no longer be exempt from this law. An amendment will kill this bill and the good it could do on behalf of many people, mostly children."

I understood why this man had been placed in the hall. "I want you to pray with me," I said suddenly, as if it were the most natural thing on earth to pray in the middle of the hall at the state house.

"Yes, ma'am," the state trooper said, bowing his head.

"Dear Father, I am asking that this amendment be stopped, that the good dogs who work with the police, the state troopers, might be protected under this law and children be saved."

The state trooper, who had bowed his head, quietly said, "Amen." The formal Episcopalian had prayed out loud, spontaneously, in the state house, and a powerful calm came over me. Elmer Borders stood quietly behind my shoulder. He and others around him had not seen praying in front of the Senate chamber before today.

"Caress," Elmer said, touching my arm, "so you know about the amendment? I've been sending notes into Lonnie Randolph all morning—he won't come out."

The well-worn raincoat looked even more disheveled around him as he shook his head. "He knows what I want," Elmer said as a wry smile at the corners of his mouth faded, turning downward in disappointment.

"There she is," came Velda's voice through the crowd as she stepped close to us. "Everything looks great. No amendment; just rush this sucker on through."

"There's going to be a try for an amendment," I told her.

"No, there's not," she said—disbelieving.

"Lonnie is going to try to place the amendment on, Velda." Elmer confirmed what I was saying by the grimness of his face.

"How do you know?" she asked me, concern starting to register.

"Teresa's office. I called about ten, and Valerie told me they'd received the paperwork." I had actually found out something at the state house before Velda.

"Is Teresa going to fight?" she asked.

"Valerie told me she was—" I said, looking at Velda who had not thought this would happen. She was not ready with her famous plan B.

For this one tactical moment I was in charge. "Kent Adams used to be a state trooper," I told Elmer, remembering the senator talking on the phone. "He could speak for the bill as a law enforcement person." Elmer's face lit up.

"He was a state trooper. I had forgotten that."

"He's Jackie Walorski's state senator and knows her," said

Velda. Senator Adams was from Bremen, in Marshall County at the top of the state where Jackie's record of success with clearing out drug dealers and their dogs was well-known in law enforcement. Velda was thinking quickly. "I'm going up to write a note using Jackie's name, asking him to defend the legislation when Lonnie finishes."

"I'd forgotten that about Kent Adams," repeated Elmer. "I'm going to talk to him too," he said, scribbling out a note and shoving it in the hands of a page.

John Hammond walked over asking, "How's it going, Caress?"

"We're trying to beat an amendment, and I think we've about done all we can do. Now we just wait and let Teresa do her part." There was a calm, resigned tone in my voice. "Lonnie Randolph doesn't want police dogs exempt from the law." John understood.

"You sure don't want anybody standing up at this point. I'm sure Teresa will fight it though, Caress."

"I'm going up and watch," I said to both men. The state trooper continued to look upon the little group clustered outside the Senate doors. There was unseen power at work within me—strange this quiet assurance. I felt it but was afraid to believe—to give up my control.

All three men seemed transfixed by the moment, watching me climb the marble stairs to the landing before I turned and walked down the hall to the Senate balcony.

Mr. Hoke opened the balcony doors. "Something going on?" he inquired.

"Senator Randolph's going to try and put an amendment on the bill."

My friend's enormous jowls drooped farther down as he rocked backward on his heels. A single, heavy "No" was uttered.

I gazed calmly at my good friend, the Senate doorman, and entered the balcony packed with supporters of the grandparents' bill. Senator Garton was calling the bills on second reading. A bill under debate was moving slowly. Hurry and finish, I thought, perversely dreading the moment when debate would start for our bill some twenty pieces of legislation away. Senator Randolph was out of his chair, pacing, debonair in his cream-colored suit. Lonnie was ready, waiting for the bill to be called. I couldn't see Teresa, for her desk was below the balcony towards the back of the chamber.

I sat down in the seat next to the railing in the first row. A motion to my right caught my attention as a sweet-faced, older woman waved at me from the center section of the balcony. One of the grandparents had noticed me. "Is your bill up today?" she asked.

"Yes, on second reading," I answered, continuing to observe Lonnie pacing below out of the corner of my eye. A soft smile came over her face.

"Good luck, Honey, we're all pulling for you," she said, turning to tell the other grandparents in her row that I was in the balcony.

Fifteen bills remained before the bill would be called. I counted them on the bright yellow sheet that listed the day's bills on second and third reading. Grasping the sheet, my fingers followed them one by one.

Senator Garton stood, gavel in hand, listening to a debate on an amendment. Tediously the arguments dragged on, minute after minute, pro and con.

Voting continued and Senator Randolph walked back to his desk. The grandparents were interested in the bill being called. A low murmur went through the balcony. Senator Garton glanced upward as the debate on the floor raged once again around grandparents' rights. He gave a stern warning— no noise in the balcony.

Mr. Hoke gingerly came down the steep, narrow stairs that were in semi-darkness. "They haven't called it yet, have they?" he whispered, placing his big hand on my shoulder.

"Not yet," I said softly.

"I'm going to sit right behind you until they do," he said,

grabbing a chair laboriously for balance.

The dog law, House Bill 1218, was seven votes away. Senator Garton looked toward the other end of the podium. Lieutenant Governor O'Bannon walked toward him and the gavel was exchanged. They must take turns, I thought, surprised. The lieutenant governor called the next bill. There were no amendments. He gaveled down quickly, calling the next two bills. Three more bills—my heart pounded along with a shiver of nerves. Sitting rigid in the front row, my hand grasped the brass rail. O'Bannon gaveled the next bill down and almost immediately the next. Another few moments passed. The gavel came down on the third and final bill as the electric board in the front of the chamber flashed "Vicious Dog." "House Bill 1218," called the lieutenant governor. There was silence, both my hands wrapped around the rail, eyes darting, searching the chamber. The lieutenant governor momentarily hesitated before calling out, "Are their any amendments for House Bill 1218?" A dead silence followed, then the thud of a gavel as he moved on to the next bill. My hands continued to clench the rail as I searched for Senator Randolph who had vanished.

The grandparents broke into applause. I turned around, amazed. Mr. Hoke was standing, the heavy, jowled face beaming as the big body shook, nearly falling over the seats in front of him, clasping his hands together over his head.

I began climbing the narrow little steps, hearing short sentences from the grandparents. "Good for you, Honey."

"One more vote," another called. Mr. Hoke held out his hand as I reached him.

"I've got to go downstairs," were the only words I could say. He squeezed my arm.

"Pretty nice that fella leaves the room." Mr. Hoke's big smile went ear to ear. Heart still pounding—I reached the hall, then the long stairs. Elmer ran towards me, raincoat flapping, the state trooper and John Hammond on his heels. Elmer was screaming.

"HE LEFT! HE MISSED IT! HE MISSED IT!"

I blurted to the state trooper, *"It was that prayer!"*

"Yes, ma'am!" he said, incredulous, big-eyed, shaking his head.

"In all my years at the state house, Caress, I have never seen anybody miss a bill they were prepared to put an amendment on. He came out in the hall to talk to someone, walking real quick—must have thought he had more time," Elmer explained, gesturing wildly with his hands. "I turned my back so maybe he wouldn't notice me and watched O'Bannon through the window—he called that bill so fast—didn't want to turn around, just wanted him to keep talkin'. He must've thought he should hurry and go back in 'cause, watchin' through the corner of my eye, I saw him turn toward the door, then it was over! *HE MISSED IT—YESSSS!*"

The door to the Senate chamber swung open as Teresa bolted out of the chamber. The petite senator ran towards us, arms outstretched. "HE LEFT THE ROOM!" she yelled in the hall. "I watched him leave," she said excitedly, bouncing up and down. "Maybe he's going to the men's room, maybe I'll just sneak in there and throw the latch on that door," she laughed, throwing an imaginary latch with her hand.

"Well, you could make a believer out of me," Velda said, not sure what to think; the praying in the hall, Caress who seemed to have this belief, chosen for this task. She smiled, thinking of Senator Randolph, probably bored, figuring he had time to see this lobbyist, then missing, just missing his moment. A coincidence, but there were a lot of coincidences, she thought, briefly, happily, as the group held hands and jumped up and down like four year olds.

"When this is all over we should have a party," John said, beaming.

"We should be quiet. We don't want to embarrass him," said Teresa softly, looking around.

"Teresa, do you know who sent him out?" I asked,

knowing the answer. I heard my friend Sarah speaking quietly to me. "Caress, give Him the Glory."

"It was God, you know, Teresa."

"That's right," Elmer said, the state trooper nodding. "She was right down here praying in the hall with this trooper. I will never forget her praying with him," he said earnestly. Teresa understood, John Hammond heard and believed. Maybe Velda heard and perhaps she saw somewhere a purpose, a magnificent sense of timing, and a mission that had been made public.

Although it was mid-afternoon and few people happened to be in the hall off the Senate chamber, we were attracting attention with the hysteria and football huddles. "I have to go back in," Teresa said, and hurried off toward the doorway. Elmer smiled, looking around the hall as the state trooper walked a few feet back to his post. John Hammond waved as he took off down the hall. My friends had experienced the drama, intensity, and euphoria I had been living with these last months. The bill had been in jeopardy, yet once again was delivered back to us free from harm.

* * *

Velda sat with me in Paul's outer office. "Now, it's not gonna be any fun at all," she bemoaned, having escaped an amendment and conference committee.

"They have to actually vote on it now, and the governor does have to sign it," I reminded her.

"Aww, that's nothin'," she said, flicking her wrist.

"Bet me," I said with a touch of sarcasm.

Paul's voice came across the loud speaker as we became quiet. He was speaking on a bill dealing with gambling and riverboats.

"Democrats are gonna' ram that one down the governor's neck aren't they?" Velda said, turning towards Cathy who was listening from her desk.

Cathy smiled, resignedly adding, "It's sure looking that way."

"Gambling and the budget for the governor to worry with, he's not gonna' spend time doin' something unpopular like not signing your bill," Velda said with assuredness. "You know, you get this law, and the easy part will be here at the state house; the real challenge will be gettin' prosecutors to use it." Velda was talking out loud, thinking far beyond today.

"We're still working on getting it voted on," I said, wanting Velda to remain on guard and thinking about her plan B's.

"You're right, nothing is certain around here 'till it's signed with the ink dry. Only thing now is time," she acknowledged. "I think that's the biggest concern if it's not called for a vote and they run out of time. Teresa will have to ask that senator—you know the cigar smoker—"

"Meeks," I said.

"Yeah, Meeks—not to speak against the bill on the floor. It could still fail," she said solemnly before quickly changing the subject. "Caress' family leaves for Grenada tomorrow but she's gonna stay here for the bill. Hangin' on—leavin' Tuesday," she explained to Cathy.

"I hope they've voted by then," I said. "They should have. Usually it's the very next day after the vote on second reading. Today's Friday, Monday's a recess day—so, *Tuesday.*"

I had until Tuesday evening at 6:00 P.M.

"Tell Paul, Cathy—tell him everything," I asked because it was getting late.

"As soon as he makes it in here, he's going to hear the whole works," she said, waving good-bye.

Velda walked with me into the hall. "Caress, I was telling Joe that if something should happen to the bill I didn't think you could handle it." I was silent, I didn't know if I could handle it either—but every promise had been kept. Velda was worried about me. "Remember, anything is possible here," she warned.

"Will you go with them to the airport tomorrow?" she asked softly, trying to lift the weight of my thoughts.

"Oh, yes, early, very early, with half of Indianapolis trying to get on planes."

"Good ol' spring vacation," said Velda. "At least they're not going to Ft. Lauderdale and throw beer on each another while waiting for you to get there," she said, smiling sweetly. "I'll bet you never did that, did you?" she teased.

"I'll bet you're right," I said.

"I *knew* it," she said dryly.

* * *

The traffic was heavy as the whole world seemed to be traveling to the airport. I remembered other vacations with little boys snorkeling and playing in the waves. Happy times, idyllic family times. Today everyone in the car was quiet as we drove in and out of traffic, finally arriving on the airport ramp where travelers were checking suitcases. I stepped out of the car along with Benjamin and Matthew to wait on the curb. The skycap took the bags and tickets as Pat came around the side of the car, handing me the keys, kissing my cheek. "Good luck, Mama," he said.

"Will you come, Mom?" asked Benjamin.

"I'll come in a few days," I said, kissing him on the cheek, then Matthew and Pat. The three of them stood silently— nothing more to say. It was time for them to go. "Have a good time," I smiled, then waved good-bye, getting back in the car, swinging the bandaged leg inside, shutting the door.

I drove down the airport ramp and around on to the interstate, heading back home. It was the end of March and the weather was still somber, but there was no sadness. I would be with them soon. Feelings of joy and expectancy rose inside of me. There was no timetable for when these wondrous feelings would finally reach their climax, only that they would.

I was on the path once again, winding down by the creek, walking with the rustling summer leaves and warm breezes, anticipating whatever was coming. I remembered the calmness during the attack. The understanding, with Sarah's words, "You are to change the law." The team of experts that formed around me. The press corps that followed me daily. The doctor who was to hear the story, Jesse's baby, Brandon, the answer of how to serve little children. I felt uplifted and light, soaring along the asphalt—probably it was angel's wings, I thought, that carried me along in a rapture.

TWELVE

Time's Up

Monday was a recess day at the state house, so I remained at home alone in the house; only Boomer and Chuck would occasionally pad into the bedroom to check on me. The bandage around my foot kept coming apart at the heel because my chief wrapper was in Grenada. Most of Pat's white athletic socks had been ruined covering my foot. I struggled to find socks and wrap the bandage these last few days.

I wanted to make contact with my doctor before I left, but what I would say to reach him was, as always, a mystery. He was frustrating—too busy thinking about what he would say instead of listening. There was so much I wanted him to hear: Lonnie missing the vote, praying with the state trooper. "I'm not a good listener," he would say, never understanding why. Perhaps it was selfish on my part, wanting him to hear the whole story. I was, after all, just an instrument.

He had time to see me, but I never trusted the schedule because patients' names and appointments were lost with regularity. So, it was no real surprise when no one expected me when I arrived that afternoon.

His nurse told me to stay; he'd want to see me, and to wait on the porch. Shortly he appeared, puffing on a little cigar. The doctor was all ears today, anxious to know what was happening, as I gave him another political update. "Tomorrow, after the vote, I want to go and be with my family in Grenada." He nodded his head and looked down at the wrapped leg.

"How's the leg?"

"It's fine except when you get gum on your sock," I said, while he laughed.

"I want to know what happens."

"I'll let you know—no matter what." He wanted the law too, not only for me, but he had also begun to believe, sometime ago, that this might happen. For whatever reason in his life, this understanding was meant for good and perhaps, someday, to assure and comfort him.

I drove toward the north side of the city to pick up my airline tickets. This was preparation day. Tomorrow my attention, time, and strength would be focused at the state house. There were a little over twenty-four hours left before time would be up; my part in the race would be over. Had I run the good race, fought the good fight? Had everything been done?

The travel agency had closed for the day, but a note was stuck to the door. My tickets were at a nearby store, where the doctor's daughter also worked. People and timing— nothing surprised me anymore. "I'm here to pick up airline tickets," I said to her.

"Where are you going? Anyplace fun?" she asked.

"Grenada, tomorrow," I answered. "I've just been to see your father," I told her, speaking almost to myself. This daughter reminded me of the doctor, and I wondered if somehow what was happening to me and told to him would also touch her. Perhaps someday her life would be aided in a way I could never imagine, for it was no coincidence in my mind that she handed me the tickets.

An empty suitcase was waiting at home for me to quickly pack. A bathing suit; Pat would help me stand in the water. A flash of the long, tender red scar, the concave leg, went through my head. I would have to try to be myself. The bathing suit went in the suitcase. Dresses, long light beach cover ups, what shoes could I walk in? The floppy black shoes would barely stay on my feet, the other shoes were too stiff. It had been so long since I'd thought about shoes. Perhaps my soft, pink moccasins? They weren't in my shoe closet or in the other closets. I needed those shoes. They were really the only ones I had that were light and would stay on my foot.

The phone rang. "It's on third reading for tomorrow," Velda's voice said excitedly. "The list just came out. The afternoon session starts at 1:30—I thought it would be there." Velda was ecstatic. "I think we're gonna do it tomorrow!"

"I'll be there, you know I will," I said happily to her.

"What you been doin' on this recess day?" she asked.

"Well, I picked up my tickets, saw my doctor, now packing the bag." I could see Velda bouncing up and down in the chair, leg swinging.

"I'll bet you're ready to go lie on the beach."

The beach, it still seemed a new idea to me. "Has the family gone?" she asked.

"On Saturday," I answered.

"I'll bet they were sorry to leave you here chasing this law."

"Well, God willing, I'm going. I want to be able to remember Grenada with them, and Benjamin and Matthew are getting older. Probably not too many more trips together," I said softly.

"When does the plane leave tomorrow, Caress?"

"Ten minutes after seven," I answered with an innate sense of finality. "If for some reason I don't go, everything has to be canceled by six o'clock: the plane, the hotel in Miami. If I don't go tomorrow, there won't be enough time for me to try and go again—it's too far."

"Well, you're gonna' make it, we're the fifth bill listed." Velda said confidently.

"I'm ready," I told her.

"Ready for this to be over with, and *soon!*" she answered with a laugh.

"No, just ready, and, Velda, I know you don't understand, but this has been one of the most *wonderful* times."

"I hope it all ends tomorrow for you. It should," she said.

"*I'll* be there, Velda."

"Goodnight, Caress," she added gently before the phone clicked down.

The suitcase lay open on the floor; back to packing. What was I doing? The shoes—still needed the soft, lightweight shoes. I looked under the bed and in Pat's closet as my thoughts wandered. What was my family doing this Monday evening? Grenada was an hour ahead; probably at dinner—Matthew would have on his blazer.

I started down the front stairs to check a downstairs closet that held old outdoor shoes and boots. A funny sensation between my toes brought me to a stop. A feeling of wet, oozing warmth, the feel of blood filling a shoe. The moccasins were gone. I had them on the day of the attack. A flashback of kicking the shoe off—sitting on the curb and blood pouring onto the asphalt. There was a young man at my side on his knees. "I watched the whole thing from my apartment. I couldn't come 'cause they'd get me too." I was going down on the elevator and lying in the grass while he was asking me for forgiveness. I hadn't understood before that he had wanted my forgiveness. He had come as I lay in the grass, running back and forth to call Pat, of course he had my forgiveness.

I turned to go back up the stairs, the leg was stiff, unable to be very flexible. Harder-soled shoes would now have to go to the Caribbean.

The packed bag was heavy, hitting each stair step with a clump. I'd packed too much. Dragging the bag down the hall and outside, with a great heave I hoisted the suitcase into the trunk of the car. There might not be time tomorrow to come back home, so everything had to be ready. I placed the tickets carefully in my purse.

In the pantry there was enough dog food for Boomer and Chuck. Geneva would check on them and the house. I had done all I could do—everything was ready.

Boomer and Chuck slept by the bed all through the night, my protectors, or did they just think they were family and belonged there with me at bedtime? Both dogs followed me downstairs early Tuesday morning, tails wagging. "You're two of the good dogs, aren't you?" I asked them as Chuck cocked his head to one side as though not sure of his status. "You know I'm going away, but I'm leaving you both in charge." Boomer plodded toward the back door, it was time to go out. Shaggy black dog hair stood up around Chuck's neck while barely covering his four skinny legs. He was not handsome, but he had dog smarts. "You've got to believe you can be good, Chuck. No more harassing the U.P.S. man or binge barking."

At noon I made one last check of the house. The little Christmas tree still stood in the den with its tiny lights and satin red ribbons. After sparkling in the darkness throughout the winter months, it was unfair to put it away now, at the very end. The tiny lights would stay on until I came back home; then there would be closure to the little tree's work.

I drove the familiar route that ran by Fall Creek over to Capitol Avenue and past Methodist Hospital. Today the route reviewed the mission for me as the tires droned a quiet hum under a blue sky.

Our business was busy as I passed, but Pat, Benjamin, and Matthew were far away. The dome of the state house appeared and the rest of the building came into view. Parking lots were full as I turned the car onto Ohio Street, looking for a spot with the pay meters. Today I was lucky and a car pulled out as I turned the corner, parking in front of the legislators' lot.

Velda was waiting at the top of the stairs in front of Gene's desk. She had the bills listed for today's Senate session. "I've been workin' my coffee breaks this morning," she smiled gleefully as I took the last step. "Saw Teresa, told her you'd be here today in the gallery, watching her defend the bill. Thinks we're okay. She talked to Senator Meeks and he's not going to vote for us but he's not going to speak against the bill either, which is important."

I could imagine the petite Senator Lubbers standing, going one on one, with the massive Senator Meeks.

"Also a case of Mannweiler's bill that's helping to quiet him—that's my thought anyway," she said, impulsively grabbing my arm. "Caress, I've said it before, but it's so much fun getting legislation with you," she squealed, green eyes flashing wickedly. "Just won't be any good times when you're not paradin' around here. I saw your friend the doorman and told him they were gonna' vote on your bill today. He's so cute, said to me, 'You mean she's not gonna' be down here anymore?' Then he said," Velda mimicked Mr. Hoke's voice, " 'Well, I'm so glad for her.' "

My good friend, the sizable, gentle guardian of the Senate, Mr. Hoke—I would miss him. Almost as if not to jinx the day I answered, "I hope it passes," as we walked toward the Senate balcony. Nothing had come without a fight. I wasn't in the celebrating mood.

The ever-present tiredness was back along with a sensation of not having much strength in my legs. Mr. Hoke stretched out his big arms. "Well, is it really the day?" he asked.

"I hope it's the day," I smiled fondly at him as I listened to Senator Garton begin the Senate session through the doorway.

"We'll miss you down here. You've gotta come and visit before I retire," he said sincerely, big jowls slightly shaking, pulling the corners of his mouth down.

"You can't retire. No one would let me upstairs," I said, nodding toward the Senate offices.

"They'd let *you* in," he said softly.

"We'll all miss her," Velda said, glancing toward the Senate doorman then at me. "They've started inside, Caress," she cautioned, noticing I was looking toward the entrance, hearing the voices over the speaker. "They've got a few bills on second reading, then we're the fifth bill down for the final vote," she informed Mr. Hoke.

"I'll be listening," he said, bending over in a semi-bow. Velda slipped into the darkened gallery.

"We're gonna sit down right in front so they'll all know the hurt little lady is here."

"How many bills on second reading?" I asked, looking at the sheet held tightly in Velda's hand as we seated ourselves close to the railing.

"About twenty but they're already on number nine," she said, glancing down at the Senate schedule and then at her watch.

It was now quarter of two by the large clock on the south wall of the chamber that was placed not far from where we sat in the balcony. Senator Garton quickly gaveled down the next bill. There were not many days left for second readings. He had to hurry and move the bills on for the final vote. There was an amendment placed on the fourteenth bill—God rest it's soul, I thought. Ten more minutes had passed. Senator Garton waited momentarily for the possibility of amendments on each of the remaining bills. There were none. The gavel hit the podium one final time; second readings were finished.

Senator Garton looked grave standing behind the podium. The clock on the wall read 2:00; four bills and then it would be our turn. "We adjourn to caucus," he said simply, without emotion.

"Oh, brother," said a disgusted Velda. "It's that damn budget or the damn taxes the governor thinks he wants." Both Republicans and Democrats were filing out of the chamber, going to their respective chambers on each side where the strategy would be laid out for whatever reasons these pow-wows were being called. *"They'll* be back. They can't talk to each other forever," she said encouragingly.

"I just hope it's this afternoon," I sighed. Velda stood up and touched the brass railing, looking down at the now empty chamber. I remembered General MacArthur and his WW II promise of "I will return." All Velda needed was little round sunglasses and a general's hat covered with braid. She *would* return the missing senators to the chamber. I continued to sit, still surprised by the sudden caucus. Velda stood up and stretched her legs.

"Caress, I've just gotta go back to the office, lotsa briefs to go over for the judge."

"I know you do, don't feel like you have to stay with me—I'm all right," I said, finally standing.

"Will you come get me when they come out? You know I've just gotta be here."

"Sure I will," I said back to her, glancing over at the clock whose minute hand continued to move.

"You're welcome to come up and sit with me while I do some work," Velda said, trying to find a way the time would pass more easily.

"I think I'll keep watch down here," I answered.

"Really, it would be *fine.*" she added with a Cheshire cat grin.

Velda headed up the steep balcony stairs. I watched her turn the narrow corner and disappear. The balcony had emptied, the chamber was silent; where had everyone gone so quickly? It was amazing, I thought, looking up at the long window that allowed senators to glance into the chamber while passing into their Senate offices.

The two parties were taking their time caucusing to discuss their strategies and listen to their leaders. Now I stood alone looking down into the Senate chamber. The dog bill was not their mission or priority, it was mine. It was now 2:30 in the afternoon. Climbing the stairs and leaving the balcony, I wandered over to the House side. I could hear the

Speaker's voice coming over the microphone, booming out in the hall as I walked closer to peer in the windows. There were lobbyists in the hall making final pitches to legislators. Time was running out for them too as they pleaded their bills to important Democrats who had access to the Speaker.

A minister from northern Indiana was in the hall to lobby for gambling. He wore his cleric's collar, talking to everyone who would listen about jobs and casino boats. Politics did breed strange bedfellows.

Inside the House, Representative Kruzan was up walking around the chamber. He waved and smiled at me through the chamber window. It was true what Velda said about him; he *didn't* miss much. I remembered his words regarding the Speaker, had the dreaded amendment happened. "What if I would talk to the Speaker?"

"Politics will always come first with him, Caress. He would have listened, and could have said if you want the bill out of conference committee have Paul Mannweiler do this, and this, and this and I will release the bill." Then he added, "That's why Paul didn't want you to approach him, for fear you would be used. The Speaker could have also politely listened to you and after a short time shown you to the door, or," and he paused, "he could have been genuinely moved and had the bill released."

I chose to believe the large man with the jutting lips at the podium would have been moved, but I remembered, "Politics come first."

A lobbyist stood next to me looking at her watch, which reminded me that it was probably past time to check the parking meter outside. Now after 3:00 in the afternoon, I had earned the red lever meter violation. It had surely popped up, because my parking time had dissolved. Like Cinderella, I scooted down the hall, grabbed the banister, and hurried down the stairs.

I rounded the corner heading toward the outside door to the parking lot. "Where you goin' so fast?" asked my friend

Rick from the desk of the Capitol Police. "You didn't park that car on the street did you?" he said, questioning me.

"I'm always chicken to bring the car in here," I said half seriously.

"Well, you're going to park in the legislators' lot today," he said with certainty. "And as a guest of the Capitol Police. Now you just give me those keys, and you wait here 'cause I'm personally parking it right up in front." I dropped the keys in his hand and watched him walk out the doors, striding toward the car, pulling it in just as he promised, filling some unknown state senator's parking spot close to the entrance.

The policeman took two steps at a time climbing the outside steps and swinging open the door, handed me back my keys. "You know those senators have to vote on my bill today," I said, laughing. "I might have lost a vote."

"Naaw. They'll just find another spot and if they throw a fit I'll tell them I parked that car there for you."

"Thank you, Rick," I said, still a little worried about infuriating some senator with a vote. "Hopefully, they'll be voting this afternoon, if they ever quit caucusing." A shiver went through me having questioned out loud the senators' reappearance.

"Well, you can bet we're all pulling for you," he said, beaming the big smile.

The marble stairs stretched out in front of me up to the third floor as I rounded the corner. Each step had acquired a familiarity, having climbed them so often. The hall in front of the Senate was empty. The caucus was still in progress and mid-afternoon was slowly passing. Now there was nothing else to do but wait, sitting in the chair behind Velda. I poked my head around Velda's office panels to see briefs piled high on her desk as she busily typed away on the computer. "No stirring yet?" she asked, as if she had eyes in the back of her head.

"Not even a mouse," I answered, quietly sitting down.

"Frustratin' bunch aren't they?" she said.

"I just hope they come back soon," I replied, hoping out loud as if it would have some positive effect. Joe came out from the inner office, wire rim glasses fixed firmly behind his ears, working on one of the judge's cases.

"I heard it's today," he said with a grin.

"It'll be today," piped up Velda. "She's gotta plane to catch to Grenada."

"I'm glad you get to go, Caress," he said, shuffling an armful of papers in his hand.

"You don't have to stop and spend time with me," I said, looking at both Joe and Velda. "I know you're busy and the judge doesn't know I'm out here, so you both better get back to work or I'll get the look. You know—silence, glasses sliding down on the end of his nose, eyes boring a hole in my side."

"Yeah, that's it," smiled Joe, looking briefly behind him as he headed back towards his desk. "I'm thinking of you, Caress."

"You oughta keep checking the Senate," Velda warned, spinning back to the computer on the swivel chair.

"Oh, I will, in a few minutes."

A clock was hung over the door directly above the picture of Elvis on the office divider. The seconds moved by one after another, not quickly or slowly, only monotonously. My eyes rested on my purse and I impulsively pulled out the yellow sheets that listed the travel itinerary, plane dates, and hotel reservation in Miami. "Hotel must be cancelled by 6:00 P.M.," read the travel agency's instructions printed in bold, black letters at the bottom of the sheet with the Miami phone number. I had gone over the various complications of leaving with the travel agent who was trying to get me to Grenada. If the hotel was cancelled, it meant I wouldn't be taking the evening flight to Miami, and my connections to Grenada would be gone. I folded the sheets of paper back in my purse and checked the tickets again. The functional black-rimmed clock on the wall showed four o'clock in the afternoon. I stood up. "I'm going to check," I said simply as Velda watched me leave her cozy enclave.

Mr. Hoke was not out in the hall and few people walked outside the doors. Not a good sign, I figured as I headed for the balcony doors and walked down the narrow aisle. This all should have been over by now, I thought to myself as I sat back down in the same chair I had vacated just two hours earlier. Senator Landske sat down at a desk visible through the window built over the chamber. The Republicans must have finished their caucus and were waiting for the Democrats. Another senator hurriedly walked by—more movement.

The large wall clock showed the minutes ticking by, now close to ten after the hour. I had around one hour and fifty minutes before my time would be up. Go or stay, the final decision would have to be made soon. All the weeks and months were coming together as I waited in my chair, alone, in the Senate balcony. There was the promise, I said to myself, watching the seconds pass.

"You know I just couldn't let you come and sit here all by yourself," said Velda, who suddenly stood in the aisle to my side. "You know me and timing—looks like they're movin'," she said with a grin as the noise of a door below opened and a lone senator entered the chamber.

Slowly, one by one, as if drawn into the chamber by a giant magnet, the senators came through the door. "I wish we could see Teresa," I said as Velda peered over the edge.

"Her desk is just too far back under the balcony," said Velda, "but I know she's ready." I had the same feeling as Senator Garton entered.

"There's the one we need," said Velda, looking over at the dapper head of the Senate as he mounted the podium. A few onlookers entered the balcony. Senator Garton looked up into the gallery. "He sees you, Caress," whispered Velda.

The senator stood staring upward towards us from the podium, looking like he remembered "Mrs. Garton." Lowering his eyes, he watched over the chamber as senators continued to come in the door for a few interminable minutes. Finally, at quarter to five, the gavel pounded and Senator Robert Garton called the first bill on third reading. The bill involved money, and whenever money was being spent there was always debate in the conservative Indiana Senate. Debate was important, but today there wasn't time. Senator Borst, head of the Finance Committee and the only veterinarian in the state house, came to the podium.

"You know this is goin' to pass if he's speaking for it," Velda whispered. "Wouldn't have gotten this far without him. He'll speak on our bill, too. Anything that has to do with an animal, he'll take a stand. That's why I showed him our bill early on—so he can kind of take credit for it."

One speaker followed another—twenty minutes passed before the vote.

Another senator was ready to introduce the next bill. The clock was moving, now a little after five, as another debate began. Senator Hellmann, the minority leader, came to the podium. "He has to have his say on everything," fumed Velda under her breath.

A senator caught my eye. He was standing by his desk, holding several papers in one hand, his reading glasses far down on his nose. He looked up towards the balcony and waved. "Who's that?" whispered Velda.

"I think it's Senator Alexa," I said quietly, looking down at him, remembering his face from the memorized legislative handbook. He was a lawyer, a Democrat, from Valparaiso, Indiana.

"Do you know him?" she asked with amazement.

"No," I answered. "He's one of the senators I never met."

"He's *hittin'* on you," she exclaimed wide-eyed, sitting straight up.

"No, he's not," I told her as I gave him a friendly wave back.

"Yes, he *IS hittin'* on you," she repeated. The senator went back to reading his papers, still standing by his desk.

Senator Garton was calling for the vote. I glanced at the clock, five-thirty in the afternoon. Staring at the minute hand, a sudden stillness came over me; they would stop at six o'clock, it was something I knew. There was no official time for adjournment; the Senate could work until late in the evening, but as I watched the hour hand come closer to six, I understood when business would finish.

"Just two more," Velda squirmed, raising her shoulders and giving me a smile. Expressionless, I nodded at my good friend. Too much to comprehend, I thought. Senators came forward to introduce the third bill. Velda occasionally muttered, "He's right, but the man likes to hear himself talk." Pro and con, one speaker after another, as she would cross and recross her legs, pulling her sweater more closely around her, waiting, as the gavel pounded down, and the vote was recorded.

In fifteen minutes, it would be six o'clock, the Senate wasn't going to vote on the bill—not today. There was a sereneness about me, no disappointment, only uncertainty as to what I was to do next. Velda was excited, "We're next," she whispered as the debate for the fourth bill had begun.

Below the balcony, Teresa Lubbers was quickly writing a note as she tapped Potch Wheeler's chair. Senator Harold H. "Potch" Wheeler was busy at his desk as the majority caucus chairman. The note was addressed to Senator Garton and Potch glanced at it before handing it up the aisle. Senator Garton was to know Mrs. Garten was in the balcony, so Teresa placed a request to call the bill today. She was uneasy and nervous waiting.

The clock's minute hand inched closer to six, and almost on cue the vote was called for and flashing lights appeared on the electronic tally board. So strange to sit and know what was going to happen and feel no emotion.

Senator Garton leaned into the microphone. "I think this is a good time to stop, and we'll adjourn the Senate until tomorrow morning," he said, as the gavel went down and he stepped off the podium.

"*They can't do that!*" Velda spit out the words of surprise and shock. She was sitting on the edge of her seat. "They can't do that," she repeated again to me, still unbelieving. Teresa Lubbers was leaping to her feet, wanting to catch the eye of Senator Garton, but it was too late, the Senate day had ended.

He never received her note. It had been noticed, then mislaid on a senator's desk while traveling to the front of the chamber.

"They can do it," I said calmly to her, remaining motionless.

"I just *can't* believe it," she continued to say. There were no words for me to tell her I had known what would happen. The chamber was quickly emptying, and we were soon going to be alone again in the Indiana Senate.

Velda was stunned; she hadn't counted on this. I was like a sailboat far out on the lake without a breeze as my thoughts drifted; ambivalent, turning without direction. Standing up in the balcony, it was time to go, but go where?

"Do you want to go back to the office with me?" asked Velda.

"I have to go with you anyway—that's where my purse is—remember?"

"Well, I'd want you purse or no purse," smiled Velda, regaining some composure. We walked into the hall; even the ivory tower seemed quiet. Past six o'clock. The nine to five employees who worked in the state house had gone home.

The judge's chambers were silent. Joe and the other law clerk were gone for the day along with the judge. "When should you go?" asked Velda solemnly.

"Now," I said, it was almost twenty minutes past six. I sat still in the wooden chair whose back rested against the century-old wall. Reaching down towards my purse, I again pulled the travel itinerary out and my eye caught the bold black sentence, "Hotel reservations must be canceled by six o'clock."

"Could I use your phone, Velda? There's someone I have to call."

"You know you can and right now," she said quickly, wanting somehow to make it all better. Perhaps there was one mortal who might help me now. Sarah, whom I had told last summer that something was coming, because everything seemed incomplete. She had told me while my eyes were closed in a hospital bed, "You're to change the law." Sarah had given me the perfect direction and immediate relief.

I dialed the number. She picked up the phone as I knew she would. "Hello," answered the pleasant voice who had no reason to expect anything but an ordinary phone call. I wanted her to provide direction from the Almighty.

"Sarah, I need your advice," I said quickly. "They were going to vote on the bill today in the Senate but adjourned right before they got to it. Now, I don't know what to do, or what I should do. Pat, Benjamin, Matthew expect me to come, and if I don't get on that plane within the hour I'll miss going to be with them—I'll break my promise," I mumbled. "I feel I have to go."

"Caress, you're the one who has moved that bill. Your presence has moved that bill," she said simply.

"I know—but it seems as if I'm out of time, as if time's up."

"They would understand if you didn't come," Sarah said softly, assuredly.

"I promised them, that's all I can say to you, Sarah, except I feel you are the only living soul who would understand this anguish."

"I do understand, for this is something that is going to save lives and you were given this task. Well," she paused, "let's pray for a minute if you feel you must go."

Sarah began one of her rich and beautiful prayers as Velda stood behind the swivel chair. Velda, who would not understand the conversation but so deeply felt the emotion. Sarah was praying flowing, gentle words about guidance and watching over us, but I started to hear a buzzing sound in my head. The concentration was gone; Sarah was praying for both of us. As the buzz continued, a picture of an operating room with a heart monitor's line gone flat appeared in my thoughts. "In your Son's name we ask this Father, Amen." Sarah had finished.

"I'll call you later, Sarah, from either Atlanta or Miami. Thank you," I said tenderly.

"Take care, Caress."

I stood up from the swivel chair and looked at Velda. "I'm going to go," I said to her.

"Well, wait just a minute." She disappeared around the outside panels and immediately reappeared.

"This is for you on the beach," she said, placing a bottle of liquid moisturizer in my hand while giving me a hug. "Just keep squirting this stuff all over your face," she told me as I took the bottle and hugged her back.

"I love you, Velda." There was no time now.

"I love you too, Caress," she told me as I hurried alone around the panels, over the dark green carpeting, and out into the hall, grasping the bottle of some elixir called Nu Skin in one hand and the flimsy yellow sheets with the itinerary in the other.

The state house was golden and warm but very still, emptied of life like the loveliest palace whose ball had ended. Cinderella had now stayed too long. Down, down the marble steps, gingerly stepping with the bandaged leg, descending from the ivory tower, making the turn on the third floor. Sarah had not given me the answer. I grasped the wooden railing rounding the massive balustrade, and passed through the doors to the outside.

The day was still beautiful, although it was past six-thirty in the evening—close to the last day of March. A breeze ruffled the tissue-thin sheets of the travel itinerary still grasped in my hand as I hesitated, ambivalently looking down at the bright yellow papers while standing by the car door. Sarah had her opinion, but she couldn't tell me with certainty to go or stay. Was this what I was to do—leave? Was this what I was to do—someone who felt this calling so deeply? There was no time—go or stay?

"I'm sorry we didn't get to your bill today," came a voice from behind, startling me. I hadn't noticed anyone in the parking lot. Senator Alexa, who had waved to me earlier from the Senate floor, came closer and stood beside me. "I thought we would," he said with a slight smile. "That's why I was waving at you. It just missed the time."

"I don't know what to do," I said, slightly lifting the papers in my hand. "I have a half an hour before the plane leaves to be with my family—I don't know whether I should go ..." The words trailed off to a silence.

"*You must leave,*" he said immediately, and then more adamantly, "I *insist* that you leave. I will go to the podium tomorrow and tell them I insisted that you leave." The senator paused and quietly but firmly began again, "I've seen you in the halls, week after week, month after month. I've watched you and now it's time for you to go."

"I won't know how it ends," I said sadly, anxiously, back to him.

"I will call you," he said. I slowly shook my head, looking down at the papers in my hand.

"I'll be too far away." The senator I had never met answered with absolute assuredness:

"I will call you *anywhere* in the world."

I ripped the travel itinerary in two, handing Senator Alexa the bottom half with the hotel's phone number in Grenada. "Now you must go," he said again, opening the car door then shutting it behind me. I started the engine and began backing up the car. My eyes were fixed on the state senator who held the torn yellow paper in his hand. "I will call you," he said again, reading my mind. Senator Alexa watched the car leave, his eyes intensely bidding me on my way from the state house.

The car raced up the interstate ramp heading toward the airport. Well, if I don't make the plane, it just wasn't meant to be, I thought as the digital car clock showed about twenty-five minutes before the plane was to be in the air; it would be close. I saw the car phone and called Sarah. "There's your answer," she said immediately to me, hearing the story of Senator Alexa in the parking lot.

She was right, I was to leave, the state senator had been placed there for me. I wove in and out of traffic. The sign appeared for the airport expressway, and I veered off the highway heading for the terminal; there was only ten minutes.

I entered the gate for the parking garage, pulled into a spot, yanked the suitcase from the trunk, and hobbled, half falling across the street. I positioned a set of electric curlers under my arm. They had been thrown into the trunk at the last minute this morning. A solitary wheelchair stood outside the doors; I heaved the suitcase on the seat as the terminal doors slid open. Shoving the wheelchair inside, I looked for the gate. Half running, pushing the wheelchair, I passed quickly through security.

An airline representative stood at the gate. There were no passengers waiting; everyone had boarded the plane. "I know who you are, and I guess we just couldn't leave without you," she smiled. "How are you doing on that leg?" she asked.

"Well, I ran through the airport," I laughed.

"It's a good thing you did because another minute and I would have been gone," she said as I picked up the boxy curler set with its long electric cord trailing behind me, finding the aisle seat that was waiting for me.

Thousands of feet high in the night sky I flew away. Higher than the hawk or eagle, higher than the great blue heron, as lights appeared below and the man-made bird sailed up and down with the currents of wind.

We landed in Atlanta, and inside the busy airport a smiling

young black woman behind a cash register in a newspaper shop offered me a paper bag with handles. "This is for the electric curlers—you really want to carry those around?"

I hadn't thought about the curlers; too many emotions going on to worry about a trailing electric cord. Strangers seemed to notice and look out for me.

Two hours later a second plane landed in Miami where it was close to midnight. This time the bag had been checked and I waited to grab it off the conveyer belt. It was still just as heavy as I remembered it back home in Indiana. Although there was a room waiting for me in the airport hotel, there were no handy little carts left or anyone else around. I dragged the bag to the elevator, fell inside, and rode up to the main lobby of the terminal.

The lights were turned off and bodies littered the darkened floor. With both the homeless and stranded passengers, the terminal was filled with sleeping people rolled up in old blankets and newspapers. I pulled the bag slowly alongside the wall. Someone cried out in Spanish while I hoped not to step on the wrong person. Turning a corner, I saw a light down the hall and a working people mover. My arms were exhausted and limp as the rubberized sidewalk took me towards a distant corridor where a sign pointed to the airport hotel.

With one last heave I pulled the bag around a bend and felt perspiration break out on my forehead. Only the presence of a bellman who hurried to help kept me from sitting down on the airport floor. The hotel room was still there and waiting, and in a few minutes more I opened the door.

The little room was a harbor in the night as I sat down on the bed and picked up the television channel selector. A comedian was going through his routine on the "Comedy Club." "Do you know what a pit bull thinks curled up by your feet? He's thinkin'— I'm gonna kill you." One pit bull joke followed another, and whether it was exhaustion or relief having finally made it to the room, he made me laugh.

* * *

The plane rolled down the runway and the door opened into the midday Caribbean sunshine and heat. The old taxi rattled over the green hills of Grenada as the turns in the road revealed glimpses of the glittering Caribbean. The driver turned down a long private lane that wove around to the hotel. Two more quick turns and there was Pat walking toward an open loggia covered with startling hues of pink frangipani.

I unrolled the window as the cab came to a stop. "Hello, sailor," I said to Pat as he broke into a big smile.

"I've been watching for you. I'd about given up thinking you'd be able to get here," he said, holding my hand as I stepped from the car, placing my head next to his chest. "We missed you," he said simply as we walked through the loggia. "What happened with the bill?" he asked.

"They haven't voted on it yet. A senator is going to call me when they do," I told him briefly as the memory and anxiety immediately came back. "Where are Benjamin and Matthew?"

"They're at the pool," he said, guiding me around a little path past a broad, green yard that rolled out like a carpet towards bright, blue waves. Up some concrete steps, and there was Benjamin lying flat down on his stomach by the pool while his brother splashed around. Benjamin lifted his head up.

"We've had an injury," Pat told me. There were sutures holding a bad cut together over Ben's right eye. "He went climbing on some rocks by the ocean," Pat explained. "I thought he was getting dressed for dinner."

Ben smiled. "You wouldn't believe what they call a hospital here," he said. "There was a guy injured with half his foot gone who tried to break the door down while this doctor stitched me up. The doctor stops, shoves him back, then slams the door."

"It was what you call an experience," Pat said. I wondered if Ben would have gone for his rock climbing adventure if I had been there to watch. Perhaps it wouldn't have happened, I thought, while Matthew told me the waves weren't up to his standards on the beach.

"Did your bill pass?" Ben asked.

"Not yet," I told him, watching his brother at the other end of the pool. With a splash he came from under the water.

"Can you come in?"

"I've got to get my bathing suit on first."

Pat walked with me down a winding path by a patio where a waiter poured tea and passed little sandwiches and pastries. "Ben and Matt have been enjoying tea-time daily," he told me with a smile. "It's like the ugly Americans take tea. They call each other 'old boy' and say 'bloody' but the waiters all like them, so they haven't been too obnoxious."

Our cottage was connected by a loggia, covered in pink bougainvillea, to where both boys stayed together in an adjoining room. A small sitting room, enclosed by screens, looked across the yard to the sea. White wicker furniture filled the little room that led to the bedroom and bath. "You go back," I said to Pat. "I'll be there in a few minutes."

"Will you be all right?" he asked. I knew he was thinking of my leg.

"I'll be all right," I promised.

A long mirror in the bathroom reflected someone new, in her bathing suit, whose legs definitely did not match. The concave leg's ugly red scar was glaring. I hadn't walked around people before without the bandage. There's an awkward, sad feeling when you look different from other people. It was something I hadn't had time to think about, and now it was time to parade around a swimming pool. My children expected normalcy. There could be no self-centeredness.

I remembered the purpose behind the leg as I walked into the bedroom and looked around the room. There was a phone by the bed. Could I call the United States from the room? I bent down looking for a phone book, but instead on the open bottom shelf was a book with two words on the cover, *Gideon Bible.* Gideon, the one who needed assurance and more assurance. It didn't look as if anyone had ever touched this Bible. I had never made the connection between the famous bibles placed in hotels across the world and my learning Gideon's story.

Placing it gently on my lap I opened the Bible randomly to the book of Joshua. "I will be with you. I will not leave you nor forsake you. Be strong and of good courage." The only words I had read: assurance and more assurance. I took the Bible onto the little porch, placed it on the table still opened and walked out into the bright afternoon light.

Ladies in linen dresses were taking tea as I walked past the patio. I looked straight ahead trying not to think about my different-looking leg as I wrapped a beach cover up around my waist.

It was mid-afternoon in Indianapolis. The Senate session would be underway, and the vicious dog bill had been next on the third reading. Perhaps there had been a call or a message for me. As I walked through the flower-scented loggia to the open air room that was the business office, a receptionist greeted me with a broad smile. "No, ma'am, there were no calls," she told me in a light sing-song voice, heard in the Caribbean.

"If one does come, please try and find me immediately or place a call through to the room no matter what time."

"Yes, ma'am," came the reply. Perhaps it was intuition, but it didn't surprise me there hadn't been a call. The incessant worry momentarily increased.

Time to go swimming. The words "Have courage for I will not forsake you," remained with me.

Matthew and Pat were in the water as I came up the stairs that led to the pool. Ben was dangling his feet in the shallow end. They were waiting for me. There was an English family leaving, so now there was no one to stare at my different leg except my own children. I could handle them, I thought.

"Now let me get my hair wet," I begged them as I always had to work myself slowly into the water. Those were my last words as I was dragged under, followed by a fierce water fight. The Ugly Americans were now in the pool, screaming and laughing. The leg didn't like the water nor the other legs that brushed up against the long scar during the water fight. I was happy, though, to be with them and in the sunshine.

I caught my breath, refusing to be dunked again and dove to the bottom of the pool to swim like a shark with Matthew. An hour later I sat by the edge of the water—it was late afternoon at the state house. I twisted uncomfortably as the pressure and anxiety of not knowing mounted. What possibly was going on? Had they voted? Momentarily, I had a sense of the Senate chamber, voices droning over the room. I felt my lack of presence in the chamber, yet I had been sent away.

Everyone was now out of the pool. "It's about time for Clyde and Neville to hit tea," Pat said as we readied to leave. A young waiter grinned as the two boys approached. He was about their age, slender, standing in his white jacket. "They get along great with the waiter, he plays snooker with them in one of the back rooms. I'm so glad you're here. We missed you, I missed you," he said, taking my hand.

"Well, I'm in the right place," I told him as we entered the flower-draped cottage. I looked at myself again in the long mirror. "It looks bad doesn't it?" Pat paused at first.

"I'm real proud of you," he then answered softly. "Give it time." I looked at the phone as he went into the little sitting room. You could make a direct international call from the room I read on the dialing instruction sheet under the phone. It was almost five o'clock in Indianapolis, and the weight of not knowing anything was terrible. I dialed the number for the United States then the area code then Velda's number at the state house. The phone was ringing then picked up almost immediately.

"Velda—it's me."

"Where are you?" she said surprised.

"In Grenada."

"You sound like you're in the office next door."

"Velda, the bill."

"There was no movement today, Caress; the bill was listed but they didn't go in order. Senators kept asking for their bills to be moved forward."

A sick feeling spread over me. There were only seven working days left in the 108th Indiana General Assembly. I wasn't there to remind anyone.

"You having a good time?" she asked cheerfully. "Using that Nu Skin all over? How's the weather?"

"Yes, not yet, and fine," I answered her. "But—Velda?"

"I know, you're worried," she answered. "What's your number there?" Rattling off the string of numbers, I thought of Senator Alexa and hoped he wouldn't forget me.

"I saw Teresa scooting down the hall … no time to talk to her though." Velda hesitated, "Say, you're supposed to have a good time, not think 'bout this—phone call must cost a fortune," she clucked, "all that way."

"I'm calling again tomorrow," I told her. "Velda, I have to know."

"I'll call you anything happens," she answered.

Velda didn't know about Senator Alexa or that Gideon had been in the little cottage in Grenada. She understood the flow and patterns of politics, not the other sense of timing that I acknowledged.

Outside, overhead, a large black frigate circled high in the blue sky with eyes so sharp the bird could see dinner swimming in the light blue water. The frigate floated in the currents of air with wings designed in perfect, sharp angles. Drawing those wings to his side, he pierced the air, falling like an arrow, finding his mark in the water. What was hidden to human eyes was clear to the frigate. So sure and accepting, he plunged into the deep Caribbean Sea.

I, too, was now in deep water, going deeper, waiting for the moment to be propelled to the surface. I had been given promises and assurances; now I was asked to wait. The human pull continued between trust and the ugly gnaw of worry. If angels do battle for us, I needed them with me because there was such exhaustion no words were forming to pray anymore.

In a crisis we are always closest to God and Sarah's words repeated in my thoughts, "He hasn't brought you this far to let you down now."

* * *

March ended and the new month of April began with sunshine in Grenada. "Do you think they'll vote on the bill today?" were my first words to Pat.

"Today's the day," he said with confidence. Pat never made statements like that about things he didn't know for a fact. He was the engineer, the scientist, but this morning he seemed certain. "I thought we might go fishing this morning," he said, looking through a small section of advertisements in the phone book. "Benjamin and Matthew want to go." Pat was trying to keep me busy. "Fishing with *Rambo,*" he said half smiling. The motorized rowboat came to take us away.

"You're kiddin', Dad," the two boys said together.

"He'll know just the right spots," Pat assured us. I liked being out in the little rowboat close to the water where flying fish raced in front of us, sailing on tiny wings. Pulling with ancient fishing rods and using chopped-up fish resting in a tin bucket, a thrashing barracuda was hauled into the boat. Rambo flashed a big, toothy grin and the morning passed in fishing heaven.

Into the afternoon my anglers casted until the words "fishing no good now," were solemnly announced.

I knew the state house was busy. "Don't worry," I prayed while the wobbling outboard motor sped us back to the hotel. Into the waist deep water we splashed, feet hitting the sandy bottom, moving slowly to shore. On the beach my leg sank into the wet sand. Pat's arm steadied me as the waves rolled in around our ankles. A man was coming down the beach close to the water. He stared at the jagged red scar and leg. As I glanced over at him he looked away, walking on past. "He just likes to look at good-lookin' 'wimmen,'" Pat told me.

At the far end of the beach two dogs played in the waves and came closer. "They don't bother me," I told him, sensing his apprehension as we both noticed the dogs at the same time. "You know my dog business happened for a reason. It's just the waiting now, the not knowing," I told him as we walked back toward the little flower-covered cottage.

* * *

Velda had arrived at the state house early; she was worried. The bill was still on the schedule for third readings but it was being shoved behind other bills. The senators were fighting over the budget, and there were rumors of a special session. She had gone over the senators in her mind, votes for, votes against. Teresa thought the vote might come today if the caucus time was kept to a minimum. Velda worried about time—which was rapidly evaporating.

She found herself in an unusual situation—she was nervous. Had she planned well enough? Senator Morrie Doll, the balancing Democrat, whom Paul had drafted to help sponsor, defend, and guide the bill, was excused from the session today. "Why today?" Velda muttered under her breath, rocking back and forth in the rolling swivel chair. Part of Plan A was gone with his absence. "Damn," she uttered. Velda's Plan B had her friend and legislator, Luke Kenley, defending the legal aspects of the bill. Luke had gone to Harvard Law and was totally capable, but he wasn't a Democrat like Senator Doll. Would it make a difference?

she wondered, for you never knew. She had stopped Teresa in the hall saying, "I'm not calling Caress, telling her this didn't work."

Velda remembered the last week and Caress whose long silences, exhaustion, and anxiety worried her. She had told her it could be killed, even now. We both believe this is gonna' work, she said to herself. Caress feels God's got it planned, and if anyone in Indiana was perfect to be bitten and come down here, it was her.

Glancing at the tacked up animal calendars on the office partitions, she whispered, "I hope God remembers Indiana is full of good old boys."

Johnny Nugent, a senator from rural Lawrenceburg, had told her, "I'm just an old country boy and won't be voting for the bill." Senator Nugent had his own business selling tractors in Indiana's heartland. "Everybody knows in the country dogs roam free anyway."

Velda remembered the dog pack and the little girl dying on the rural Paoli, Indiana, road.

"Where's my friend?" asked Mr. Hoke outside in the hall as the Senate's session began.

"She's in Grenada," Velda told the Senate doorman.

"Where?" he asked as the big frame quivered like jello for a moment.

"You know, where we fought the war," she explained. "Didn't want to go—had to though, for her family. She's real worried 'bout the law—what's happenin'— not being here while they vote."

"It's gotta pass. They wouldn't think of not passing that bill," Mr. Hoke said, his voice lowered with concern.

"Well, neither Teresa nor I want to be calling her if they don't," she said as the good Senate doorman worried about his friend.

* * *

The little cottage in Grenada had been made ready for our return with fresh flowers in the vases. The Bible still remained opened on the table. I touched the words on the page for assurance and looked at the phone. The little red light that signaled a message was dark. The ending of another day as I remembered Pat's words this morning, "This is the day." In the bedroom I dialed the numbers to reach Velda. The rings began immediately and continued one after another—no one answered the phone. Odd, she should have been there because it was only four in the afternoon. None of the law clerks picked the phone up in the judge's chambers. I dialed Teresa's Senate number where Valerie answered the phone. "Valerie, it's Caress, is Teresa there?"

"They're in session, Caress; are you where I think you are?" she asked.

"I think I probably am, Valerie. Do you know about the bill?"

"I don't think there's been any movement, Caress, but I don't know what's going on down there now. Is it beautiful in Grenada?" she asked pleasantly.

"Oh, yes, beautiful," I responded, half listening. My thinking started to take on the quality of a poor phone connection, momentarily clear then distant, disconnected.

"I'll tell Teresa you called and want to know about the progress of a vote," she told me.

"Tell her I need to know what's going on," I said.

"I will, Caress, I'll place this right on her desk." The voice came through with secretarial efficiency. "Now you have a good time," she said soothingly into the phone.

Velda was correct. I won't be able to handle it if it doesn't pass. Why hadn't she answered her phone? It was so unlike her not to be right at that desk or to have a law clerk answer. Maybe they were afraid to tell me bad news over the phone, I thought negatively. No, that couldn't be—wouldn't be— they were all busy finishing the race for me. I could no longer see the runners but felt the urgency of their finishing.

The pit in my stomach grew as I ran water for a bath. My preoccupation was becoming all-consuming.

* * *

Velda had watched the debates on the floor as she sat in the Senate gallery. Back and forth she traveled from the judge's chambers, constantly checking on the bill still listed for third reading on the daily Senate agenda. The afternoon dragged on as both parties caucused then contentiously debated. The judge himself was preoccupied with work, but after twenty years of working with Velda, he had a familial sense when something, although he never asked what, was so important to her she had to know what was going on. He had noticed the twitching leg at her desk and the hurried walk as she passed the outside door to his chambers. Whatever this was, it had her nervous, concerned. He hoped it ended soon.

Velda watched the clock move in the Senate chamber while the same senators had to get their two cents in on everything. On the House side they would heckle you for continuing to come to the podium and blab, Velda thought disgustedly as one speaker rose after another. Senator Garton would *never* allow heckling, she affirmed with a smile. He announced they would recess for the afternoon but return for an evening session. The senator noted the 108th Indiana General Assembly was running out of time. "No kidding," she echoed worriedly.

She walked past Mr. Hoke in the hall and shrugged her shoulders. "Nothing yet," she said to him, shaking her head and sighing as she treaded the well-worn path back to her desk.

"Well, by God," Velda said out loud as she headed toward the court of appeals, *"I'm not going home 'till they vote on that bill."*

The office was empty; the clerks had left early. The judge walked slowly around his office, hands in his pockets. He was not driving home to northern Indiana tonight. He had decided to spend the night in his office curled up on the hideaway bed folded away in the tall cabinet next to the hanging deer horns.

The judge noticed Velda had returned and was walking toward his office. He guessed she wasn't leaving the state house for home either. "Want to go eat dinner?" she asked him, eyes avoiding the animal heads around the room.

The Greek Islands restaurant was close and filled with hungry legislators. "I'm glad they don't serve ouzo 'cause it tastes just like battery acid," she cheerfully told the judge as they waited at their table.

"Following a bill tonight?" the judge responded dryly.

"Yep," she acknowledged, "and tonight *better* be the night," she added.

"I can't pronounce most of the things on the menu," he said, smiling.

"I always have the same thing and I know how to pronounce it," she said, smiling beguilingly.

"Oh, you do?" he said to her.

"Yes, I do," she said, smugly enjoying the sibling-like snarling. The waiter appeared.

"I'll have the Spanakotiropita," she said quickly, syllables rolling off her tongue before momentarily pausing. "And he'll have the Greek potatoes and beer."

* * *

The tree frogs had begun to sing in Grenada; it was the Caribbean's serenade into evening. Benjamin and Matthew had appeared from their room, wearing their navy blue blazers and khaki pants. It was time for dinner, six-thirty in Grenada, five-thirty at the state house. Velda's phone rang again and again—no answer. She must have left for the day, I thought as we went out the door.

The judge and Velda walked back into the state house together after dinner. The main floor was busy even though it was approaching seven in the evening. They entered the elevator filled with legislators as the brass doors closed. "We're gonna pass some bills tonight," laughed a senator as the little elevator jolted up to the third floor. The legislators were in a good mood, Velda thought, having had their dinner and, yes, they had better pass some bills tonight. She was pleased with the energy she felt.

Senator William Alexa entered the Senate chamber and walked to his desk; the ragged piece of travel itinerary was safely placed in his coat pocket. He was anxious now to have this vote and to make the call to Grenada. Surely it would pass, but you never knew until the lights went on the board. If there was a problem, he would go to the podium and give it his best shot. He would do that for her as he had promised in the parking lot. She had looked lost two days ago, worried and torn—her family or what she felt so compelled to see completed. He imagined the worries that followed her into the Caribbean.

There were some Democrats against the bill, but there had been no party move to kill the legislation. The senator looked through the bills to be voted on this evening. Piles of legislation were stacked on his desk. How many would they pass? There were bills that died at the end of the session because they were never called; too many other issues pushed them to the end of the line. On the last session day at midnight it was over, the uncalled bills were dead, vanishing like hot embers drowned in ice water. He wanted it over for her; she was counting on him.

Velda had returned with the judge to his chambers. The old high-ceilinged office could actually be made to look quite homey as a table lamp spread its light on the early American sofa and well-worn coffee table. The judge had reading to do that evening. Opening the tall cabinet, he unfolded the narrow bed as Velda popped her head in. "I'll see you later," she said, grimacing at the thought of his sleeping under animal heads gazing off into space around the room. She left the lights on in the outer office and closed the door to the hallway, protecting the judge from anyone who might not belong, and walked quickly toward the Senate balcony.

The upstairs hall was empty outside the Senate balcony. Mr. Hoke had retired for the evening. "Don't expect too many in the peanut gallery tonight," she whispered to herself as she opened the heavy doors. Velda worked her way down the steep stairs to the brass railing, sitting down in the first row. Senator Garton had promptly begun the evening session and the chamber was already voting on the first piece of legislation. Senators sauntered back and forth to the podium. "Some of this we could do without," she muttered.

She thought about the dogs at home and the five kitties. If Joe hadn't fed them by now, they would be giving him no peace. Mozart, her sassy cat, would have batted his little dish into the kitchen, and the dogs would be panting behind Joe and stepping on his heels. This bill would make her forever more careful of the dogs around children.

"The real work is getting prosecutors to use it after we pass this bill," she had confidently told Caress. Now she just hoped it would pass. She thought it might help to pray but didn't believe anyone was really listening. An image of the little boy in Florida, the picture Caress had trouble looking at, returned to her mind. A baseball cap covered the parts of his head where hair no longer grew, thick scars ran down the left side of his face, part of the nose was gone, and wisps of light hair appeared where an ear had been. The little boy had one eyebrow gone with only a jagged scar that pulled at his left eye. Terrible scars covered his neck. The results of a child in the jaws of a pit bull.

The first time she had seen Caress had been in a newspaper picture. I wonder what she looks like now? had been her thoughts. Caress believed she had been spared the facial disfigurement so people could look at her as she told her story at the state house and through the press. That was a point—she would never have been as effective if people were uncomfortable talking to her. Maybe there was a plan. She mulled the thought over for a minute, waiting for the next bill to be called.

* * *

I had not reminded Pat of the words he had spoken this morning, "Today's the day." I was mentally drifting, even though at dinner everyone laughed and we wondered how barracuda tasted. Pat smiled at me across the table while people talked as I did with those they loved. I wanted to be cheerful while the weight of a concrete block settled in my chest.

"What time is it in Indianapolis?" I asked some time later back in the room. Pat picked up his watch from the dresser where it lay conveniently forgotten for a week.

"It's seven-thirty," he said. "Eight-thirty here," he told me, sitting down, returning to his book.

I left him for the phone in the bedroom, dialing a string of numbers to Velda's home.

"We can't come to the phone right now," chirped the familiar voice. "Please leave a message and we'll call you back just as soon as we can." The obnoxious beep for a message started.

"Velda, if you're there—and alive—it's Caress. Call me." My purse had a crumpled piece of paper with Teresa Lubbers' home phone number.

Another answering machine with one of her little girl's politely phrasing, "You have reached the Lubbers' residence. We can't come to the phone ..." Perhaps Teresa was at the state house or was she just too busy with her children to answer?

The phone in Velda's empty office at the state house would be quiet, alone in a dark room. Out of nervous frustration I called the number—just to hear it ring. "Hello," answered a male voice on the other end of the line.

"Judge, it's Caress," I said, surprising myself by speaking to him in the familiar tone of two people who knew very well who the other was but who had never spoken.

"Hello, Caress," he said quietly to the woman who had tried to avoid his displeasure for months. I had never heard his voice before. My hand began to squeeze the receiver.

"The judicial and the legislative bodies must remain separate," Velda had preached, but I had to know what was happening. "Judge, I need to speak with Velda."

"I think she's down listening to the legislature, Caress," he answered as if I was someone he had always known.

"Judge, you know I'm sorry to bother you," I stammered. "Velda told me sometimes you spend the night up there, and right now I'm a very long way away in Grenada, so I can't just come down."

The judge was quiet, listening. Velda would not have mentioned anything about me. He would only know what he read in the papers.

"I wonder if I might call back later?" I asked as if it were midnight instead of eight-thirty in the evening. The judge had to figure it was important and about the legislation. Velda wasn't down at the state house this late at night without a good reason.

"Sure, that would be fine," he said calmly, sounding like one of his law clerks. I said good-bye.

They were burning the midnight oil at the state house. Velda was still there, so was Teresa, they must expect the vote tonight. My heart started to pound.

* * *

Senator Lubbers sat at her desk in the Senate chamber and listened to the speakers as they came to the podium. She did expect the vote to come tonight. She went over in her mind what she would say when the bill was called. The waiting made her nervous, but she had prepared and hopefully the vote would be positive. Valerie had passed on the message that Caress had called from the Caribbean. She didn't want to think about the bill not passing for Caress' sake and also for her sake. This was the first piece of legislation her name would be remembered with—one she would never forget.

She glanced to her left where Senator Meeks was sprawled out in the large, leather desk chair. His size dominated even the furniture. I hope he remembers he wasn't going to the podium, she thought. The Republican Caucus was busy with so many other battles it was good Caress had made her case. Too bad, but for a fluke, it would have been voted on two days ago.

Now everyone was nervous, including Velda, who had told her that afternoon she would be waiting for the vote in the gallery. Senator Garton held the Republicans together as a voting unit on casino gambling, taxes, the budget, but on other bills Republicans disagreed publicly. Her bill had its detractors, but hopefully she could handle the debate. She watched the speakers go to the microphone and glanced at the wall clock whose small hand now pointed to nine.

* * *

The wicker chair creaked as my back pressed against the soft pillows. Our room was quiet as was the hotel. It was quarter after ten in the Eastern Caribbean, and the subdued British atmosphere of the hotel lent itself to families that played all day and were exhausted at night. Pat had fallen asleep in the bedroom while Benjamin and Matthew were noiseless in their room.

I had tried the judge once again at ten Caribbean time. Velda had not returned so there was no news for me. I sat in darkness on the little porch as a breeze gently moved the clusters of bougainvillea. The *Gideon Bible* remained in front of me. Pat had not asked me nor had I told him about the passage on courage, for I felt so weak. Faithless, I was drowning, the shore was still out of reach, my feet felt no soft sandy bottom. Nothing to be done but sit and wait. Courage, it was gone; energy, ability to pray, gone. I wondered again if Senator Alexa still remembered or perhaps he had lost the paper. Maybe he wouldn't call if the bill failed. The sound of waves washed in on the beach, continuous and eternal, adding to the night noises as the chair back creaked again where my head rested as I waited for the phone to ring.

* * *

Velda's foot wiggled back and forth as she sat in her front row balcony perch. Arms folded around her, she wondered at the passing hours that seemed to always elude the bill. She was getting tired, and the muted light of the chamber added to the heaviness she felt. Senator Randolph walked down the aisle to the podium. There's a vote I wonder about, she said to herself. But the man sure can dress, she thought, watching the dapper senator.

Dinner seemed a decade ago as she remembered the judge who was spending a quiet evening just down the hall. Her eyes moved around the chamber because the senator who had done that waving at Caress glanced momentarily up at the gallery.

The gavel had pounded down again as the umpteenth vote was taken that evening. Her eyes were glazing over when, in a moment, everything changed. "House Bill 1218," called Senator Garton from the podium. "Senator Lubbers." The electronic board at the front of the chamber printed out "Vicious Dog." Velda sat straight in the chair, alert, a shot of adrenaline ripped through the tired body as her hand went unconsciously to her heart.

"This is a bill that is personally important to me." The freshman senator paused, the chamber was listening. They all knew something of the story, for some senators reviewed the legislation while she spoke. "It has passed the House with little opposition and came out of committee unanimously." She glanced quickly back at Senator Meeks. "In order to close a loophole in the law, this legislation would hold the owner of a dog responsible for an unprovoked attack on an individual off the dog's property. Both this bill and

the woman it represents have come a long way, and tonight
I urge the passage of House Bill 1218." Teresa stepped away
from the microphone for other senators to speak. Velda craned
her neck over the brass railing, expecting Senator Randolph
to make a point about the use of police dogs in crowd control,
but the senator remained seated. Instead, Senator Hellmann
stood and took over the microphone.

Velda's foot shook again. That man always has to have his
say, she thought, glaring down. "I'm going to vote no on this
legislation because it introduces something new in the law.
Something we haven't seen before in Indiana, and that is having
an owner be responsible for the actions of an animal."

Velda understood what he was saying, but Indiana did
need the law, and he obviously didn't know the extent of the
problem. She muttered and folded her arms about her again
as she began to rock back and forth. She hadn't thought of
Hellmann and now wondered why he hadn't crossed her mind
as someone for Caress to go see. Caress had seen a lot of the
legislators below. It would have been hard on her if she were
here listening to him. Paul Mannweiler had not said anything
when she had mentioned Hellmann as a possible sponsor of
the bill in the Senate. Perhaps there was something between
the two men? The senator from the blue-collar town of Terre
Haute, Indiana, continued on about the seriousness of adding
to the content of the law.

Teresa stood by the podium as another senator waited to
speak and Senator Hellmann finally stopped talking.

Senator Borst was one vote Velda thought she had taken
care of weeks before. Concerning money or animal issues
you had better have the senator with you. Each respected
the other for their knowledge. Both had carefully watched
years of animal legislation. The tall, silver-haired senator
didn't let her down.

"This is a new piece of legislation, and I am going to
vote for it," he said slowly as if to make a statement. Velda
relaxed a moment, sitting back in her balcony chair and

watching the senator. Senator Borst had his veterinarian hat on and was now explaining his knowledge of dogs to the Senate. He had also been an ally in not allowing greyhound racing in Indiana. Arguably, Senator Borst was the most powerful man in the state house because as finance chairman he held the legislative purse strings of Indiana. He had been powerful for a long time. He was respected. Velda smiled to herself; he also listened to her.

Teresa remained by the microphone. A senator in the back of the chamber called out a question, snapping Velda's attention immediately to the floor. Teresa hesitated for a moment before speaking. This was a legal question. Not being a lawyer or familiar with Indiana Code, Teresa couldn't answer. One of Velda's Plan B's had been tripped, and Senator Luke Kenley immediately came to the front of the chamber. The former city judge from Hamilton County was needed for the absent Senator Doll. Velda smiled from the balcony, for she had seen the need for a lawyer to defend the bill. Senator Kenley answered the question that there was a need for a state provision for physicians to report a bite rather than a local requirement. Teresa scanned the chamber, wondering who else would question the legislation.

Ed Smith watched through the big plate glass window from the second floor. The Senate doorman had drawn duty this evening and he expected a busy night. He watched for latecomers in the hall who were interested in the evening Senate session. Ed had strolled the hallway to break the monotony, standing in front of the heavy doors. By chance he had peered through the plate glass window the very moment "Vicious Dog" flashed on the screen. Ed looked around the empty hall. There was no press, no television, and no Caress.

Where was Caress at this moment when all the months of work were to be voted on? Anxiously, he watched the debaters as he worried, for she would want to know what happened. He remembered her in the halls and pushing through the crowds, now the vote was coming. Ed's hands touched the smooth glass of the window as he watched a senator walk towards the front of the chamber.

This senator had seen pit bulls, teeth clenched, hanging from tires. She had been chased on top of her car by dogs while campaigning. Senator Kathy Smith, a Democrat from New Albany, down by the Ohio River, was for the bill. Ed smiled, for Senator Smith was one of his, he thought fleetingly. She passed through his door daily.

Senator Garton asked the question, "Are we ready for the vote?" as Senator Lubbers returned to her seat and Ed peered through the window, listening to the loud speaker reverberate in the empty hall. The debate had ended, the vote was called and little green and yellow lights appeared on the voting board. Ed counted the yellow nays through the window then ran for the phone book he kept below the wooden desk with the paper message pads.

Velda held her breath and her heart as she watched the innocuous little voting lights that would affect four million lives. She quickly counted the yellow lights, watching them come on one after another like lightn'n bugs in the early Indiana dusk. She leaned forward out of the chair, standing at the last moment before almost falling over the rail. They had won. Relief and a quick thank you swept over her, being carried to someone somewhere, she wasn't sure whom or where. Joy helped her tear up the stairs and out of the balcony down to the second floor.

Teresa Lubbers quickly left her chair for the outer hall, a personal victory, and proof the senator could hold her own.

Senator Alexa's hand touched the thin paper waiting in his coat pocket while the vote was taken. He watched the lights appear and quickly counted the yeas and nays. More Republicans had voted against the bill than Democrats. To the surprise of those around him, he scooted back in the heavy desk chair and left the chamber, for he had to make a late phone call, one that he had promised to make, and one that no distance was too far.

Teresa pushed open the heavy oak door and ran on her toes out to the main hall where Velda waited and screamed, "Yes!"

"*How'd* I *do? How'd* I *do?*" she asked excitedly as both women grabbed each other and shook in delight. "I didn't want Caress Garten to commit suicide on me down in Grenada," she laughed in relief.

"Maybe not suicide," smiled Velda, "but it would have been hard."

"Where's Caress?" A man's voice by the doorman's desk yelled. "I'm calling every Garten in the phone book, just to tell her; she'd want to *know,*" he said, waving the receiver in the air. Ed spoke as the phone was dialing another unrelated Garten in Indianapolis.

"*She's in Grenada,*" the two women answered together then laughed again.

"You did a *great* job, Teresa, a *great* job. Hellmann almost gave me a heart attack but it worked anyway. The whole thing's incredible, first bill I've ever seen go through the state house just like the textbooks say it should," Velda said, eyes sparkling, before a slight gasp. "*I've got to go call her!*" she said, grabbing the state senator's arm.

"She left a message for me this afternoon," added Teresa. "I've got to get back," she said reluctantly, not wanting to give up the moment yet not wanting to miss another vote.

"I'll talk to you later. Good job again." Velda waved and Teresa smiled as she reentered the chamber; a ton of bricks had been removed from her shoulders.

Velda momentarily looked at the little brass elevator to carry her back upstairs to the judge's chambers, then turned to the flight of stairs and started to run.

* * *

The moon had slipped from behind a cloud, and soft light covered the manicured lawn, outlining more clearly the banana trees bending gracefully next to the sea. Their palms rustled in the unseen breeze that flowed through the screens, gently bringing to life the little room in which I quietly sat. Mentally exhausted, there would be no sleep. I waited for the sound of a ringing phone in the room. A biblical promise and fading hope were there in the room with me as I waited.

The phone by Pat was still, and now it was quarter of eleven when the porch door creaked open. Matthew appeared. "Mom, there's a phone call for you in our room," he said with half-closed eyes, standing in the doorway. For a brief moment I stood still by the chair then ran past him outside and into the boys' bedroom. Benjamin was asleep, but the light on the bedside table glowed. I picked up the receiver.

"Hello," I said quickly into the phone.

"This is Senator Alexa," a man's voice began, "and your bill just passed out of the Senate, thirty-nine to eight. Congratulations, Caress," he said genuinely, "enjoy the rest of that vacation."

"Thank you for calling, Senator," I told him joyously.

"You're welcome," he answered simply, and, "Good job."

He hung up the phone with a soft click, and I looked down at Matthew who was again sound asleep and then at Benjamin. I ran into our bedroom and leaned over Pat. *"It passed, the bill passed!"* Pat heard me and from a deep sleep, said gently, "I'm glad, I'm glad," before drifting back to sleep.

The phone by our bed rang and I snatched the phone.

"It *passed*," were the first words Velda said.

"I *know!*" I said jubilantly back to her.

"You mean I'm not the first one to tell you?" she said somewhat crestfallen.

"Senator Alexa just called me!" I fairly screamed.

"You're *kiddin'*," she said. "That bill was voted on not fifteen minutes ago."

I cried, "I *can't believe it! I can't believe it's over. I'm so glad!*"

"You always thought it was supposed to be," Velda said. "You should've seen Teresa—we were both dancing in the halls."

"Best phone call I've ever had, Velda." Pure happiness welled up inside of me. "I've been talking to the judge tonight," I told her.

"That's what he just called out to say, that you'd been askin' about me."

"I had to know what was going on, Velda."

"I didn't call you because there was no way to know if they'd put the vote off again. I was worried," she said.

"I was worried too," I told her.

"I somehow guessed that," she drawled. "So, when you comin' home now that we got you out of town so you could worry most of the time?"

"Day after tomorrow," I told her.

"Well we're gonna be ready for a celebration," she said with glee.

"Thank you, Velda,—thank you for being a very good friend to someone who was a stranger."

"We all wanted this, Caress, and then you happened to be so good at what you did, so much fun. Hey, what are we going for next year?"

"Something good I know," I told her.

"Well this was great," she said. "What's the weather like in paradise?"

"Well, nice, always nice, bright, even at night," I told her, watching the moonlight filter through the screens.

"Makes you not miss this place I bet?"

"I feel like I never left you."

"Well, gotta start 'cause there's not much time left."

"I'll start breathing easier now, Velda."

"I know you will, Caress."

"I should let you go, Velda."

"Good night, Caress, sweet dreams."

With a click she was gone and I placed the phone down. I started to speak to Pat but stopped. He was sound asleep. I was radiant, joyous. Everyone was asleep while the promise had come true! I ran out of the little cottage onto the rolled lawn and stood under millions of stars. Arms wrapped around me, I felt only lightness as I spun around on the grass. I stopped spinning and looked at the sea. A deep voice came from the darkness, "Are you all right, ma'am?" An enormous man, a security guard, stood close to me on the little winding path. His dark skin melted into the night, and only his voice with the soft British undertone of Grenada told me he was of this world.

"I'm *fine,*" I said ecstatically back to him. "I just changed the law in a place called Indiana—ever heard of Indiana?"

"No, ma'am," he said slowly, politely.

"It's in the United States," I said, sensing he didn't understand, "in the middle. Chicago, ever heard of Chicago?"

"No, ma'am," he said again more tentatively.

"The Final Four, basketball, ever heard of that?" The big man in his white uniform shook his head no.

"Do you know about God?" I asked him suddenly. He grinned in the darkness and nodded his head.

"Yes, I know about Him," he said with a smile.

"Well, God wanted me to do something for Him in a place called Indiana," I said, "and He promised if I would try, only try, it would happen."

"Yes, ma'am," the security guard said sincerely, his voice more upbeat, coming out of the shadows.

"You must be happy," he added knowingly. I nodded back at him.

"It's all true you know," I said to him, looking up at the stars. The security guard stood silent with me for a moment as the tree frogs sang and we gazed at the sky.

"Tomorrow Grenada and Pakistan for the championship —West Indies Cricket—are you going?" he asked expectantly.

I had never watched a cricket match, but then he didn't know about basketball.

"No, I'm not going," I said, "but I'm rooting for Grenada." The big smile reappeared on his face.

"I'm glad you changed the law in—," he stopped.

"In *Indiana*," I added. He gave a slight bow and walked down the path into the night, leaving me with the stars and sea and a glowing inner peace that no one could ever take away.

Epilogue

April, 1993

There was to be no signing ceremony in the governor's office where the governor posed for photographs and handed pens to those present. Mark "the cruiser" Kruzan had made his way to the office to ask for the honor. He was told by Governor Bayh's press secretary, Fred Nation, there would be no ceremony for "Paul Mannweiler's sister-in-law." "The cruiser" explained that Caress Garten was no relation to Paul Mannweiler but was a friend of his. The answer remained the same—no. Paul's "slick Willy" comment had gotten some revenge.

November 5, 1993, 3:00 P.M.

I was sitting at my desk in the mayor's office having worked all afternoon. I had been hired to implement the project I had finished a year ago to the day—the day of my attack. The anniversary, with its morning sunshine, didn't bother me. I remembered some typing the secretary in the main reception area was doing for me. Joanne was busy at her desk. I passed a woman sitting nearby, waiting to see the mayor. Windows lined the room high on the twenty-fifth floor. The day had turned gray and there were spatters of rain against the glass. *It was like the day.* Grabbing the wood rail that surrounded the desk, I noticed the clock—3:15 P.M. *It was the time.* Stunned, my head dropped, my balance became shaky.

"How is your leg?" asked the stranger waiting to see the mayor. Frozen, I didn't answer. "How is your leg?" the voice repeated with authority. Joanne stopped typing. I turned toward the visitor.

"It's fine—a little stiff. I've lost some motion." The stranger gazed intently at me.

"Always remember the good you accomplished for others," she said. Drawn toward her, I hesitated.

"Thank you for saying something to me," I told her, feeling as if an angel had caught me before a fall.

"You're very welcome," she said while I left the room knowing I continued to be watched over.

January, 1994

In the 1994 Indiana legislative session, an amendment was added quietly to a major crime bill. The amendment added one word—animals—to the state's deadly weapon statute. The word was added on behalf of the woman in Fort Wayne who had been sexually assaulted then seriously injured by her attacker's pit bull whom he commanded to "sic" her. Paul Mannweiler placed the amendment on the crime bill with permission from Governor Bayh's office. Criminal offenses committed with a weapon raise the charge to a more serious felony, making prison likely. Indiana became the first state in the union to add animals to its deadly weapon statute.

I was asked not to appear at the state house so no attention would be brought to the amendment.

Belinda Lewis and the Fort Wayne prosecutor were delighted.

* * *

In November of 1994, Paul Mannweiler once again became Speaker of the Indiana House of Representatives, holding on to the Speaker's position for two years before the Republicans once again lost control of the house in 1996.

Paul returned to the role of minority leader until the fall of 2000 when he stepped down from his leadership role.

Michael Phillips, Paul's old nemesis, was caught by the press not attending sessions of a national convention of legislators held in New Orleans in 1994. Taxpayers had paid for the trip, and undercover cameras found the Speaker playing golf and visiting riverboat casinos instead of attending sessions. He lost his House seat in the 1994 election. Mike Phillips went to work as an attorney and lobbyist at the state house.

Mark "the cruiser" Kruzan became House majority leader in 1996 when the Democrats regained control. Prosecutor Jeffrey Modisett was elected attorney general of the state of Indiana in 1996. Lieutenant Governor Frank O'Bannon became governor of Indiana in 1996. He was re-elected governor in 2000. Jesse Villalpando retired from the House in 2000 and was appointed a judge in Lake Superior Court by Governor O'Bannon. Senator Lonnie Randolph retired from the Senate and was appointed a judge in East Chicago City Court by Governor O'Bannon. Sue Anne Gilroy left her position as state director for Senator Richard G. Lugar and was elected Indiana secretary of state in 1994. She was re-elected in 1998 and lost a 2000 election attempt to become mayor of Indianapolis.

Belinda Lewis remains the head of Fort Wayne, Indiana, Animal Control, still one of the most effective in the United States. Sally Allen continues to head U.S.A. Defenders of Greyhounds, rescuing dogs around the United States from racing tracks. Linda Worsham, media expert of the dog dream team, became chief of staff to United States Congressman Steven Buyer. She founded the first humane society in Indiana's Tipton County.

Sandy Rowland remains the head of the Great Lakes Chapter of the Humane Society of the United States. Senator Teresa Lubbers and Senator William Alexa are still effective legislators in the state Senate. Senator Robert Garton continues to hold his power as Senate president.

Mr. Leroy Hoke remained as Senate doorman until the spring of 1998 when he suffered a heart attack while on duty at the state house. Rick Harris of the Capitol Police now works for the Lawrence, Indiana, Sheriff's Department. Gene Cummings continues as the chief bailiff of the Indiana Court of Appeals. Randy Rollings, the assistant bailiff, won sixteen million dollars in the Indiana Lottery and retired.

Sarah Spearman, my friend with the "direct line," who told me what my mission would be, teaches school in Indianapolis. Dr. Frank Kik is a professor at Reformed Theological Seminary in Charlotte, North Carolina.

Velda Boenitz remained with "The Judge" in the ivory tower of the court of appeals until they both retired in 2000. Velda remains a friend, rescuer, and preserver for all creatures great and small.

Our gentle Boomer died of old age in the winter of 1999. Chuck remains the guardian of his home and last year welcomed Gerdie, another rescued dog, to his domain.

In the spring of 1993, I was hired by Indianapolis Mayor Stephen Goldsmith to create a program to honor volunteers in the neighborhoods and churches of Indianapolis. The Mayor's Volunteer Partnership Awards were formed in conjunction with United Way and became part of Mayor Goldsmith's Front Porch Alliance program. This program became the basis for President George W. Bush's Faith Based Alliance, and Stephen Goldsmith is a key volunteer in managing this initiative.

I left the mayor's office in 1998 to finish writing *On Behalf of Innocents.*

* * *

Children injured in dog attacks and their families have become my friends. I remember them as I speak to groups regularly about the mission, the state house, and the prosecution of irresponsible dog owners.

I did go to physical therapy for many months after the

legislation was passed to rebuild the muscles in my leg while learning to walk again using the heel of my foot. The facial scars on my forehead are very slight. Most people never notice them at all.

I am not afraid of dogs and, in fact, love and enjoy my own. The dogs who attacked me were very unusual animals due to their strength, viciousness, breeding, and training.

I have no emotional scars from the attack. I believe this is due to the knowledge that I was used in a very special way to help other people. All things happen for a reason, and even the most terrible events can end up being purposeful, positive, and even wonderful.